He said unto his disciples,
Gather up the fragments that remain,
that nothing be lost.

JOHN 6:12

Prophetic Fragments

††

Cornel West

WILLIAM B. EERDMANS PUBLISHING COMPANY
GRAND RAPIDS, MICHIGAN

AFRICA WORLD PRESS, INC.
TRENTON, NEW JERSEY

To my marvelous parents
IRENE AND CLIFTON WEST
whose lives of love and sacrifice give
so much joy and happiness to us

Copyright © 1988 by Wm. B. Eerdmans Publishing Co.
This edition published jointly by
Wm. B. Eerdmans Publishing Co.,
255 Jefferson Ave. SE, Grand Rapids, Mich. 49503
and Africa World Press, Inc.,
P.O. Box 1892, Trenton, N.J. 08608
All rights reserved
Printed in the United States of America

Library of Congress Cataloging-in-Publication Data:

West, Cornel.
    Prophetic Fragments / by Cornel West.
        p.   cm.
    Eerdmans ISBN 0-8028-3653-4
    Africa World ISBN 0-86543-085-3
      1. United States—Religion—1960-
      2. Afro-Americans—Religion.
  I. Title.
  BL2525.W42   1988
  291'.0973—dc19   88-1403
                            CIP

Contents

77103

CONTENTS

Part 2: Religion and Culture

Part 3: Religion and Contemporary Theology

Foreword

From the inception of thought humans have grappled with the question of their substantive existence. Though we all face this dilemma, precious few of us have the "seed of engagement": an inner drive, an unquenchable thirst, perhaps even a DNA-determined heartset that hears the beckoning call of those who suffer. An even more precious few among those who hear the call actually yield to it.

Although we are all wrapped and bound up in packages of individuality, through the efforts of such as these we once again awaken to the collective nature of our existence. As individuals, we strive to explore, question, and consequently reconstruct the everchanging horizons of our individual actualizations. But we must also do so as a collective body. Cornel West is one of those "vehicles" whose visceral travels transport us ever closer to a protective light whose rays illuminate places that yearn for light. In doing so, he enhances the quality of our lives.

There is really no more appropriate way for me to comment on this text than to speak of how it reflects the fabric of the person who wrote it. Three issues dwell at the very core of this text and its author. The first issue is *faith*. As I have heard my brother say on occasion, "Faith is stepping out on nothing and landing on something." It is more than just the stuff from which dreams are made. It is the inevitable source that enables them to become reality.

The second issue is *hope*. Not the passive, laissez-faire variety that one is reduced to in buying a lottery ticket. This is a hope born out of discipline and fueled by preparedness, a hope ready to seize opportunity.

The third issue is *love*. Love—the foundation upon which faith and hope must be built. Love—as basic as the birth of a new day, yet as complex as the varied conditions under which we find God's children living today.

As you travel through the text and are reminded of its author, you should know that herein lies the obsession of truly one of the most compassionate thinkers of our time. Herein lies the product conceived in a most special marriage between an inexhaustible discipline and a raw but talented passion. Herein lies the testament of personal conviction—a conviction of *faith*, an addiction to *hope*, and a profession of *love*.

CLIFTON L. WEST III

Acknowledgments

This work was made possible—as are all of my writings—by my precious family and friends: my inimitable parents, Clifton L. West, Jr., and Irene Bias West; my steadfast brother, Clifton L. West III; my supportive sisters, Cynthia West Cole and Cheryl West Gaston; my close confidants, James Melvin Washington, Professor of Church History at Union Theological Seminary in New York City, and Anders Stephanson; and my wonderful son, Clifton Louis West. Lastly, I am grateful for the incredible inspiration and deep love of a very special lady who sustained me in putting these fragments together in this published form.

C.W.

INTRODUCTION
The Crisis in Contemporary American Religion

The crisis in contemporary American religious life is profound and pervasive. The crisis is profound in that it deepens as Americans turn more desperately toward religion. The crisis is pervasive in that it affects every form of religiosity in the country—from Christianity to Buddhism, from reform Judaism to Islam. To put it bluntly, American religious life is losing its prophetic fervor. There is an undeniable decline in the clarity of vision, complexity of understanding, and quality of moral action among religious Americans. The rich prophetic legacies of Sojourner Truth, Walter Rauschenbusch, Dorothy Day, Abraham Heschel, and Martin Luther King, Jr., now lay nearly dormant—often forgotten—and the possession of a marginal few. Political and cultural conservatism seems to have silenced most of the prophetic religious voices and tamed the vast majority of churches, temples, synagogues, and mosques. Prophetic religion indeed is at the crossroads in present-day America.

The principal aim of this book is to examine and explore, delineate and demystify, counter and contest the widespread accommodation of American religion to the political and cultural status quo. This accommodation is suffocating much of the best in American religion; it promotes and encourages an existential emptiness and political irrelevance. This accommodation is, at bottom, idolatrous—it worships the gods created by American society and kneels before the altars erected by American culture.

American religious life—despite its weekly rituals and everyday practices—is shot through with existential emptiness. This emptiness—or lack of spiritual depth—results from the excessive preoccupation with isolated personal interests and atomistic individual concerns in American religious life. These interests and concerns unduly accommodate the status quo by mirroring the privatism and careerism rampant in American society. Like so much of American culture, exorbitant personalistic and individualistic preoccupations in American religion yield momentary stimulation rather than spiritual sustenance, sentimental self-flagellation rather than sacrificial self-denial. Needless to say, these accommodationalist forms of religion fit well with the thriving consumerism, narcissism, and hedonism in the country. And religion becomes but one more stimulant in a culture addicted to stimulation—a stimulation that fuels consumption and breeds existential emptiness. In this way, postmodern American culture attempts to eliminate spiritual depth, disseminate stimulatory surfaces, flatten out transcendence into titillation, and replace the sense of the mystery of existence with that of the self's feelings of intensity (usually of the orgiastic sort). Accommodationalist forms of religion usually aid and abet this postmodern condition, thereby surreptitiously prohibiting the very existential state they claim to promote—namely, spiritual depth.

Furthermore, American religious life—notwithstanding its vast philanthropic networks and impressive charitable record—lacks a substantive social consciousness. This is so because, like so much of American life, it suffers from social amnesia. American religious people have little memory of or sense for collective struggle and communal combat. At the level of family and individuals, this memory and sense lingers. But at the level of larger social groups and institutions, this memory and sense of struggle evaporates. This social amnesia prevents systemic social analysis of power, wealth, and influence in society from taking hold among most religious Americans. Instead, the tendency is to fall back on personalistic and individualistic explanations for poverty, occupational mobility, or social catastrophe.

For instance, moralistic acts are often conflated with moral actions. Yet the former proceed from sheer sentimental concern—for example, pity—whereas the latter flow from an understanding of the larger context in which the action takes place and of the impact of the action on the problem. In short, moralistic acts rest upon a narrow, parochial anti-intellectualism that sees only pitiful individuals, whereas moral action is based on a broad, robust prophetism that highlights systemic social analysis of the circumstances under which tragic persons struggle. It is no accident that the moralistic, anti-intellectualistic forms of American religion thoroughly trash modernity and secularity yet revel in the wonders of technology and in the comfortable living of modern prosperity. This flagrant hypocrisy—simply highlighted in the events in recent months yet true for all of the big-time, narrow TV evangelists—is overcome only when one adopts a principled prophetism; that is, a prophetic religion that incorporates the best of modernity and secularity (tolerance, fallibilism, criticism), yet brings prophetic critique to bear upon the idols of modernity and secularity (science, technology, and wealth).

This book purports to set forth the contours of a principled prophetism in the form of essays, articles, reviews, and fiction. I live, work, and write out of a particular religious perspective—namely, that of the prophetic stream of the Christian tradition. I first encountered this stream in the bosom of the black Baptist heritage in America, and this stamp is still felt and seen in my own religious outlook. Yet I am concerned with the prophetic potential of all religions (such as Buddhism, Hinduism, Judaism, and Islam) and the progressive possibilities of all secular ideologies (including feminism, Marxism, anarchism, and liberalism). My prophetic outlook is informed by a deep, historical consciousness that accents the finitude and fallenness of all human beings and accentuates an international outlook that links the human family with a common destiny; an acknowledgment of the inescapable yet ambiguous legacy of tradition and the fundamental role of community; a profound sense of the tragic character of life and history that generates a strenuous mood, a call for heroic, courageous moral action always against the odds; and a biblically motivated focus on and concern for the wretched of the earth that keeps track of the historic and social causes for much (though by no means all) of their misery.

On the one hand, I assume that religious traditions are, for the most part, reactionary, repressive, and repulsive without heavy doses of modern formulations of rule of law, gender and racial equality, tolerance, and, especially, substantive democracy. On the other hand, such modern formulations can be based on or derived from the best of religious traditions. To be a contemporary religious intellectual—and person—is to be caught in this creative tension on the boundary between past and present, tradition and modern—yet always mounted in the barricades on this battlefield on which life is lived and history is made. Prophetic thought and action is preservative in that it tries to keep alive certain elements of a tradition bequeathed to us from the past and revolutionary in that it attempts to project a vision and inspire a praxis which fundamentally transforms the prevailing status quo in light of the best of the tradition and the flawed yet significant achievements of the present order. These fragments—which feebly reflect the Christian faith that shores me up against the ruins in our world—are linked together by my response to one basic question: How does a present-day Christian think about and act on enhancing the plight of the poor, the predicament of the powerless, and the quality of life for all in a prophetic manner?

PART ONE
Religion and Politics

first—and most important—source was *the prophetic black church tradi-tion* that initially and fundamentally shaped King's worldview. The sec-ond consisted of a *prophetic liberal Christianity* King encountered in his higher education and scholarly training. The third source was a *prophet-ic Gandhian method of nonviolent social change* that King first encountered in a sermon by Mordecai Johnson (president of Howard University) and that he later used in his intense intellectual struggle with the powerful critiques of the Christian love ethic by Karl Marx and Friedrich Nietzsche. The last source was that of *prophetic American civil religion* that fuses secular and sacred history and combines Christian themes of deliverance and salvation with political ideals of democracy, freedom, and equality. I shall argue that these four religious sources constitute the major pillars of Martin Luther King, Jr.'s, thought. Let us start at King's beginnings—that is, in the bosom of the black Baptist church.

The black church—a shorthand rubric that refers to black Christian communities of various denominations that came into being when Afri-can-American slaves decided, often at the risk of life and limb, to "make Jesus their choice" and to share with one another their common Chris-tian sense of purpose and Christian understanding of their circum-stances—is unique in American culture. This is so because it is the major institution created, sustained, and controlled by black people them-selves; that is, it is the most visible and salient cultural product of black people in the United States. The profound insights *and* petty blind-nesses, immeasurable depths *and* immobilizing defaults, incalculable richness *and* parochial impoverishment of that complex hybrid people called Afro-Americans surface most clearly in the black church.

And let us be very clear and let us never forget that the great Ameri-can prophetic figure of our time, Martin Luther King, Jr., was a child of the black church—an individual product of the major institutional prod-uct of black people in this country. The black church was created under economic conditions of preindustrial slavery and socioeconomic cir-cumstances of "natal alienation" (Orlando Patterson's term in *Slavery and Social Death* to describe a form of social death in which people have no legal ties of birth in both ascending and descending generations, no right to predecessors or progeny). Hence black people were *confined* to a perpetual and inheritable state of domination and *defined* as dishonored persons with no public worth, social standing, or legal status—only economic value, mere commodities to be bought, sold, or used. In this regard, the black church signified and signifies the collective effort of an exploited and oppressed, degraded and despised, dominated and downtrodden people of African descent to come to terms with the ab-surd *in* America and the absurd *as* America. The black church was a com-munal response to an existential and political situation in which no penultimate reasons suffice to make any kind of sense or give any type of meaning to the personal circumstances and collective condition of Afro-Americans. With the "death of the African gods" (to use Albert Raboteau's phrase in his book, *Slave Religion*), black people creatively appropriated a Christian worldview—mainly from such dissenters in the American religious tradition as Baptists and Methodists—and thereby transformed a prevailing absurd situation into a persistent and present *tragic* one, a kind of "Good Friday" state of existence in which one is seemingly forever on the cross, perennially crucified, continuously abused and incessantly devalued—yet sustained and empowered by a hope against hope for a potential and possible triumphant state of affairs. The ground of this hope was neither rationally demonstrable nor empirically verifiable. Rather, it was existentially encountered in an intense *personal* relationship with Jesus Christ, whose moral life, agonizing death, and miraculous resurrection literally and symbolically enacted an ultimate victory over evil—collective slavery and personal sin—a victory that had *occurred* but was not yet *consummated*, with evil *conquered*, but not yet *abolished*. The Christocentric language of the black church—of Jesus as the bright and morning star against the backdrop of the pitch darkness of the night, as water in dry places, a companion in loneliness, a doctor to the sick, a rock in a wearied land—exemplifies the intimate and dependent personal relationship between God and individual and between God and a world-forsaken people.

The important point here is not simply that this is the broad black Christian worldview that King heard and adopted at his father's church, Ebenezer Baptist Church in Atlanta, Georgia, but also that this worldview put the pressing and urgent problem of evil—the utterly and undeniably *tragic* character of life and history—at its center. Furthermore, the major focus of the *prophetic* black Christian worldview was neither an escapist pie-in-the-sky heaven nor a political paradise on earth. Rather, the stress was on marshaling and garnering resources from fellowship, community, and personal strength (meditation, prayer) to cope with overwhelmingly limited options dictated by institutional and personal evil. In short, this black Christian perspective indeed affirmed a sustaining eschatology (that is, a heaven-orientation) and a moral critique of pervasive white racism—but its emphasis was on survival and struggle in the face of an alternative of absurdity and insanity.

The principal African resources in black Christianity were threefold. First, a *kinetic orality* permeated black sermons and songs, black prayers and hymns. A sense of community was constituted and reinforced by an invigorated rhetoric, rhythmic freedom, and antiphonal forms of interaction. Fluid, protean, and flexible oral stylizations of language gave black church life a distinctively African-American stamp—a stamp that flowed from black cultural agency in a society that tried to deny and downplay any form of black agency and black creativity. Second a *passionate physicality* accented black control and power over the only social space permitted to them in American society—that is, their bodies. Self-assertion of *somebodiness* enacted by bodily participation in stylized forms of spiritual response in black church liturgy signified a sense of *homefulness* for an exilic people. Last, a *combative spirituality* was promoted and promulgated by the central roles of preacher, deacon, and choir. Each had to meet a weekly challenge of feeding the flock, encouraging the discouraged, and giving hope to the downhearted. This stress on the performative and the pragmatic, on pageantry and the histrionic put a premium on prospective moral practice or forward-looking ethical struggle for black Christian parishioners. This sense of struggle paradoxically cultivated a historical patience and subversive joy, a sober survival ethic and an openness to seize credible liberation opportunities.

The theology of the black church was, for the most part, traditionally Augustinian with an African-American difference. It accented the traditional Protestant Christian doctrines of divine majesty, sovereignty, mystery, sin and grace, forgiveness and love filtered through the black experience of oppression. This filtering linked God's plan of salvation to black liberation—inseparable though not identical—and bestowed upon black people a divine source for self-identity—for example, as children of God—that stood in stark contrast to the cultural perceptions and social roles imposed upon them by a racist American society.

This African-American difference not only highlighted the dignity of a people (as unique individuals) denied such dignity in their surroundings but also accented the strong universalist and egalitarian Christian *imago dei* notion of all persons having equal value and significance in the eyes of God. In this way, the black church put forward perspectives that encouraged both individuality and community fellowship, personal morality and antiracist political engagement, a grace-centered piety and a stress on Christian good works. To put it crudely, the black church attempted to provide a theological route through the Scylla of a quietistic, priestly American Christianity that legitimated racism and the Charybdis of a secular (self-righteous) Promethean view that elevated human powers at the expense of divine grace and divine aid. The black church tried to hold together both the dignity and depravity of persons in such a way that God—like Yahweh with the children of Israel—identifies with the disinherited and downtrodden, yet even the disinherited and downtrodden are sinners in need of conversion and sanctification. Human beings can change and be changed—both individuals and societies—yet no individual and society can *fully* conform to the requirements of the Christian gospel, hence the need for endless improvement and amelioration.

This complex dialectical interplay of human finitude and human betterment in predominant black church theological perspectives makes Afro-American Christianity more evangelical than fundamentalist. This is so because fundamentalist Christianity is preoccupied with the claims of science and historical criticism of biblical texts; it views the Bible not only in literalist terms but more importantly in the form of propositions in light of a notion of *closed* revelation—only certain biblically derived propositions constitute divine revelation. By contrast, black evangelical Christianity is primarily concerned with human fallenness, including our readings of the Bible. Biblical texts indeed remain the authoritative guide to Christian life, yet the focus is on moral conduct and spiritual development in light of *continued* revelation—that is openness to divine purpose, especially through the Holy Spirit—grounded in the Bible *and* appropriated by individuals and communities in the present. In short, fundamentalist Christianity is *rationalistic* in orientation and *legalistic* in effect, hence it leans toward bibliolatry; whereas black evangelical Christianity is *dramatic* in orientation and *moralistic* in effect, hence it affirms a biblically informed perspective.

My claim is that black church viewpoints not only fundamentally shaped King's thought but also regulated the themes and motifs, aspects and elements he accentuated in his encounters with liberal Christianity at Morehouse College, Crozer Theological Seminary, the University of Pennsylvania, Boston University, and Harvard University; Gandhian conceptions of love and social change and American civil religion. In this way, the black church's influence on King's views is the most *primordial* and *decisive* source of his thought. In his own writings and sermons, he simply presupposed this influence and always assumed that his being a black Baptist minister spoke for itself regarding this black church influence. For example, his choice of Georg Wilhelm Hegel as his favorite philosopher was not because King was convinced of the necessary developments of the *Weltgeist* put forward in *The Phenomenology of Spirit*, but rather because Hegel held that "growth comes through struggle"—a view King was quite disposed to, given his formation in the black church. Furthermore, King's preferred method of looking for partial truths in opposing positions, in rejecting extremes and affirming a creative synthesis of opposing views in a tension-ridden harmony is, on the surface, Hegelian. But it is, on a deeper level, rooted in the dialectical mediation of the dualistic character of the self (spirit/nature) and world (history/eternity)—a mediation both King (in an Afro-American context) and Hegel (in a German Lutheran context) inherited from Christian thought. The point is not that King did not learn much from Hegel, but rather that Hegel was a *supplement* to King's black church influence.

This supplementary character of intellectual sources subsequent to King's black church formation can be seen quite clearly in his encounter with liberal Christianity in his formal higher education and training. For example, at Morehouse College, King's concentration in sociology re-inforced his theological and moral condemnation of the hypocrisy of white racist southern Christians and their alleged adherence to the Chris-tian gospel. Walter Chivers, his sociology professor, conducted detailed empirical investigation of lynchings in the South in light of a self-styled ethical critique of American capitalism. More pointedly, under George D. Kelsey (head of the Department of Religion) and Dr. Benjamin Mays (Morehouse College president), King's black church prospectives were refined. By avoiding fundamentalist traps, shedding parochial images of mere cathartic preaching and linking sophisticated intellectual pursuit to serious Christian commitment, King became convinced at Morehouse that his vocation lay in becoming a minister in the black Baptist tradi-tion.

King's response to the Euro-American Christian academic world was to select those viewpoints that gave philosophical and theological artic-ulation to deeply held themes and beliefs he acquired in the black church. The four central religious themes were the dignity and sanctity of human persons; the moral obligation and social responsibility of Christians to resist institutional evils such as racist segregation; the significance of per-sonal immortality; and the power of Christian love to make a difference in personal *and* social life. At Crozer, King took nearly one-third of his courses under George Davis. In a way similar to black church perspec-tives, Davis conceived of God as a deity intimately and intricately in-volved in human history—a "working, toiling God" who labors through human beings to realize the ultimate end and aim of history. This end and aim was the recognition and appreciation of the value of human per-sonality and the brotherhood of man. Influenced by the social gospel of Walter Rauschenbusch, Davis linked his personalism to political and so-cial engagement. Yet it was the work of L. Harold DeWolf at Boston University that provided the liberal Christian resources most congenial and amenable to King's refined black church perspectives. In his six courses with DeWolf and in writing his doctoral dissertation (on the conception of God in Paul Tillich and Henry Nelson Wieman) under the guidance of DeWolf, King found an acceptable and respectable academic theology that best expressed the major themes and beliefs of his black church background. DeWolf's personalism provided King with a pro-fessional theological language that put forward the four basic themes King had inherited from the black church tradition. During his years in graduate school, King did tentatively adopt limited liberal Christian ideas about the natural goodness of people and the progressive direction of human history. Yet later in the heat of battle, King fell back on more classical Christian ideas of sin, grace, and hope within the context of the black struggle for freedom. In short, Davis and DeWolf *supplemented* King's black church viewpoints—supplements that resulted in slight revisions, emendations, and new academic forms for his evangelical content. King indeed called himself an evangelical liberal—an apt description after adopting Kelsey's nonliteralist, dramatic reading of the biblical texts, Mays's Christian modernist view of educated and engaged black ministers, Davis's stress on human history as the crucial terrain for divine activity, and DeWolf's full-blown personalism that undergirded a social gospel.

The major challenges to King's black church formation came from the critiques of religion put forward by Karl Marx and Friedrich Nietzsche as, for example, Marx's claim (based on Ludwig Feuerbach's views) that religion was the opiate of the people—the instrument of those who rule in that it disinvests people of their own powers by investing God with all power and thereby rendering them submissive and deferential toward the status quo. Furthermore, Marx's claim of the vast economic disparity between the rich and poor—for instance, the *class inequality* in America between 1 percent of the population who owned 28 percent of the wealth and the bottom 45 percent of the population who owned 2 percent of the wealth—made an important impact on King. King's black church formation led him to conclude that many forms of religion did render people submissive, but also that *prophetic* Christianity could *empower* people to fight against oppression and struggle for freedom and justice. King remained convinced all of his life that there was a need for a redistribution of wealth and a deemphasis on material possessions in a profit-oriented capitalist society. And later in life, King endorsed some forms of (indigenous) American democratic and libertarian socialism that preserved a constitutional rule of law and protected individual liberties in order to secure and promote a "person-centered rather than property-centered and profit-centered" economy. In regard to his response to Marx, King wrote:

> I read Marx as I read all of the influential historical thinkers—from a dialectical point of view, combining a partial yes and a partial no. Insofar as Marx posited a metaphysical materialism, an ethical relativism, and a strangulating totalitarianism, I responded with an unambiguous "no"; but insofar as he pointed to weaknesses of traditional capitalism, contributed to the growth of a definite self-consciousness in the masses, and challenged the social conscience of the Christian churches, I responded with a definite "yes."

In short, King succumbed to neither a knee-jerk negative reaction to Marx without reading and grappling with him nor an uncritical acceptance of Marx's atheism that overlooked the contribution of prophetic religious people to struggles for freedom.

Nietzsche's view of Christian love as a form of resentment and revenge of the powerless and impotent toward the powerful and the strong led King briefly to "despair of the power of love in solving social problems." Following both the black church tradition and liberal Christianity, King had concluded that the Christian love ethic applied only to individuals' relationships—not to group, nation, or class conflicts. And if Nietzsche was correct, even individual relationships of love were but power struggles masquerading as harmonious interactions. The Gandhian method of love-motivated (agapic) nonviolent resistance provided King with a response to Marx and an answer to Nietzsche. The love ethic of Jesus Christ was a moral and practical method—a way of life and way of struggle in which oppressed people could fight for freedom without inflicting violence on the oppressor, humiliating the opponent and hence possibly transforming the moral disposition of one's adversary.

For King, this method of nonviolent resistance required more internal *moral discipline* than that of Marxist revolutionaries because one had to accept suffering without retaliation, to receive blows without striking back. For him, this was not cowardice but courage, not fear but fortitude. Nonviolent resistance also went beyond Nietzschean resentment and revenge in that resistance was directed at the forces of evil rather than against persons who commit the evil. The enemy is injustice and oppression, not those who perpetuate the injustice and oppression.

Needless to say, this Gandhian viewpoint goes against our common instincts and moral intuitions. In this sense, the application of the love ethic of Jesus Christ in the social sphere requires not only tremendous moral discipline and fortitude, but also *profound trust* in the redemptive power of love and in the salvific plan of God. This trust presupposes that the unearned suffering of agapic nonviolent resisters can educate, transform, and even convert one's opponents. The aim is not simply to rely on the moral sense or conscience of the adversary but, if need be, to force the adversary to develop such a sense and conscience. And if one concludes that no such development is possible, then we simply must admit that we are doomed to an unending cycle of violence and oppression—with the old victims of violence soon to become new perpetrators of violence. Such a nightmare—an inevitable conclusion for Marx and Nietzsche in King's view—radically calls into question the very power of the love ethic of Jesus Christ. For King, if one accepts such a nightmare, then only self-destruction awaits us. To accept such a view—for individuals, groups, or nations—is to acquire and preserve "power without compassion, might without morality, and strength without sight."

The last major resource for King's thought was American civil religion—that complex web of religious ideals of deliverance and salvation and political ideals of freedom, democracy, and equality that constitute the evolving collective self-definition of America. This first new nation—born liberal, born modern, and born bourgeois—gave birth to a grand social experiment unprecedented in human history. Its Declaration of Independence constituted, for King, a great moral event and document. King's appropriation and interpretation of American civil religion led him creatively to extend the tradition of American jeremiads—a tradition of public exhortation that joins social criticisms of America to moral renewal and calls America back to its founding ideals of democracy, freedom, and equality. King was convinced that despite the racism of the Founding Fathers, the ideals of America were sufficient if only they were taken seriously in practice. Therefore, King's condemnation of and lament for America's hypocrisy and oppression of poor whites, indigenous peoples, Latinos, and black people was put forward in the name of reaffirming America's mission of embodying democracy, freedom, and equality. King did not support and affirm the bland American dream of comfortable living and material prosperity. Rather, he put forward his own dream—grounded and refined in the black church experience, supplemented by liberal Christianity, and implemented by Gandhian methods of nonviolent resistance—rooted in the American ideals of democracy, freedom, and equality.

King's thought remains a challenge to us principally in that he accented the anticolonial, anti-imperialist, and antiracist consequences of taking seriously the American ideals of democracy, freedom, and equality. He never forgot that America was born out of revolutionary revolt and subversive rebellion against British colonialism and imperialism and that while much of white America viewed the country as the promised land, black slaves saw it as Egypt; that just as Europe's poor huddled masses were attracted to America, the largest black mass movement (led by Marcus Garvey) was set on leaving America! Through his prophetic Christian lens, King saw just how far America had swerved away from its own revolutionary past. In its support of counterrevolution in Vietnam, Guatemala, Colombia, Jamaica, and South Africa—and today we can add Chile, Nicaragua, and South Korea—the United States betrayed its own ideals. King acutely observed in 1968:

> The greatest irony and tragedy of all is that our nation, which initiated so much of the revolutionary spirit of the modern world, is now cast in the mold of being an arch anti-revolutionary. We are

engaged in a war that seems to turn the clock of history back and perpetuate white colonialism.

King's universal and egalitarian religious and moral commitments, as well as his historical consciousness, led him to *internationalize* the American ideals of democracy, freedom, and equality and thereby measure not only domestic policies but also U.S. foreign policy by these ideals. And he found both sets of policies wanting. He knew some progress had been made—yet so much more progress was needed, and even present gains could be reversed, as we have witnessed in the past few years. Regarding the domestic front, King proclaimed:

If the problem [of injustice to the poor and blacks] is not solved, America will be on the road to its self-destruction.

And on the eve of his murder, he again warned regarding the international scene,

And also in the human rights revolution, if something isn't done, and in a hurry, to bring the colored peoples of the world out of their long years of poverty, their long years of hurt and neglect, the whole world is doomed.

The unique status and legacy of Martin Luther King, Jr., is that as a black Baptist minister, he embodies the best of American Christianity; as an organic intellectual, he exemplifies the best of the life of the mind involved in public affairs; as a proponent of nonviolent resistance he holds out the only slim hope for social sanity in a violence-ridden world; as an American prophet he commands the respect even of those who opposed him; and as an egalitarian internationalist he inspires all oppressed peoples around the world who struggle for democracy, freedom, and equality. What manner of man was he, this child and product of the black church open enough to learn from others and rooted enough in his own tradition to grow, who now belongs to the nation and the world—a nation and world still "not able to bear all his words" even as they try to honor him?

Religion and the Left

Notwithstanding the secular sensibilities of most leftist intellectuals and activists, religion permeates and pervades the lives of the majority of people in the capitalist world. And all signs indicate that the prevailing crisis in the capitalist world is not solely an economic or political one. Recent inquiries into the specificity of racism, patriarchy, homophobia, state repression, bureaucratic domination, ecological subjugation, and nuclear exterminism suggest that we need to understand this crisis as that of capitalist civilization. To extend leftist discourses about political economy and the state to a discourse about capitalist civilization is to accent a sphere rarely scrutinized by Marxist thinkers: *the sphere of culture and everyday life*. And any serious scrutiny of this sphere sooner or later must come to terms with religious ways of life and religious ways of struggle.

In this chapter I shall pose three crucial questions to contemporary Marxism regarding religion. First, how are we to understand the character and content of religious beliefs and practices? Second, how are we to account for the recent religious upsurges in Latin America, the Middle East, Asia, Africa, Eastern Europe, and the United States? And third, in which ways can these upsurges enrich and enhance—or delimit and deter—the international struggle for human freedom and democracy? In the present historical moment, these queries strike me as inescapable and important.

Religion and Marxist Theory

The classical Marxist understanding of religion is more subtle than is generally acknowledged. Crude Marxist formulations of religion as the opium of the people in which the religious masses are viewed as passive and ignorant objects upon which monolithic religious institutions impose fantasies of other-worldly fulfillment reveal more about Enlightenment prejudices and arrogant self-images of petty bourgeois intellectuals than the nature of religion. Contrary to such widespread crypto-Marxist myths about religion, Marx and Engels understood religion as a profound human response to, and protest against, intolerable conditions.

From *Monthly Review* (July-Aug. 1984).

For Marx and Engels, religion as an opium of the people is not a mere political pacification imposed from above but rather a historically circumscribed existential and experiential assertion of being (or somebodiness) by dehumanized historical agents under unexamined socioeconomic conditions. Marx and Engels characterized religion as alienation not primarily because it is "unscientific" or "pre-modern," but rather because it often overlooks the socioeconomic conditions which shape and mold its expression and thereby delimits human powers and efforts to transform these conditions. In short, the classical Marxist critique of religion is not an *a priori* philosophical rejection of religion; rather it is a social analysis of and historical judgment upon religious practices.

For Marx and Engels, religion often overlooks the socioeconomic circumstances which condition its expression, principally because the religious preoccupation with cosmic vision, ontological pronouncements on human nature, and personal morality hold at arm's length social and historical analysis. Hence religion at its worst serves as an ideological means of preserving and perpetuating prevailing social and historical realities and at its best yields moralistic condemnations of and utopian visions beyond present social and historical realities—with few insights regarding what these realities are and how to change them. The Marxist point here is not simply that religion alone is an impotent and inadequate form of protest, but also that without a probing and illuminating social and historical analysis of the present even the best-intentioned religionists and moralists will impede fundamental social and historical transformation. In stark contrast to crude Marxists, Marx and Engels do not claim that only a substitution of a rigid Marxist science of society and history for false religion and glib moralism can liberate humankind, but rather that a Marxist social and historical analysis can more effectively guide transformative human praxis motivated, in part, by moral and/or religious norms of human freedom and democracy.

This more nuanced understanding of religion has rarely surfaced in the Marxist tradition, primarily owing to the early Eurocentric development of Marxism. In Europe—where the Enlightenment ethos remained (and still remains) hegemonic among intellectuals and the literate middle classes—secular sensibilities were nearly prerequisite for progressive outlooks, and religious beliefs usually a sign of political reaction. The peculiar expression of critical consciousness in Europe focused on a corrupt and oppressive feudal order which the institutional church participated in, firmly supported, and buttressed. And though the advent of Marxism itself bears traces of this Enlightenment legacy, the deep sense of historical consciousness nurtured and promoted by Marx and Engels led them to understand religious beliefs as first and foremost cultural practices generated from conflictual and contradictory socioeconomic conditions, rather than as ahistorical sets of philosophical arguments. Of course, Kant, Fichte, and especially Hegel and Feuerbach contributed to such an understanding.

The Marxism of the Second International—with its diverse forms of economic determinism, Kantian moralism, and even left social Darwinism—viewed cultural and religious issues in a crude and reductionist manner. Karl Kautsky's monumental work *The Foundations of Christianity* (1908) is an exemplary text in this regard. The major antireductionist voices in this deterministic wilderness were those of the Italian Marxist Antonio Labriola and the Irish Marxist James Connolly. Lenin and Trotsky indeed undermined the crudity and reductionism of the Second International, but they confined their efforts to the realms of politics and the arts. Neither provided serious and sustained antireductionist formulations in regard to ethics and religion. In fact, the Third International remained quite reductionist on such matters.

The centrality of morality and religion loom large in the works of Antonio Gramsci. For the first time, a major European Marxist took with utter seriousness the cultural life-worlds of the oppressed. Though still tied to a rationalist psychology which neglected unconscious impulses, and a revolutionary teleology which uncritically privileged industrial working-class agency, Gramsci highlighted the heterogeneous elements which comprise the cultural ways of life of oppressed people and the fragile, ever-changing character of these elements in response to contradictory socioeconomic circumstances.

Gramsci understood culture as a crucial component of class capacity. Like James Connolly before him and Raymond Williams in our own time, Gramsci examined the ways in which cultural resources enabled (and disenabled) political struggle among the exploited and excluded in capitalist societies. While Lukács disclosed the reified character of contemporary capitalist culture—the way in which processes of commodification and thingification permeate bourgeois thought, art, and perception—Gramsci focused on the cultural means by which workers and peasants resisted such reification. While Karl Korsch enunciated his principle of historical specificity—the need to acknowledge the materiality of ideology and the diversity of conflicting social forces in a particular historical moment—Gramsci applied this principle and specified the nature of these conflicting social forces with his complex notions of hegemony and historical blocs.

Ironically, the major figures of so-called Western Marxism were preoccupied with culture—but none was materialist enough to take religion seriously. Whether it was Adorno and Marcuse on the subversive character of highbrow music and poetry, Sartre and Althusser on the

15

progressive possibilities of avant-garde prose and theater, or Benjamin and Bakhtin on the revolutionary potential of film and the novel—all rightly viewed the cultural sphere as a domain of ideological contestation. Yet none highlighted religion as a crucial component of this cultural sphere.

It is important to note that it has been primarily third world Marxists—for whom issues of praxis and strategy loom large—who have confronted the religious component of culture in a serious way. Peru's José Carlos Mariátegui, China's Mao Tse-tung, and Guinea-Bissau's Amilcar Cabral were trailblazers on such matters. All three shunned the reductionism of the Second International, eschewed the excessive hostility toward religion of the Third International, and transcended the Enlightenment prejudices of the Western Marxists. Mariátegui, Mao, and Cabral—whose cultural concerns inspire black Marxists, feminist Marxists, gay and lesbian Marxists in the first world—recovered and refined the classical Marxist insights regarding the materiality and ambiguity, the relative autonomy and empowering possibilities of cultural and religious practices by grasping the existential and experiential content of such practices under capitalist conditions. In our own time, such Marxist historians as Christopher Hill and E. P. Thompson in England, W. E. B. Du Bois and Eugene Genovese in the United States, Marc Bloch and Henri Lefèbvre in France, Manning Clarke in Australia, and Enrique Dussel in Mexico have begun to come to terms with the complex relation of religious practices to political struggle. In other words, the age of crude Marxist reductionist treatments of religion—along with the European secular condescending attitudes which undergird them—is passing. Concrete social and detailed historical analyses of the relation of religion to revolutionary praxis is now a major issue on the agenda for contemporary Marxism.

Religion and Marxist Politics

The fundamental challenge of religion for Marxist politics is how we should understand religious practices as specific forms of popular opposition and/or subordination in capitalist societies. Recent religious upsurges around the world—in postindustrial, industrial, and preindustrial capitalist countries—call into question bourgeois theories of secularization and crude Marxist theories of modernization. The world-historical social processes of rationalization, commodification, and bureaucratization have generated neither a widespread "disenchantment with the world," a "polar night of icy hardness and darkness," nor a revolution-

ary class consciousness among industrial workers. Instead, we have witnessed intense revivals of nationalism, ethnicity, and religion. Modern
capitalist processes indeed have transformed traditional religious worldviews, intimate *Gemeinschaft*-like arrangements, and customary social
bonds; but these processes have not eliminated the need and yearning
for such worldviews, arrangements, and bonds. Recent nationalist,
ethnic, and religious revivals constitute new forms of these worldviews,
arrangements, and bonds, with existential intensity and ideological fervor.

There are three basic reasons for this. First, the culture of capitalist
societies has, for the most part, failed to give existential moorings and
emotional assurance to their inhabitants. The capitalist culture of consumption—with its atomistic individualism, spectatorial passivity, and
outlooks of therapeutic release—does not provide meaningful sustenance for large numbers of people. So in first world countries, religious responses—often in nostalgic forms but also in utopian ones—
are widespread. Given the relative lack of long-standing ties or
traditional links to a religious past, these responses are intertwined with
the prevailing myths of European modernity: nationalism, racism, anti-
Semitism, sexism, anti-Orientalism, and homophobia. This is why religious (as well as nationalist and ethnic) revivals are usually dangerous—
though they also can be occasions of progressive opportunity. Such
opportunity is significant in that religious impulses are one of the few resources for a moral and political commitment beyond the self in the capitalist culture of consumption. These impulses often require commitments to neighbor, community, and unknown others—though such
commitments are ideologically circumscribed.

The second reason religious revivals emerge is that they constitute
popular responses to intense capitalist domination of more traditional
societies. This is especially so in third world countries in which the cultural forms are either indigenous or colonial and the capital is primarily
external or international. The boom-town character of industrialization,
urbanization, and proletarianization demands that cultural ways of life,
usually religious, provide strategies for new personal meaning, social adjustment, and political struggle.

The emergence of the most important third world development in religious practices—the liberation theology movement—consists of such
strategies of new personal meaning, social adjustment, and political
struggle. This movement began in Latin America primarily in response
to rapid capitalist penetration, quick yet painful industrial class formation, rampant state repression, and bloated urbanization. This response
was not only rooted in Christian thought and practice, it also flowed
from the major "free" space in these repressive regimes, the church. And

given the overwhelming Roman Catholic character of this movement—
with the monumental reforming impetus of Vatican II (1962–65) and
the ground-breaking counterhegemonic posture of the Medellín Latin
American Bishops' meeting (1968)—these new strategies became more
open to personal meanings, social adjustments, and political struggles informed by prophetic elements in the Scriptures and ecclesiastical tradition as well as progressive social and historical analyses.

Liberation theology in Latin America—embodied in the works of
Gustavo Gutiérrez, Reubem Alves, Hugo Assmann, José Miguez-
Bonino, Victorio Araya, Ernesto Cardenal, Paulo Freire, Elsa Tamez,
José Miranda, Pablo Richard, Juan Luis Segundo, Enrique Dussel,
Beatrice Couch, and others—is generated and sustained by popular re-
ligious opposition to the consolidation of capitalist social processes in
Latin America. It is, in part, an anti-imperialist Christian mode of
thought and action. Similar liberation theology outlooks—with their
own contextual colorings—are found in Africa (especially South Africa),
Asia (especially the Philippines and South Korea), the Caribbean (especially Jamaica), and the United States (especially among blacks and feminists). Yet in terms of widespread concrete praxis, none yet rivals that of
Latin America.

The last reason such religious revivals emerge is that they constitute
anti-Western forms of popular resistance to capitalist domination. This is
especially so in those third world countries (or pockets in the first world,
as with indigenous peoples) in which a distinct cultural and religious
way of life still has potency and vitality compared to Western modes of
religion. For example, in the Middle East and parts of Asia and Africa,
Islam, Buddhism, Hinduism, or traditional religions still have substance
and life. Hence these religions serve as cultural sources against not simply Western imperialism but also much of Western civilization—especially Western self-images, values, and sensibilities. Such resistance, like
all forms of resistance, can be restorative and reactionary (as in Iran) or
progressive and prophetic (as among many Palestinians).

In short the religious revivals, along with nationalistic and ethnic ones,
fundamentally result from the inability of capitalist civilization to provide contexts and communities wherein meaning and value can be found
to sustain people through the traumas of life. And since there can be no
potent morality without such contexts and communities, these religious
revivals represent an ethical challenge to Marxism. Instead of the promised autonomy and progress of the European Enlightenment, the modern West has bequeathed to the world—besides ingenious technological
innovations, personal liberties for some, and comfortable living for the
few—mere fragments and ruins of a decaying and declining civilization.
This decay and decline owes much to the captivity of its ways of life to

class exploitation, patriarchy, racism, homophobia, technocratic rationality, and the quest for military might. Of course, many of these remarks—and even more so in the realm of personal liberties—can be made of "actually existing socialist" civilization. But our focus here is the capitalist world. And as this capitalist world continues its deterioration, religious revivals will more than likely persist. The great question is: Will such revivals enable or disenable the left in its struggle for human freedom and democracy?

Religion and Marxist Strategy

Religious upsurges in the third world (and second world, as in Poland) may quite clearly contribute to the building of a left movement. As we have seen in Latin America—where over two hundred thousand base Christian communities exist as concrete praxis-centers for social change, communal support, and personal sustenance—and parts of Africa and Asia, religion plays an important role in liberation struggles. The prophetic church in Nicaragua, with its tensions (both healthy and unhealthy) with the state, is the best recent example of this crucial role.

The major contribution religious revivals can make to left strategy is to demand that Marxist thinkers and activists take seriously the culture of the oppressed. This fundamental shift in the sensibilities and attitudes of Marxists requires a kind of desecularizing and de-Europeanizing of Marxist praxis, a kind of laying bare and discarding of the deep-seeded Enlightenment prejudices that shape and mold the perspectives and perceptions of most Marxists. This shift does not demand a softening of critical consciousness but rather a deepening of it. It does not result in an antiscience stance but rather in antiscientism (the idolizing of science). It does not yield an antitechnology viewpoint but rather an antitechnologism. Nor does it produce a rejection of reason but rather a specifying of liberating forms of rationality.

Such a shift is necessary because after over a century of heralding the cause of the liberation of oppressed peoples, Marxists have little understanding and appreciation of the culture of these people. This means that though Marxists have sometimes viewed oppressed people as political or economic agents, they have rarely viewed them as *cultural* agents. Yet without such a view there can be no adequate conception of the capacity of oppressed people—the capacity to change the world and sustain the change in an emancipatory manner. And without a conception of such capacity, it is impossible to envision, let alone create, a socialist society of freedom and democracy. It is, in part, the European Enlightenment legacy—the inability to believe in the capacities of oppressed people to create cultural products of value and oppositional groups of value—which stands between contemporary Marxism and oppressed people. And it is the arrogance of this legacy, the snobbery of this tradition, which precludes Marxists from taking seriously religion, a crucial element of the culture of the oppressed.

Needless to say, shedding the worst of the Enlightenment legacy does not entail neglecting the best of this European tradition. Relentless criticism and historical consciousness remain the crucial ingredients of any acceptable emancipatory vision—just as protracted class struggle and an allegiance to socialist democracy remain indispensable features of any recognizable Marxism. So the call for an overcoming of European bourgeois attitudes of paternalism toward religion does not mean adopting religious viewpoints. Religious affiliation is neither the mark of ignorance nor of intelligence. Yet it is the mark of wisdom to understand the conditions under which people do or do not have religious affiliation. In this sense, science neither solves nor dissolves the issue of religious beliefs. Instead history provides us with traditions against which we must struggle yet in which we must critically abide. The grand quest for truth is a thoroughly historical one which takes the form of practical judgments inseparable from value judgments upon, and social analytical understandings of, prevailing socioeconomic realities. There indeed are standards of adjudication, but such historically constituted standards include multiple viewpoints worthy of adoption. Hence, the quest for truth continues with only human practice providing provisional closure.

If Marxists are to go beyond European bourgeois attitudes toward the culture of the oppressed, without idealizing or romanticizing these cultures, it is necessary to transcend a hermeneutics of suspicion and engage in hermeneutical combat. In other words, Marxists must not simply enact *negative* forms of subversive demystification (and, God forbid, more bourgeois forms of deconstruction!), but also *positive* forms of popular revolutionary construction of new personal meanings, social adjustments, and political struggles for human freedom and democracy. These new forms can emerge only after traversing, transforming, and building upon the crucial spheres in society—religion, family, labor process, state apparatuses—in order to consolidate and unite multiple organizational groupings for fundamental social change.

So to take seriously the culture of the oppressed is not to privilege religion, but to enhance and enrich the faltering and neglected utopian dimension of left theory and praxis. It is to believe not simply in the potential of oppressed peoples but also to believe that oppressed people have already expressed some of this potential in their actual products, their actual practices. To be a person of the left is not only to envision and fight for a radically free and democratic society; it is also to see this society-in-the-making as manifest in the abilities and capacities of flesh-and-blood people in their struggles under conflictual and contradictory socio-economic conditions not of their own choosing. This is the fundamental message regarding the relation of religious practices to a revolutionary praxis beyond capitalist civilization.

Religion, Politics, Language

The relation of religion to politics is now at center stage in American public discourse. I find this phenomenon both salutary and frightening. It is salutary in that the role of religious faith and ecclesial institutions in public life has been unduly neglected. What is frightening is the ideological narrowness and intellectual naiveté on display in the discussion.

The discourse has been dominated by mainstream democrats and republicans, establishmentarian Catholics and Protestants. For the most part, the quality of discussion has been low and its purpose transparently manipulative. What has been more striking to me, however, is the awkward and equivocal stances put forward by the interlocutors. All seem to speak out of both sides of their mouths.

Ronald Reagan, the Hollywood religionist, fans and fuels dogmatic Christian incursion into politics, yet guards against wholesale examination of his own slack church attendance, personal habits, and familial relations. Walter Mondale, the preacher's kid, presents himself as pious and diplomatic, while diluting religious faith to privatistic sentiments and weekly practices. George Bush, the whimsical Yale product, defers to the cantankerous religious constituency by uncomfortably reversing many of his earlier positions. Geraldine Ferraro, the Italian Catholic posing as a feminist and undergoing fierce media assault, governmental harassment, and ecclesial attack, claims loyalties to a fair press, trustworthy government, and authentic church. Mario Cuomo, the elected official turned public intellectual, reconciles Catholic dogma and prevailing practices by appeals to common consensus, thereby reducing the function of religion from that of thermostat to mere thermometer. Lastly, the Roman Catholic hierarchy—present-day hierophants confronting issues of public concern on a highly selective basis—appear to speak boldly and clearly to the nation. But their lay parishioners continue to engage in practices their bishops condemn—with little change in sight. In short, there is much hypocrisy and hot air in this hyperbolic discourse about religion and politics.

Ironically, the black church experience is often invoked as an example of the religion/politics fusion, but rarely as a source to listen to or learn from. Instead, it is simply viewed as an instance that confirms the particular claims put forward by the respective sides. The black experience may

From *Christianity and Crisis* (Oct. 15, 1984).

no longer be invisible, but it remains unheard—not allowed to speak for itself, to be taken seriously as having something valuable to say.

The position of the prophetic black church—exemplified by Martin Luther King, Jr., and Jesse Jackson—is a complex one. First, like the Moral Majority, it affirms that the Christian faith mandates a public and political presence in society—though it differs greatly from the followers of Jerry Falwell with regard to what kind of presence this should be. Hence the prophetic black church unequivocally rejects the privatistic conceptions of Christian faith found in the views of Mondale, Ferraro, and Cuomo. Unlike the Moral Majority, the prophetic black church holds that Christian intervention into the public arena must speak the common moral language of the society as a whole: namely, the language of rights.

This is so because the crucial doctrine of the separation of church and state is precious for the prophetic black church. As a people for whom, for more than a century, it was a legal *crime*—punishable by torture and even death—to worship God together without white supervision, freedom of religion is a serious existential matter. And as a people who disproportionately opted for the Baptist and Methodist denominations—both religious dissenting groups with deep roots in the notion of religious liberty—freedom of religion is a crucial theological matter.

Adoption of the language of rights as the medium for moral discourse in modern nations had the effect of secularizing discussion and thereby cooling the heated, often violent exchanges between people whose rights in general were either unacknowledged, denied, or flagrantly violated. Like the Huguenots in Catholic France, black Christians have been forced to employ a mode of moral discourse through which they could make their plight understood in terms the rest of the nation could grasp. Unlike the Huguenots, black Christians found a language of rights already in place. The problem became that of extending and enriching this language by deepening its moral basis and enlarging its legal scope. It is no accident that the U.S. Constitution and the Declaration of Independence (as opposed to the Bible) have served as the major resources for appeals against injustice by evangelical black church–led protest movements.

Rights Include, Dogmas Divide

These movements have avoided calls for a "Christian nation" to live up to its religious creeds or for authoritarian imposition of "Christian" values upon non-Christians in the public sphere, steps leading inevitably

23

to the trivialization of religious faith. Cognizant of the brute fact that the only modern nation to constitutionally designate itself a "Christian nation" was (and is) the Republic of South Africa, prophetic black Christians have understood the xenophobic substance of the designation. And given the realities of persecution experienced by American Catholics, Jews, socialists, communists, anarchists, and atheists, prophetic black Christians could identify with their plight.

Contrary to widespread myths regarding the civil rights movement, black Christian leaders did not call for an authoritarian imposition of "Christian" values upon a recalcitrant racist South. Rather, these Christians, motivated by their religious values, struggled through legal and political channels to reinterpret the law of the land. This radical reinterpretation called for the acknowledgment of black people as citizens with rights in America. In stark contrast to proposed constitutional amendments regarding abortion and prayer in public schools which produce new victims (women, especially poor women, and non-Christians), the civil rights movement promoted new laws to empower victims. Furthermore, the Moral Majority employs the divisive language of "Christians vs. Others" (e.g., modernists, pagans, homosexuals, etc.), whereas prophetic black Christians used the language of rights and common good. Of course, some argue that the civil rights movement produced victims. But to compare violating property rights of restaurant owners with violating reproductive rights of over half the country's citizens is ludicrous.

Although prophetic black Christians shunned religious language to couch their public concerns, they refused to trivialize their Christian faith by relegating it to mere private affairs. Instead they knew that their role as public Christians in a pluralistic capitalist democracy required a language of rights that permitted and protected other life-styles as well as their own. Far better than the most visible interlocutors in the present public conversation, prophetic black Christians have understood that to be religious, especially Christian, is to be political; and to be political in modern nations is to be moralistic in rhetoric, legalistic in impact. And the empowerment of the downtrodden has been at the center of their vision. Unfortunately, most prophetic black Christians still employ an inadequate social analysis of power, wealth, and influence in American capitalist society, but this shortcoming requires but one step forward, whereas the prevailing public dialogue is two steps backward.

On Michael Harrington's
The Politics at God's Funeral

Michael Harrington is the socialist evangelist of our time. He is the bearer of the mantles of Eugene Debs and Norman Thomas. Unlike Debs and Thomas, Harrington is a serious intellectual. His first book, *The Other America* (1962)—aided by Dwight Macdonald's famous review in the *New Yorker*—prompted the Kennedy administration's campaign against poverty. His works *Socialism* (1972) and *The Twilight of Capitalism* (1976) are insightful, though far from original, texts on the history of Western socialist movements and contemporary analyses of capitalist societies. Harrington's most ambitious works, *The Accidental Century* (1965) and, now, *The Politics at God's Funeral,* take the prevailing crisis of Western civilization as their point of departure and put forward a vision of a new order.

Harrington's vision is, in part, anchored in his Irish Catholic roots. Though an atheist, he remains obsessed with what he perceives as the disappearance of God and the decline in community. Harrington is a Pascalian Marxist who wagers on the ability and capacity of men and women to create a democratic and libertarian socialist future. This perspective permits Harrington to sidestep the scientism of elitist Leninists, the rigid pseudo-Marxism of the authoritarian USSR, and the diluted Marxism of social democrats. Harrington is a Marxist in the American grain: experimental in method, moral in motivation, and optimistic in outlook. Like Emerson, Whitman, and Dewey, he believes in the possibility of social betterment by means of creative intelligence, moral suasion, and political struggle. Yet his Marxism is of an orthodox variety: he considers the working class to be the major agent of fundamental social change. Unlike American new left thinkers, such as C. Wright Mills and Herbert Marcuse, who said farewell to the proletariat decades ago, Harrington remains tied to the (waning) progressive wing of the labor movement and, therefore, continues to subordinate cultural and social concerns to economic issues.

In *The Politics at God's Funeral,* Harrington focuses on the political consequences of what he calls the disappearance of God in the West. For Harrington this disappearance is neither the historical decline of belief

From *Christianity and Crisis* (Dec. 12, 1983); review of Michael Harrington, *The Politics at God's Funeral* (New York: Holt, Rinehart & Winston, 1983).

in God nor the absence of metaphysical grounds for this belief; rather it is the inability of the Judeo-Christian God to serve as the major source for the normative integration of Western civilization. Harrington devotes the central sections of the book to examining this disintegration in influence. In a competent though predictable manner, he charts his journey from Kant's reduction of God to a postulate of morality, through Marx's attack on all gods as a precondition for human emancipation, to Nietzsche's catastrophic atheism. On the religious front, Harrington reviews Schleiermacher's dilution of religion to a particular feeling of absolute dependence, Kierkegaard's relegation of religion to private decision, and Barth's *Deus absconditus* as tacit theological acknowledgments of the inability of Christianity to serve as the major force for the "normative integration of Western civilization," that is, as the conceptual and cultural source of one's view of the self, society, world, and God which holds communities together.

Harrington propounds a *normative* version of the secularization thesis which claims not that religious beliefs are fading away and secular humanism looms large, but rather that religious beliefs (whether increasing or decreasing) *ought* to play a secondary role in determining how we organize our society and culture. On the surface, this claim may be disturbing to devout Christians and religious thinkers; but upon further reflection, it is nothing but the Huguenots' proposal for resolving political and religious disagreements—better known as the secularization of public discourse. This proposal to decenter authoritarian religious belief-systems and thereby create a public sphere for civil dialogue and discourse is not only desirable but indispensable for pluralistic societies and cultures that include irreconcilable religious creeds and clashing ideologies. Therefore, Harrington's normative version of the secularization thesis is the least controversial claim in the book.

What is disturbing is Harrington's move from this normative claim to descriptive ones concerning the de facto atheism—the hedonistic individualism and aimless amorality—of contemporary capitalist societies. This move is disturbing not because Harrington is descriptively wrong, but rather because he does not provide a full account of why so much of late capitalist culture is vapid and sterile. Instead of a sustained historical analysis of the emergence and development of the culture of consumption, we are given a stimulating yet inadequate intellectual history of the modern masters of Western thought. Needless to say, the de facto atheism Harrington rightly identifies has more to do with radio, television, motion pictures, the automobile, and credit cards than with the profound ruminations of Kierkegaard, Nietzsche, and Barth. In other words, just when a Marxist analysis would be helpful, Harrington opts for idealistic history-telling.

26

This refusal to explain the origins and presence of late capitalist culture precludes Harrington from making the subtle connection between the desirable secularization of public discourse and the undesirable commodification of modern culture. The secularization of public discourse indeed prevented large-scale religiously motivated bloodshed, but it left us with no overarching conception of the common good or public interest. This vacuum was filled with decrepit nationalisms shot through with corporate interests and popular demands. And as economic growth escalated, even nationalism could not contain the instability and upheaval generated by economic inequality, social disparity, and cultural degradation. The commodification of culture—with its outlook of therapeutic release through consumption—yielded a new mode of legitimating the capitalist order. Hence the de facto atheism Harrington denounces is an effect, albeit an unintended one, of the secularization process he cherishes.

The conservative response to the commodification of culture, especially with regard to sexuality and education, is to attack the secularization process itself. But this attack is both foolhardy and dishonest: foolhardy because it attempts to reverse the Huguenot resolution of religious disagreement and thereby impose religious values on others in an authoritarian fashion; dishonest in that it surreptitiously revels in the culture of consumption (often offering it as the prosperity God promises for the elect) and partly survives owing to the manipulative orientation of its managerial ethos (e.g., religion as packaged commodity and liturgy as dramatic television commercial).

The liberal response is to accept the commodification of culture and attempt to find some kind of authentic human existence within it. This response is naive and self-defeating. It is naive because it refuses to see this cultural process as a modern structure of domination and hence wrongly equates it with "progress." It is self-defeating in that it manages only to tease out of this culture some semblance of authenticity within a process that parades a new "style" of authenticity for each succeeding market-season.

To his credit, Harrington chooses neither the conservative nor the liberal response. This is so because he is aware of the basic challenge of the culture of consumption: the eclipse of utopian energies in the West; that is, the eclipse of the very conditions for the possibility of prophetic vision and progressive practice, and specifically the collapse of morality and lack of concern for ethical values. Therefore, almost out of sheer desperation, Harrington calls for a united front of progressive secular humanists and prophetic religious people to keep alive utopian visions and ethical values—to preserve internationalism and egalitarianism in the West.

This ambitious project rests upon the "hope that the values of Judeo-Christianity will indeed survive the dying of God—*but not in religious form.*" For Harrington, these values consist primarily of a deep hatred of oppression and exploitation and engaged compassion for the wretched of the earth. So he strongly endorses the first world liberation theologies of Jurgen Moltmann (whom Harrington wrongly dubs a Catholic), Johann Metz, and Dorothee Sölle, who put forward "a political-spiritual project for all of Western society," though these religious communitarian visions must unite with similar secular humanist movements.

Harrington's project is global in scope yet Western in focus. He does not deal with the energizing emancipatory visions of either third world liberation theologies or first world black and feminist liberation theologies. This is so principally because he deliberately confines his analysis to the spiritual crisis of first world middle-strata people in late capitalist societies. This self-limitation is permissible since it includes most people in the U.S. (at least in self-perception and behavior) and a significant segment of Europe. Yet it also is blinding. A more international perspective would have led him to place less emphasis on spiritual sterility and hedonistic fanfare and more on spiritual awakening and oppositional religious practice. Such awakenings and practices are often dangerous, as with politicized Muslims in Iran or orthodox Judaic sects in Israel. But they can also be quite promising, as with the basic Christian communities in Chile.

Harrington's book is challenging and courageous. Its spiritually concerned socialist vision is admirable and attractive. This book signifies an American Marxism-coming-of-age in its genuine effort to speak to the realities of spiritual malaise and to engage in dialogue with religious thinkers on contemporary emancipatory possibilities in the West. The deepening of this dialogue in itself is a sign of hope. Yet ultimately the book falls short of the mark. On the practical front, it remains a voice crying in the wilderness, reluctant to take seriously the enormous obstacles that confront its political projects; this makes it vulnerable to cheap shots from the overconfident right. More pointedly, Harrington's rhetoric and vision seem slightly anachronistic. This is so not because Marxist analysis and socialist politics are irrelevant, but rather because they are not relevant enough to our postmodern realities.

An Incomplete Vision

The major point here is not simply that Marxism and socialism are contaminated with popular images of the repressive regime in the USSR or the crushing of a democratic movement in Poland. More importantly, neither Marxism nor socialism encompass the emancipatory visions and practices of the most visible and salient movements in the U.S. and Western Europe, movements that evolve around the issues of nature, race, gender, sexuality, and peace. Marxist analyses of late capitalist societies remain insightful, yet these societies render old-style socialist movements innocuous and outdated. In fact, to believe that the working class is the central agent of social change in late capitalist societies is equivalent to believing that Christianity can be the integrating force in the West: both claims bespeak noble though nostalgic visions.

This does not mean that socialism is politically and morally bankrupt, but rather that even democratic and libertarian socialism provides an incomplete social vision, at once indispensable and inadequate. It is indispensable because the attempt to uphold and extend the democratic ideal into crucial service-oriented and corporate-dominated spheres of the economy should be an essential element of any acceptable social vision. It is inadequate because even this grand ideal does not speak seriously to the complex realities of ecological imbalance, patriarchal institutions, racial and sexual freedom, and nuclear annihilation.

To put it bluntly, promoting democratic socialism as an acceptable program for late capitalist societies is like appealing to liberal theology in our postmodern times: both constitute creative projects of an era now past. Of course, both democratic socialism and liberal theology are crucial stepping-stones to new projects and have much to teach us. Yet just as experiences of dread and despair eclipsed liberal theological sensibilites, so our struggles against racism, sexism, ecological disaster, and nuclear catastrophe eclipse mere socialist sentiments. Just as Karl Barth and Reinhold Niebuhr understood that neoorthodoxy must remain in close conversation with liberal theology, so in creating a new social vision we must remain in close contact with Marx and Gramsci.

What is required now, in other words, is neither warmed-over Marxism, vulgar anti-Marxism, nor superficial post-Marxism. Rather we need a new social emancipatory vision that takes seriously Marxism, feminism, Garveyism, ecologism, and antimilitarism. There are some of us who still believe—and I think Harrington would agree—that the Christian gospel provides invaluable resources for such a vision. Yet unlike Harrington, some of us also believe that such a vision would remain a *religious* vision and retain *Christian* spirituality.

The New Populism: A Black Socialist Christian Critique

Populism is the most indigenous form of American radicalism. Therein lies its strengths and weaknesses, its paradoxes and contradictions, its amorphous character and often vacuous content. I shall argue that the contemporary versions of populism promoted by Harry Boyte, Sara Evans, Frank Riessman, and others represent creative, gallant, yet inadequate attempts to keep alive the radical tradition in America. I shall suggest that the two major ideological pillars of this country's self-definition—namely, cultural conservatism (nativism, sexism, and, above all, racism) and Lockean liberalism (the sanctity of individual rights, private property, capital accumulation, and economic growth)—strongly mitigate against neopopulism emerging as a potent radical force. This is especially so in a period of closely-knit international interdependence, national decline as a world power, and internal cultural decay. In such a period, a full-scale American populism would move much further to the right than to the left.

The strengths of populism constitute the best of the democratic tradition of a rural, preindustrial, pastoral America: local control, decentralized economic relations, small-scale political institutions, limited property ownership, and intimate, face-to-face interaction and asssociation. This important stress on local activism, politics of everyday life of ordinary people, and discernible, credible, and visible forms of peoples' empowerment is rooted in the homespun American ideologies of Jeffersonian and Jacksonian civic republicanism. It represents an oppositional yet nostalgic form of radical plebeian humanism which is antibourgeois yet not anticapitalist. To put it crudely, populists tend to want modern liberal capitalist democracy without impersonal forms of bureaucracy, centralized modes of economic and political power, and alienating kinds of cultural practices in pluralistic urban centers.

The weaknesses of populism consist of the worst of the xenophobic and jingoistic tradition of a European settler society: racism, sexism, homophobic, inward and backward-looking, preoccupied with preserving old ways of life, defensive, provincial, and, at times, conspiratorial. This seamy side of populism is grounded in the cultural conservatism of a

From Harry C. Boyte and Frank Reissman, eds., *The New Populism: The Politics of Empowerment* (Philadelphia: Temple University Press, 1986).

30

deeply isolationist people, a conservatism and isolationism reinforced by geographical autonomy, economic prosperity, and cultural insularity. Yet it is this side of populism which looms large in the eyes of Afro-Americans.

A central paradox of American populism is that it invests great confidence in the goodwill of the American people. Yet, from a black perspective, it has been primarily when the federal courts and government has "imposed" its laws upon the American people that there has been some black progress. It is important to note that the two major public acts associated with black progress—the Emancipation Proclamation (1863) and the *Brown v. Board of Education* case (1954)—were far removed from the collective will of the American people. In fact, Congress would not have passed either if consulted and both would have lost in a national referendum.

Another paradox of American populism is that its attractive theme of empowerment rarely is inclusive enough to take black interests seriously. This is so not solely because of the racist sentiments of populist activists but, more importantly, because these activists must pursue their many goals within the American political system which forces populists to prioritize their goals and demands. Given this political context of limited options, populists (even those with the least racist sensibilities!) tend to sacrifice the interests of minorities to that of the majority. The strange career of Tom Watson—from left populist to the Ku Klux Klan—is exemplary in this regard. And less dramatic examples dot the landscape of American history. I do not deny that black interests overlap with the interests of other powerless people. But I do hold that there are specifically black concerns (e.g., lynching at the turn of the century, police brutality in our own time) which are not identical with the concerns of powerless nonblacks in America.

The dominant ideology of American populism is highly contradictory. On the one hand, it is opposed to Big Business, Big Government and Big Labor. This opposition is put forward in the name of decentralized control and steep declines in the quality of life. On the other hand, populism is locked into the mainstream American quest for economic growth in order for more Americans to get in on the high standard of living in the country. Yet this growth presupposes the high levels of productivity and efficiency of Big Business, Big Government, and Big Labor. And given the deeply American character of populists, most would more than likely opt for a higher standard of living with bigness and the concomitant maldistribution of wealth over a lower standard (yet possibly higher quality) of living with the decentralization they cherish. Needless to say, such a preference reveals the class composition of most American populists: middle class and stable working class.

The new populists intend to focus their message more and more on the minorities—the poor, women, gays and lesbians, and labor. But such culturally heterogeneous constituencies would only create even more contradictions—especially given the cultural conservatism of most American populists. As a black democratic socialist I welcome and support such a focus. Yet I believe that an honest effort in this direction will undermine the basic assumptions of populism: namely, relative cultural homogeneity and persistent economic growth of the U.S. capitalist economy. To take seriously the plight of the above constituencies means accenting and promoting, not simply acknowledging and tolerating, vast cultural differences and calling into question the conditions under which U.S. capitalist growth persists. This latter issue shifts the weight from populist concerns about consumption of goods and services to more socialist concerns about production and distribution of wealth. To question the growth of the capitalist pie is not to promote less consumption but rather to focus on how it gets baked in the first place and who more disproportionately benefits behind the mask of economic growth.

This issue of economic growth in populist ideology leads us to its major blinder: the international character of the U.S. capitalist economy. In the past, American populism has supported the most vicious forms of U.S. imperialism. The new populism remains quite vague on its foreign policy pronouncements. Yet U.S. involvement in Latin America, Africa, Asia, and Europe are not simply matters of geopolitical and ideological concern. They also relate, in complex ways, to whether U.S. economic growth can be sustained.

Furthermore, the nature of these involvements shapes the perceptions of the potential populist constituencies in various ways—such as the impact of the Middle East conflict on Jews and Arabs in America, Ireland on labor (especially its leadership), Africa for black people, Philippines and South Korea on Asians, Chile and Nicaragua on Hispanics. Again, the cultural conservatism—especially the uncritical nativism and naive patriotism—of most U.S. populists does not allow dealing candidly with the devastating critiques of U.S. past and present practices in much of the world. And to take seriously such critiques may result in the loss of a significant number of the original neopopulist constituencies. Yet these international issues cannot be avoided or downplayed.

These potential troubles partly account for the amorphous character of U.S. populist movements. The passionate promotion of localism shuns sustained international and national considerations such as foreign policy, the role of the state, and bureaucracies. The imprecise message of decentralization tends to overlook crucial issues of productivity, efficiency, and the inescapable presence of some forms of centralization and bigness. Lastly, the slippery conception of democracy indeed serves as a desirable standard to criticize present societal realities, but it remains unclear what positive and constructive content it possesses.

For those of us from black America, symbolically and sometimes literally on the outside looking in, this amorphous character and often vacuous content represents the agonized conscience of the liberal white middle class and stable working class upset with their tenuous and uncertain niches in the corporate-dominated U.S. economy, an unresponsive conservative U.S. government, and a disintegrating U.S. culture. On the one hand, this agonized conscience is to be supported and encouraged for it may lead to more fundamental issues such as organized attacks on class inequality, patriarchy (in the private and public spheres), and institutionalized racism. On the other hand, these fundamental issues which speak more directly to the needs of the black working poor and underclass would scatter the liberal white middle class and stable working class—and thereby leave the populist space to be filled by xenophobic demagogues.

This is the basic dilemma of the relation of populism to black America. And the black instincts of survival tend to lead toward deep suspicion of a movement with such negative potential. Of course, white instincts of survival tend to do the same—as seen in the white distance from the Jackson campaign partly owing to Minister Louis Farrakhan's anti-Semitic demagogery.

With the absence of a potent leftist tradition and social presence, the black political class, for the most part, remains locked into a self-serving liberalism—a liberalism increasingly under attack from the right in both the Republican and Democratic parties. Black conservatives, be they intellectuals supported by right-wing thinktanks or preachers associated with Jerry Falwell's Moral Majority—are trying to take advantage of the vacuum created by the relative lack of organized black radicalism and the crisis of liberalism. Yet right-wing populism has little chance of broad success in black America, despite pervasive black conservative convictions regarding abortion and gay/lesbian life-styles. This is so because right-wing populism's close association with racism is simply undeniable.

What then is an appropriate black attitude toward the new populism? In light of the highly limited progressive alternatives on the political scene, neopopulists should be supported in their attacks on corporate power and encouraged in their defenses of human rights of downtrodden people here and abroad. They are to be congratulated in their attempts to take culture seriously as a ground for local political activism. But the widespread cultural conservatism in the neopopulist movement must be opposed. Black progressive people should resist the sexism in American families, the racism and patriarchalism in American churches, the pseudoreligiosity creeping into our schools, and the exclusivism in our neighborhoods. The political struggle over cultural ways of life should be waged under the ideals of pluralistic self-determination and self-realization through diversity. Lastly, black activists within and outside the neopopulist movement must highlight the age-old American problems of racism and U.S. intervention in third world countries. No matter how tired white Americans become regarding white and American supremacist practices here and around the world, it is the responsibility of black progressives to admonish each emerging wave of American radicalism that racism and ethnocentrism must be resisted in their old as well as new forms.

Winter in Afro-America

There is an artic chill across the country, especially in those urban centers and rural pockets inhabited by people of African descent. It is often said that when America sneezes, Afro-America catches a cold, and when America catches a cold, Afro-America catches pneumonia. Even the moderately liberal magazine *Black Enterprise* (Jan. 1984) concluded in its first annual economic survey that black America is in a state of deep crisis; hence, "business as usual" is no longer acceptable.

The crisis in Afro-America is threefold. First, the black community is undergoing profound *economic* crisis which most visibly takes the form of unprecedented levels of unemployment, new cutbacks and speedups for industrial workers, and persistent career ceilings for professional employees. Second, Afro-Americans are facing a *political* crisis that demands redefining relations with the Democratic party. Third, black people are experiencing a pervasive *spiritual* crisis as mutual distrust among blacks intensifies and the incidence of black suicides and homicides rises. In short, Afro-America is at a crossroads.

The economic crisis in Afro-America is an effect of the international crisis of capitalism. This crisis primarily consists of a falling rate of profit for U.S. multinational corporations, an increasing maldistribution of wealth, an expanding centralization of political power, and the consolidation of subtle cultural and repressive legal mechanisms of control. Under such conditions, class inequality deepens, racist and sexist policies intensify, and interventionist ventures abroad thrive. The Reagan program of reconstituting U.S. capitalism, supported by repressive cultural sensibilities and antidemocratic political restructuring, has one basic thrust: vicious attacks and assaults on the fragile gains of working people and poor people. These attacks and assaults are disproportionately targeted at people of color, especially black women and children.

The political crisis in the black community is manifest in its captivity to the Democratic party. The refusal of black politicians to explore outside the Democratic party new forms of political empowerment has produced paralysis and powerlessness among black voters. Black captivity to the Democratic party results from black captivity to liberalism. The break from prevailing forms of paralysis and powerlessness must begin with a break from liberalism. Fortunately, there are signs that some black

From *Christianity and Crisis* (Jan. 23, 1984).

leaders are ready for such a break. The election of Harold Washington as mayor of Chicago revealed the limitations of reliance on the Democratic party and the strengths of community mobilizing and organizing. The presidential candidacy of the Rev. Jesse Jackson may point in a similar direction, if he is willing to go beyond liberalism and thereby challenge the democrats. With the election of Washington and the vast registration drives of the NAACP, PUSH, and various churches, political momentum is gaining.

The spiritual crisis in Afro-America results principally from new class and strata divisions, the impact of mass culture, and the invasion of drugs in the black community. The slow but sure polarization among the growing black middle class, the working poor, and the underclass creates immense problems of black communication and organization. These problems have spiritual consequences in that distrust and disrespect for one another are rising among blacks, producing widespread frustration and cynicism.

The impact of mass culture, especially through radio and television, has diminished the influence of the family and church. Among large numbers of black youth, it is black music that serves as the central influence regarding values and sensibilities. Since little of this music is spiritually inspiring, black people have fewer and fewer spiritual resources to serve them in periods of crisis. With the invasion of drugs in the black community, a new subculture among black youth has emerged which thrives on criminal behavior and survives on hopelessness. The black rap music of Grandmaster Flash and the Furious Five's "The Message" and "New York, New York" makes this point quite clear. For the first time in Afro-American history, large numbers of black young people believe that nobody—neither God, Mom, nor neighbor—*cares*. This spiritual crisis cannot go unheeded; for there can be no economic empowerment or political struggle without spiritual resources.

The prophetic black church can play a crucial role in the prevailing crisis in Afro-America. First, it can move toward more sophisticated social analyses of the economic depression in Afro-America. Such analyses should highlight the corporate stranglehold on the economy which delimits the capacity of local, state, and federal governments to address the basic needs of poor people and the public interest of the populace. Second, prophetic religious people can push black politicians beyond their unthinking allegiance to the Democratic party and project a more independent black politics. Needless to say, such an independent black politics would be guided by an emancipatory vision encompassing and embracing the needs of white working and poor people, Latinos, Asians, ecologists, peace activists, anti-interventionists, and women. Third, prophetic black church persons must forge a spiritual awakening throughout the country. For too long, only conservative preachers have addressed the crucial spiritual issues of our time. The richness of the prophetic tradition of Afro-American Christianity must be recovered, as Martin Luther King, Jr., did so well, if the frosty winter in Afro-America is to be transformed into a better future.

The Prophetic Tradition
in Afro-America

Prophetic modes of thought and action are dotted across the landscape of Afro-American history. I understand these modes to consist of protracted and principled struggles against forms of personal despair, intellectual dogmatism, and socioeconomic oppression that foster communities of hope. Therefore the distinctive features of prophetic activity are Pascalian leaps of faith in the capacity of human beings to transform their circumstances, engage in relentless criticism and self-criticism, and project visions, analyses, and practices of social freedom. In this chapter I shall attempt to characterize and criticize—hence try to reactivate—the prophetic tradition in Afro-America.

The American Terrain

It is impossible to characterize adequately prophetic activity among Afro-Americans without understanding the specific circumstances under which these practices occur. So it is necessary to put forward a brief sketch of the specificity of American society and culture—highlighting the ideological, political, and economic spheres.

The most crucial brute fact about the American terrain is that the USA began as a liberal capitalist nation permeated with patriarchal oppression and based, in large part, upon a slave economy. Born modern, born liberal, and born bourgeois, the USA's relative absence of a feudal past gave way in the northern states to an agrarian utopia of free independent farmers on "free" land. In the southern states, the thriving economy of slavery underscored an aristocratic ethos and an entrepreneurial ethic. These beginnings facilitated the ideological predominance of an American-style liberalism which, on the one hand, promoted the sanctity of private property, the virtue of capital accumulation, and the subordination of women; and, on the other hand, encouraged the flowering of a slave-based society principally upon the ideological pillar of the inferiority of non-Europeans, especially Africans.

This native form of liberalism was engendered not by opposition to

From *The Drew Gateway* (winter 1984–spring 1985).

feudalism as in Europe but rather by securing property-owning white male consensus in order to maintain social stability. Motivated by notions of new beginnings, Edenic innocence, and exemplary performance, the anticolonial sentiments of the nation entailed an abiding distrust of institutional power, bureaucracy, and, above all, the state. Despite unprecedented proliferation of voluntary associations, American political discourse placed great emphasis on the welfare of propertied persons as atomistic individuals rather than as community dwellers or citizens of a republic.

This liberal ideology of Americanism embodied the ideals of bourgeois freedom (such as the freedom to own property, accumulate capital, speak one's mind, and organize to worship) and formal equality (equal treatment under the law)— circumscribed by racist, sexist, and class constraints. These ideological viewpoints indeed have undergone change over time, yet their traces strongly persist in contemporary American life. To put it crudely, most Americans even now—be they of the right or the left—are highly individualistic, libertarian, and antistatist as well as racist and sexist.

The ideals of bourgeois freedom and formal equality became a beacon to oppressed social classes and ethnic groups around the world. Widespread immigration to the USA contributed to the first ecumenical, multiethnic, and multiracial working class in the world and the most complex heterogeneous population in modernity. In addition, the boomtown character of American industrialization—urban centers which appeared virtually overnight—set the context for the flourishing of nativism, jingoism, anti-Semitism, the already entrenched sexism, and, above all, racism.

In the political sphere, the infamous "gift of suffrage" to the white male component of the working class without the need for organized proletarian organization—in fact prior to widespread industrialization hence substantive modern class formation—yielded deep allegiance of the white male populace to the existing political order. The political arrangement of coalitional politics and political machines within the framework of a two-party system channeled organizational efforts of class, race, and gender into practical interest group struggles and thereby relegated oppositional movements to either ill-fated third parties or political oblivion. Furthermore, harsh state repression has been exercised against perceived extremists who threaten the tenuous consensus which the liberal ideology of Americanism reinforces.

This ingenious political setup encourages diverse modes of interest group articulation and permits incremental social change; it also domesticates oppositional movements, dilutes credible wholesale programs of social change, and encourages sustained organizational efforts at undermining the liberal consensus. The political predicament of all prophetic practices in the USA has been and remains that of ideological purity and political irrelevance or ideological compromise and political marginality.

Extraordinary American productivity principally owing to tremendous technological innovation (motivated, in part, by labor shortages), abundant natural resources (secured by imperialist domination of indigenous and Mexican peoples), and cheap labor (usually imported from various parts of the globe) has enabled social upward mobility unknown in the modern world. The availability of goods, luxuries, and conveniences—which has made comfort an American obsession—to significant segments of the population gives the appearance of a widely fluid social structure. This perception provides credence to the Horatio Alger dimension of the liberal ideology of Americanism: the possibility of rags-to-riches success for all. Even the lower classes remain enchanted by this seductive ideological drama.

High levels of productivity, with uneven expressions across various regions of the country, have made the commitment to economic growth an unquestioned national dogma. From the far right (for whom growth is a symptom of liberty) to the sophisticated left (for whom growth makes easier redistribution), Americans remain captive to the notion of economic expansion. This dogma undergirds the consensus of American-style liberalism and thereby views *as natural necessity* the close partnership of the state, banks, and large corporations and their coordinated expansionist activities abroad—often with repressive consequences for the native populations. This partnership, along with its imperialist extension, is the linchpin of the American terrain.

On Black Prophetic Practices

These distinctively American circumstances have produced *truncated* prophetic practices, especially among Afro-Americans. Such practices—be they populist, feminist, trade-unionist, socialist, or Red, Green, and Black politics—are truncated in that they are rendered relatively impotent if they fall outside the liberal consensus and irreparably innocuous if they function within this consensus. In other words, if prophetic practices radically call into question the orthodoxy of American-style liberalism they are either repudiated or repressed; and if they accept the perimeters of this orthodoxy they are effectively domesticated and absorbed by the powers that be. This clever American way of dealing with prophetic critiques has produced a marvelously stable society; it also has reduced the capacity of this society to grow and develop. In fact, it can be said with confidence that American society is one of the few to move from innocence to corruption without a mediating stage of maturity. In short, American society has been and remains unable to face its systemic and structural problems.

A major problem perenially facing black prophetic practices is that only in brief historical moments have basic black concerns—such as institutional racism—gained a foothold in American public discourse. Hence, most black prophetic practices have had minimal impact on American society and culture. This is ironic in that a strong case can be made that black Americans are the most American of all Americans; that is, they not only cling most deeply to the ideals of Americanism as enunciated in the Declaration of Independence and the Constitution but they also are the most hybrid of Americans in blood, colors, and cultural creations.

Black prophetic practices best exemplify the truncated content and character of American prophetic practices; they reveal the strengths and shortcomings, the importance and impotence, of prophetic activities in recalcitrant America. Black prophetic practices can be generally characterized by three basic features: *a deep-seated moralism, an inescapable opportunism,* and *an aggressive pessimism.* This deep-seated moralism flows from the pervasive influence of Protestant Christianity—unmatched among other modern industrial and postindustrial nations. Afro-American prophetic practices have been and, for the most part, remain ensconced in a moralistic mood: that is, they are grounded in a moralistic conception of the world in which the rightness or wrongness of human actions—be they individually or collectively understood—are measured by ethical ideals or moral standards. Like the Puritans, the first European Americans, black prophetic Americans have tended to assume that such ideals and standards ought to make a difference in regard to how individuals act and how institutions operate. In short, black prophetic practices assume that—after the most intense scrutiny—some ultimate sense of a morally grounded sense of justice ought to prevail in personal and societal affairs.

The inescapable opportunism—or the unprincipled scrambling for crumbs—of black prophetic practices is largely a function of both the unmet needs of black Americans and, more importantly, the design and operation of the American social system. The needs of black Americans are similar to those of most Americans: more control over their lives and destinies, better living conditions, health care, education, and the extension of liberties for the effective exercise of their unique capacities and potentialities. The satisfaction of these needs are rooted in the quest for more democratic arrangements—in the political, economic, and cultural spheres—which facilitate more self-realization.

41

The design and operation of the American social system requires that this quest for democracy and self-realization be channeled into unfair competitive circumstances such that opportunistic results are unavoidable. In fact, in an ironic way, opportunistic practices become requisite to sustain the very sense of prophetic sensibilities and values in the USA. This is so primarily because deliverance is the common denominator in American society and culture—and a set of practices of whatever sort cannot be sustained or legitimated over time and space without some kind of delivery-system or some way of showing that crucial consequences and effects (such as goods and services) flow from one's project. This "delivery prerequisite" usually forces even prophetic critiques and actions to adopt opportunistic strategies and tactics in order to justify themselves to a disadvantaged and downtrodden constituency.

This situation often results in a profound pessimism among prophetic black Americans regarding the possibilities of fundamental transformation of American society and culture. The odds seem so overwhelming, the incorporative strategies of the status quo so effective—and the racism so deeply entrenched in American life. Yet most prophetic practices among black Americans have given this pessimism an aggressiveness such that it becomes sobering rather than disenabling, a stumbling block rather than a dead end, a challenge to meet rather than a conclusion to accept.

In the remainder of this discussion, I shall try to defend my general characterization of black prophetic practices by presenting persuasive interpretations of three central sets of these practices in Afro-America: prophetic black Christian practices, prophetic black womanist practices, and prophetic black socialist practices. Although I may highlight certain individuals within each set of practices, I intend to view these individuals as but embodiments of the set they best represent.

Prophetic Black Christian Practices

The institutional roots of the prophetic tradition in Afro-America lie in black churches. Although never acquiring a majority of black people within its walls, black churches have had a disproportionate amount of influence in Afro-America. These institutions were the unique products of a courageous and creative people who struggled under excruciating conditions of economic exploitation, political oppression, and cultural degradation. Owing to a lower ratio of African to European Americans—as well as laboring in smaller plantations with much less absentee ownership—than that of Latin America, black people in the USA interacted more intensely and frequently with white Americans. And with an inhumane stress on slave *reproduction*—as opposed to slave *importation* in the Caribbean and Latin America—it was more difficult for young generations of Afro-Americans to preserve their ties to African customs and rituals. It is important to keep in mind that only 4.5 percent of all Africans imported to the New World—427,000 out of 9.5 million—came to North America. In stark contrast, 3.7 million Africans were imported to Brazil, 748,000 to Jamaica, and 702,000 to Cuba.

The African appropriation of Euro-American Christianity was, in part, the result of the black encounter with the absurd; that is, an attempt to make sense out of a meaningless and senseless predicament. With the generational distancing from African culture—hence the waning of African traditional religions among the new progeny of slaves—Afro-Americans became more and more attracted to religious dissenters in American culture. White Methodists and especially white Baptists seized the imagination of many black slaves for a variety of reasons. First, black people found themselves locked into what Orlando Patterson has coined "natal alienation"; that is, the loss of ties at birth in both ascending and descending generations. Hence, they experienced a form of social death as dishonored persons with no public worth, only economic value. Dissenting Protestant Christianity provided many black slaves with a sense of somebodiness, a personal and egalitarian God who gave them an identity and dignity not found in American society. It also yielded a deep sense of the tragic—not accented in West African religions—while holding out the possibility of ultimate triumph.

The Baptist polity—adopted by a majority of black Christian slaves—provided a precious historical possession not found among other groups of oppressed black people in the New World: control over their own ecclesiastical institutions. The uncomplicated requirements for membership, open and easy access to the clergy and congregation-centered mode of church governance set the cultural context for the flowering of Africanisms, invaluable fellowship, and political discourse. In fact, this setting served as the crucible for not simply distinctive Afro-American cultural products but also for much of the unique American cultural contributions to the world—including the spirituals, blues, and jazz.

Black churches permitted and promoted the kinetic orality of Afro-Americans—the fluid and protean power of the Word in speech and song along with the rich Africanisms such as antiphonality (call-and-response), polyrhythms, syncopation, and repetition; the passionate physicality, including the bodily participation in liturgical and everyday expressions; and the combative spirituality which accents a supernatural and subversive joy, an oppositional perseverance and patience. Some of these churches served as the places where slave insurrections were planned—such as those of Gabriel Prosser, Denmark Vesey, and Nat Turner. And legal sanctions against black people worshiping God without white supervision were pervasive throughout the southern USA. In short, black churches were the major public spheres in Afro-America where strategies of survival and visions of liberation, tactics of reform and dreams of emancipation were put forward. Black Christian discourse became the predominant language wherein subversive desires and utopian energies of Afro-Americans were garnered, cultivated, and expressed.

Yet, as it has been noted, Afro-American Christianity did not produce a militant millennialist tradition. This does not mean that there was no prophetic tradition among Afro-American Christians; only that this prophetic tradition did not promote explicitly revolutionary action on a broad scale. This was so for three basic reasons. First, the American status quo, especially in the South, was too entrenched, too solid. A black Christian millennialist revolt would only result in communal or personal suicide—as evidenced in the executions of Prosser, Vesey, Turner, and those who followed them. Second, the Afro-American Christian accent on the tragic sense of life and history precluded perfectionistic conceptions of the kingdom of God on earth—conceptions which often fuel millennial movements. Third, militant millennial movements usually result from the complex tension generated from a clash of two distinct ways of life in which an exemplary prophet calls for a return and recovery of pristine origins that yield ascetic sensibilities and revolutionary action. Afro-American Christian slaves—despite harsh domination—shared too much in common with Euro-American slaveholders in regard to culture and civilization. Notwithstanding deep dissimilarities, these differences were not deep enough to give cultural credence and existential authenticity to claims about Afro-Americans and Euro-Americans inhabiting two distinct and different ways of life. Subsequent black nationalist movements have attempted to authenticate such claims—but usually to no avail in regard to revolutionary action. In fact, most black nationalist movements have been Zionist, as with Chief Sam or Marcus Garvey, or explicitly apolitical as with Elijah Muhammad's Nation of Islam. Maulana Karenga's US—owing to his creative leadership and openness to criticism—is the major black nationalist organization which serves as an exception.

The inability of Afro-American Christianity to produce a millennialist tradition is a tribute to black Christians—for as great and heroic it may sound in books, it would have resulted, more than likely, in either wholesale genocide for black people or disenabling despair and overwhelming self-destruction among black people. In fact, the latter has been in process since the sixties among young poor black people given the high, almost millennial, expectations generated by the civil rights and Black Power movements and the inadequate response of the American powers that be. In stark contrast, the Afro-American prophetic tradition has remained more pessimistic—and realistic—regarding America's will to justice and thereby preserved a more tempered disposition toward quick change. Such a disposition indeed may buttress the status quo, yet it also resists suicidal efforts to revolt prematurely against it.

Martin Luther King, Jr., is a unique figure in Afro-American Christianity in that he represents both a heroic effort to reform and a suicidal effort to revolutionize American society and culture. In the early years of his prophetic Christian leadership of the civil rights movement, King attempted to bring oppressed black southerners into the mainstream of American life. In a crypto-fascist, underindustrialized racist American South, even these efforts at minimal reform could cost one's life. Yet as King moved into the urban North, reassessed U.S. presence in the Dominican Republic, South Africa, and South Vietnam, he concluded that only a fundamental transformation of American society and culture—a democratic socialist USA which promoted nonracist life-styles—could provide black freedom. This latter conclusion moved King far out of the mainstream of Afro-American Christianity and of American public discourse. Such a prophetic vision of America proved too threatening to America from one whose prophecy was not simply words but, more importantly, action. In this regard, King and his ability to mobilize people of different races and groups was far more dangerous than a library full of black liberation theology texts or a room full of black liberation theologians who remain distant from peoples' resistance movements. Yet King's deep moralism rooted in his black Christian convictions, his inescapable opportunism as enacted in his deal with President Johnson to exclude Fannie Lou Hamer and the black Mississippi democrats at the Democratic National Convention (1964) in Atlantic City and his aggressive pessimism, as seen in his later depiction of American society as "sicker" than he ever imagined, bear out the predicament of black prophetic practices in the USA.

Prophetic Black Womanist Practices

The first national articulation of black prophetic practices in the USA rests with black women. The first nationwide protest organization among Afro-Americans was created by black women. Predating the National Urban League (1900) and the National Association for the Advancement of Colored People (1909), the National Federation of

Afro-American Women (1895) brought together black women across denominational, ideological, and political lines. Inspired by the militant anti-lynching and womanist spokeswoman, Ida Wells-Barnett, black women's clubs around the country came together in order to focus on two major issues: the humiliating conditions of black women's work, especially the sexual abuse and degrading images of black women in domestic service (in which a majority of black women were employed) and the debilitating effects of Jim Crowism, especially the unique American institution (literally invented here) of lynching—which victimized two black persons a week from 1885 to 1922. Furthermore, the black women accented the subtle connection between black sexuality and white violence by acknowledging the fact that lynching was justified often as a way of protecting white women against rape by black men.

Building upon the heroic action of the underground railroad revolutionary Harriet Tubman, the outspoken abolitionist Marie W. Stuart, the exemplary nineteenth-century womanist Sojourner Truth, and the Sorbonne-educated teacher and writer Anna Cooper, the national organizations of black women raised their voices in unison against institutional racism in the country and institutional sexism in the country and in the black community. In her texts, *Southern Horrors* (1892) and *A Red Record* (1895), Ida Wells-Barnett delineated, in excruciating detail, the figures and facts of southern lynchings—including the white male and female victims—as well as put forward a broad account of why the lynchings systematically occurred—an account that acknowledged the sexual and economic motivations for lynching. And in Anna Cooper's important yet neglected book, *A Voice From the South* (1892), a sophisticated case was made linking again both racism in American society and sexism in Afro-America.

The long and winding career of Ida Wells-Barnett is illuminating for an understanding of the power and pitfalls of black prophetic practices. Beginning as editor of *Free Speech and Headlight,* a Baptist weekly in Memphis, Tennessee, Wells-Barnett was run out of town by racist whites after an article of hers presented a scathing critique of the city's silence concerning the lynching of her three close friends. She served briefly as a columnist for T. Thomas Fortune's renowned *New York Age* and then moved to Chicago where she founded and edited (along with her militant lawyer-husband, Ferdinand Barnett) the *Chicago Conservator.* Famous for her devastating criticisms of accommodationist black clergy and her bold support of black self-defense, Wells-Barnett engaged in a lifelong battle with Booker T. Washington and his ubiquitous machine. Recent works on Washington have disclosed the extent to which he controlled, connived, spied on, and manipulated the major black institutions and movements of his day. And his opposition to Wells-Barnett—principally owing to her militancy— exemplifies such behavior. For example, Washington's wife, Margaret, not only headed the first national black women's organization, she also joined the other major leader, Mary Church Terrell, in blocking Wells-Barnett from holding high office. Furthermore, Washington's control of the Chicago NAACP branch cut off valuable funding for Wells-Barnett's settlement house. Even W. E. B. Du Bois curtailed Wells-Barnett's presence on the national level of the NAACP—an organization she, along with Du Bois and others (mostly white liberals and socialists), founded—by excluding her from the board of directors. In short, Wells-Barnett employed a moral standard and found the black male clergy wanting, fell victim many times to Booker T. Washington's rapacious opportunism, and found herself abandoned by the very organizations she helped found and build. Her career ended with a similar aggressive pessimism to that of Martin Luther King, Jr.— yet hers was directed not only at the "sickness" of American society but also at the sexism of Afro-America.

This sense of aggressive pessimism can be seen in subsequent prophetic practices of black women. It is apparent in the efforts of Bonita Williams, Eloise and Audley Moore—all black women members of the Communist Party USA in the thirties—who in the midst of the least racist organization in the USA during the depression still objected to its subtle racism. In their attempt to promote a ban on the rampant interracial marriages in the party, they were forced to ask a black male comrade from Kansas City, Abner Berry, to make the motion at the Central Committee meeting only to discover later that he was married to a white woman. Similar experiences of marginality in the labor movement can be seen in the gallant struggles of Victoria Garvin—the first black woman to hold a high elected office in American trade-unionism, as vice president of the Distributing, Processing and Office Workers (DPOWA-CIO)—and Octavia Hawkins, the leader of UAW Local 453 in Chicago—both of whom were major figures in the National Negro Labor Council, the foremost black protest group in the early fifties which was soon crushed by McCarthyism.

In the recent black freedom struggle, the list goes on and on. From the legendary Fanny Lou Hamer of the National Welfare Rights Organization, Miranda Smith of the Tobacco Workers Union, Frances Beale of SNCC (now of Line of March), Ericka Huggins of the Black Panther Party, to Angela Davis of the Communist Party USA. Although each case is quite different, the common denominator is protracted struggle against the effects of race, class, and gender oppression in the USA and those of class and gender combination in Afro-America. The contemporary writings of Gayl Jones, Toni Cade Bambara, Alice Walker, Toni Morrison, Sonia Sanchez, Lucille Clifton, and Audre Lorde—though constituting both a grand literary upsurge and a dim hope for black women's enhancement—repeat the cycle of black prophetic practices: initial moralism, inescapable opportunism, and combative pessimism.

Prophetic Black Socialist Practices and the Future

Black prophetic practices as manifest in black socialist thought and action, though in my view the most important set for political purposes, requires less attention and scrutiny than the black prophetic church and black womanism. This is so, in part, because socialism as a modern tradition is less indigenous to black prophetic practices than the other two. Socialism—different from African communalism or agrarian cooperativism—is preeminently a European discourse and practice which remains far removed from both Afro-American and American life. Unlike Euro-American Christianity and white feminism, socialism has not been seriously appropriated by black people and rearticulated within an Afro-American context and language. This does not mean that there have been no noteworthy black socialists—yet none have had the will, vision, and imagination to *Afro-Americanize* socialist thought and practice. Yet, recently, rudimentary efforts have been made—such as Manning Marable's *Blackwater,* Maulana Karenga's *Kawaida Theory,* my own *Prophesy Deliverance!* and Cedric Robinson's *Black Marxism.*

The cultural distance from socialist thought and action have forced most black socialists to shun the very riches and resources of Afro-American culture, especially its deep moralism, combative spirituality, and aggressive pessimism. The results have been mere emulations and bland imitations of Euro-American socialists, who themselves possess a weak tradition of theory and practice. It is no accident that the disproportionate number of black socialist intellectuals in the USA since WW II have yet to produce a major black socialist theorist (I consider neither Du Bois nor Oliver Cox major theoretical thinkers). Or that there has been but one serious black socialist leader in this century—and he, a Baptist preacher during the Debsian phase of American socialism, Rev. George Washington Woodbey.

The major challenge of the prophetic tradition in Afro-America in the last decades of this century is to build upon the best of the black prophetic church, to promote the further flowering of black womanist practices, and to indigenize socialist thought and practice in conjunction with ecological concerns. This latter endeavor consists of reinscribing and rearticulating the specific forms of class exploitation and imperialist oppression *and* the violent destruction of the biosphere, nature, and

48

potentially the planet within the context of the Afro-American past and present.

This challenge is both intellectual and practical. It is intellectual in that it requires new forms of theoretical activity from black thinkers who are in close dialogue with European, Asian, African, Latin American, and Native American intellectuals yet rooted in the best of the Afro-American intellectual past. These new forms of theoretical activity must learn from Marxism (class and imperialist oppression), populism (local peoples' empowerment), civic republicanism (decentralized democratic control), liberalism (individual liberties, due process of law, separation of church and state, and checks and balances), and womanism (women's control of their bodies and destinies) as well as ecologism (communion with rather than domination of nature) and elements of Garveyism (dignity of African peoples). Similarly, it is a practical challenge in that it must be feasible and credible to a majority of the populace; that is, it must have organizational expressions with enough support, potency, and power to transform fundamentally the present order. In this regard, black prophetic practices are not simply inseparable from prophetic practices of other peoples: they also hold a crucial key to the widespread impact of prophetic practices upon prevailing retarding ones.

Therefore black prophetic practices will remain truncated—as with all other American prophetic practices—unless the struggles against forms of despair, dogmatisms, and oppressions are cast on a new plane—a higher moral plane, a more sophisticated and open-ended theoretical plane, and a more culturally grounded political plane. The higher moral standard must make the all-inclusive ideals of individuality and socialist democracy the center of a prophetic vision. The more sophisticated and open-ended theoretical activity must reject unidimensional analyses and master discourses yet preserve intellectual rigor and complexity. And the more culturally grounded political plane must be deeply rooted in the everyday lives of ordinary people—people who have the ability and capacity to change the world and govern themselves under circumstances not of their own choosing.

Contemporary Afro-American Social Thought

Afro-American intellectual activity is alive and well in the 1980s. This is especially so in regard to social and political thought. Gone are the passionate ideological manifestos of the 1960s and the staid self-effacing tracts of the mid-1970s. In the present decade, we have witnessed a kind of black social and political thought coming-of-age. Serious and sustained Afro-American social thought spans the ideological spectrum. In this brief chapter I shall try to provide an overview of the most important and influential texts in contemporary black social and political thought.

A distinctive feature of Afro-American social thought in the past decade is the emergence of visible and unashamed conservative thinkers—notably, Thomas Sowell. His prolific production, of which *Race and Economics* (New York: McKay, 1975) is the most noteworthy, constitutes a constant bombardment upon the dogmas of black liberal leaders. Sowell mercilessly attacks liberal notions such as the positive effects of government intervention to alleviate black oppression, the desirability of affirmative action (or preferential hiring) programs for black employment advancement, and the reluctance to highlight the debilitating habits and values of black people that deter upward social mobility.

Sowell's intellectual mentor is the distinguished conservative economist Milton Friedman, and his political perspective echoes the self-reliant strategies of Booker T. Washington. Comfortably supported by the right-wing think tank, Hoover Institute at Stanford University, and eagerly endorsed by leading neoconservatives such as Irving Kristol and Edward Banfield, Sowell has made quite a splash. Even the dyed-in-the-wool liberal Christopher Jencks went "soft" on him in a lengthy two-part review of Sowell's books, *Ethnic America* and *Markets and Minorities* (both from Basic Books) in *The New York Review of Books* (March 3 and 17, 1983).

Yet this new black conservatism has not gone unchallenged. At the forefront of the black left-liberal response has been William Julius Wilson. His controversial book, *The Declining Significance of Race: Blacks and Changing American Institutions* (Chicago: University of Chicago,

---

From *Over Here: An American Studies Journal* (autumn 1985).

1978), has received more attention than any other recent text on contemporary U.S. race relations. Although it does not explicitly attack Sowell—and, in fact, does not even mention him!—there is little doubt that Wilson's perspective provides crucial intellectual ammunition against black conservatism.

Wilson's basic argument is that "class has become more important than race in determining black access to privilege and power." He claims that an elaborate black class structure has emerged in the past few decades and that consequently class-based rather than race-based politics are required to alleviate the basic forms of Afro-American oppression. This black class structure roughly consists of three discernible groups— an underclass primarily composed of unskilled laborers, domestic workers, and welfare recipients; a stable working class principally of semi-skilled blue-collar workers; and a middle class of skilled blue- and white-collar workers. The underclass constitutes about 35 percent, the working class about 30 percent, and the middle class about 35 percent of black people in the USA.

In sharp contrast to Sowell, Wilson does not promote market mechanisms and cultural readaption as the most desirable ways to overcome black hardship. Rather he argues that because a fundamental change in the U.S. economy has produced this black class structure, the solution is not one of simply removing racist institutional barriers to the marketplace nor solely helping black people to acquire habits of hard work and patience to facilitate movement up the social ladder. Thus the basic challenge is to overcome the structural constraints of the U.S. economy that relegate the underclass to permanent status—a status reflected in rising levels of unemployment, declining labor-force participation rates, escalating numbers of female-headed households, and growing welfare recipients. This permanent status is reinforced and reproduced by a contracting manufacturing sector in the labor force and an expanding service sector, with the latter requiring levels of education and training outside of the reach of poorly educated and often functionally illiterate members of the black underclass. Hence the only jobs available to 35 percent of the black U.S. population are menial jobs with no union protection and very little hope for advancement.

Wilson has often been misunderstood by black liberals and leftists. They interpret him to be claiming that racism is no longer a crucial factor in Afro-American life. And misguided news articles have buttressed this interpretation. Yet a careful reading of the book will show that Wilson holds racism to be pervasive in American society—especially in the social, cultural, and political spheres. It remains a factor in the economic sphere, yet it has less potency and presence than it once had. The process of deracialization in the economic sphere provides a basis for considering

class issues to be as important as, or even more important than, race issues in regard to public policy and black economic progress. Wilson's
rather sensible (and tame) thesis created great controversy, especially
among black politicians and leaders who have a vested interest in keeping racism as the most visible issue to promote black progress. Yet
whereas Sowell scolds these black elites for not focusing on the "self-
imposed" impediments to black progress, Wilson criticizes these leaders
for upholding a myth of black Americans as a monolithic socioeconomic
group bereft of growing class divisions and status differentiation. Wilson
admonishes these black spokespersons to promote policies that transcend racial discrimination and combat class subordination. Unfortunately, Wilson's policy recommendations are highly undeveloped. To
date, they amount to support for a highly unpopular full employment
bill tabled years ago by Congress.

The major theoretical and political shortcomings of Wilson's left-
liberal perspective are disclosed in my *Prophesy Deliverance! An Afro-
American Revolutionary Christianity* (Philadelphia: Westminster Press,
1982). These shortcomings consist mainly of a limited Weberian conception of class, a reluctance to relate the U.S. economy to the world
capitalist division of labor, and a refusal to come to terms with the complex relation of culture to political struggle. I do not provide an adequate
answer to any of these issues, yet I raise the questions in a manner that,
I believe, requires that they be taken seriously.

In a rather peculiar, eclectic, and at times undisciplined text, I reject a
Weberian view of class (defined as financial remunerations at the workplace) in favor of a Marxist conception of class in which the population's
relation to the mode of production is understood in terms of their role
or lack thereof in decision-making processes for effective control over investment choices. This viewpoint, though fraught with messy empirical
problems concerning the exact class location in a complex capitalist
mode of production, permits me to accent the ideal of blacks' empowerment over and democratic participation in crucial economic decisions
that shape their destinies. This ideal stands in stark contrast with the
basic index for social well-being for Weberians like Wilson, namely, high
incomes. These radical democratic and libertarian ideals—derived from
a provocative interpretation of Protestant Christianity and an idiosyncratic relation to Marxist thought—hold that access to basic decision-
making processes enhances the quality of life in ways irreducible to mere
rising standards of living.

Furthermore, I emphasize an international perspective that links the
black class structure in the USA to fundamental changes in the world
capitalist economy. Hence, I highlight the various forms of dependent
development (usually coupled with harsh political repression and anti-

democratic regimes) and U.S. corporate domination of subaltern national economies. This issue leads to a stress on the complex relations of black political struggle to anti-imperialist efforts in Western and Eastern bloc countries.

Last, I acknowledge that the overdetermined articulation of racial, class, and gender forms of oppression requires not simply economic and social analysis but also cultural investigation. Following the pioneering work of Antonio Gramsci and Michel Foucault, I suggest, in a rather rudimentary way, that the oppositional potential of Afro-Americans—always in conjunction with that of other progressive Americans—must be, in part, rooted in black cultural practices and institutions. Historically, the prophetic wing of the black church has provided such a basis. The concrete programmatic dimension of this viewpoint amounts to a vague gesture toward democratic socialism embodied in disparate organizations. Yet my attempt to put flexible Marxist analysis on the agenda of black churches is a pioneering endeavor.

The issue of oppositional cultural practices looms large in the work of black American feminists. Foremost among them is Bell Hooks, whose two books, *Ain't I A Woman: Black Women and Feminism* (Boston: South End Press, 1981) and *Feminist Theory: From Margin to Center* (Boston: South End Press, 1984), have caused a stir among feminists and black progressives. Critical of the racism of the white feminist movement and the sexism of the black freedom struggle, Hooks examines the emerging forms of black women's consciousness. Mindful of the degree to which both white feminists and black male activists are captives of liberalism, Hook promotes cultural transformations in present-day patriarchy in American society and in the black community, and links them to structural changes in the U.S. economy. Like Alice Walker and Audre Lorde in literature, Hooks is one of the few black thinkers grappling with the complex relation to race, class, and gender oppression.

I save for the end comments on the most prolific Afro-American social thinker—Manning Marable—and the most profound of black social theorists in America—Orlando Patterson. Marable's writings, which include five books in the past five years, are reminiscent of the sixties. His most recent book, *Black American Politics: From the Washington Marches to Jesse Jackson* (London: Verso, 1985), combines indefatigable investigation with passionate commitment to fundamental social change. As in his solid study, *Race Reform and Rebellion: The Second Reconstruction in Black America, 1945–1982* (London: Macmillan, 1984), Marable is best at detailed historical narrative. Unlike Cedric Robinson whose ambitious work *Black Marxism: The Making of the Black Radical Tradition* (London: Zed, 1983) provides an impressive reconstruction of Western capitalist civilization accenting the role of Africans, yet whose grasp of the internal dynamics of black resistance remains vague, Marable is well-grounded in black cultural resistance but continues to search for a coherent and consistent theoretical framework. Similar to Maulana Karenga—the most resilient and sophisticated black cultural nationalist, whose works such as *Kawaida Theory: An Introductory Outline* (Los Angeles: Kawaida Press, 1980) and *An Introduction to Black Studies* (Inglewood: Kawaida Press, 1982) deserve more attention—Marable brings together oppositional elements in Afro-American culture with an internationalist socialist outlook.

Jamaican-born Orlando Patterson is the most profound black social thinker in the USA. His unduly neglected book *Ethnic Chauvinism: The Reactionary Impulse* (New York: McKay, 1977) and his magisterial work *Slavery and Social Death* (Cambridge: Harvard, 1982) employ theoretical strategies and empirical research that stand head and shoulders above the aforementioned texts. A self-styled existentialist and humanistic socialist who uses a rich dialectical, neo-Marxist analysis, Patterson's struggle with the origin, nature, and causes of modern ethnicity and his monumental investigations into the content and character of diverse forms of slavery over vast stretches of time and space provide some of the most fruitful results to date regarding the role of race in the modern world. Rivaling the contributions of such contemporary Marxist thinkers as Eugene Genovese and Stuart Hall and liberal scholars such as David Brion Davis and C. Vann Woodward, Patterson's subtle reflections on culture and social structure, status, and class position and his fecund notion of "natal alienation" as a form of psychic and social domination serve as a landmark in contemporary Afro-American social thought.

Assessing Black Neoconservatism

The publication of Thomas Sowell's *Race and Economics* in 1975 marked the rise of a novel phenomenon in the United States: a visible and aggressive black conservative assault on traditional black liberal leadership. The promotion of conservative ideas is not new in Afro-American history. The preeminent black conservative of this century—George S. Schuyler—published a witty and acerbic column in the influential black newspaper, *The Pittsburgh Courier,* for decades and his book *Black and Conservative* is a minor classic in Afro-American letters. Similarly, the reactionary essays (some of which appeared in *Readers' Digest*) and Republican party allegiance of the most renowned Afro-American woman of letters, Zora Neale Hurston, are often overlooked by her contemporary feminist followers. Yet Sowell's book still initiated something new—a bid for conservative hegemony in black political and intellectual leadership in the post–civil rights era.

This bid is as yet highly unsuccessful though it has generated much attention from the American media. The most salient figures are Thomas Sowell, a senior fellow at the Hoover Institution on War, Revolution, and Peace at Stanford University; Glenn C. Loury, a professor at Harvard's Kennedy School of Government; Walter E. Williams, a professor of economics at George Mason University; J. A. Parker, president of the Lincoln Institute for Research and Education Inc.; Robert Woodson, president of the National Association of Neighborhood Enterprises; and Joseph Perkins, editorial writer for *The Wall Street Journal*. Despite minor differences between them, these major figures of the new black conservatism are all supportive of the basic policies of the Reagan administration, such as its major foreign policies, opposition to affirmative action, abolition or lowering of adult minimum wage, the establishment of enterprise zones in inner cities, and the vast cutbacks in social programs for the poor.

These black publicists are aware of the irony of their positions; that is, their own upward social mobility was, in large part, made possible by the struggles of the liberal civil rights movement and more radical black activists they now scorn. They also realize that black liberalism is in deep crisis. This crisis, exemplified by the rise of Reaganism and the decline

From *The Christian Century* (July 16-23, 1986).

of progressive politics, has created the new intellectual space that their black conservative voices (along with nonblack ones) now occupy.

The emergence of the new black conservatives is best understood in light of three fundamental processes in American society and culture since 1973: the eclipse of uncontested postwar U.S. predominance in world markets and military power, the structural transformation of the American economy, and the breakdown of the moral fabric in communities throughout the country, especially in black working poor and underclass neighborhoods.

The end of the unprecedented postwar economic boom in 1973 resulted in the decline of American hegemony around the world on the economic and military fronts. The symbolic events here were the oil crisis, principally owing to the solidarity of OPEC nations, and the loss of the Vietnam War. In addition, increasing economic competition from Japan, West Germany, and other nations brought an end to unquestioned U.S. economic power. The resultant slump in the American economy undermined the Keynesian foundation of postwar American liberalism: economic growth along with state regulation and intervention on behalf of disadvantaged citizens.

The principal argument of American conservatives, both black and white, holds that state regulation and intervention on behalf of disadvantaged citizens (as opposed to military buildup or corporate contracts in agricultural production) stifles economic growth. As the economic slump deepened and liberal solutions failed, conservative views seemed to be the only alternatives. Needless to say, more radical democratic socialist perspectives are too marginal in American political culture to be even seriously entertained by politicians.

With the loss of the Vietnam War, self-doubts about U.S. military might provoked conservative rhetoric about the need for a renewed military buildup and reevaluation of foreign aid to U.S. allies. This rhetoric surfaced during the Carter administration with regressive tax policies supporting escalating military budgets. The major beneficiaries were domestic weapons-producing corporations and countries such as Chile, Honduras, Afghanistan, and, above all, Israel (after the fall of the Shah in Iran).

The impact of the end of the postwar economic boom on Afro-Americans was immense. To no surprise, it more deeply affected the growing black working poor and underclass than the expanding black middle class. Issues of sheer survival loomed large for the former; while the latter continued to seize opportunities in education, business, and politics. Most middle class blacks consistently supported the emergent black political class—elected black officials on the national, state, and local levels—primarily to insure black upward social mobility. But a few began to feel uncomfortable about how their white middle class peers viewed them—mobility by means of affirmative action breeds tenuous self-respect and questionable peer acceptance for many middle class blacks. The new black conservatives voiced these feelings in the form of attacks on affirmative action programs (after they had achieved their positions by means of such programs), thereby joining a louder chorus of nonblack neoconservatives.

This quest for full-fledged middle-class respectability on meritorious rather than political grounds cannot be overestimated in the new black conservatism. Their failure or success to gain respect in the eyes of their white peers deeply shapes certain elements of their conservatism. In this regard, they simply want what most Americans want—to be judged by the quality of their skills not the color of their skin. Surprisingly, they overlook the fact that affirmative action policies were political responses to the pervasive refusal of most white Americans to judge black Americans by the quality of their skills rather than the color of their skin.

Furthermore, the new black conservatives assume that without affirmative action programs white Americans will make meritorious choices rather than race-biased ones. Yet they have adduced absolutely no evidence for this. Hence they are either politically naive or simply unconcerned with black mobility. Most Americans realize that job-hiring choices are both meritorious *and* personal choices. And this personal dimension often is influenced by racist perceptions. Therefore the pertinent question is never "merit vs. race" regarding black employment but rather merit and race-bias against blacks *or* merit and race-bias with consideration for blacks. Within the practical world of U.S. employment practices, the new black conservative rhetoric about race-free meritorious criterion (usually coupled with a dismantling of enforcement mechanisms) does no more than justify actual practices of racial discrimination against blacks. And their claims about self-respect should not obscure this fact. Nor should such claims be separated from the normal self-doubts, insecurities, and anxieties of new arrivals in the American middle class. It is worth noting that most of the new black conservatives are first generation middle-class persons—offering themselves as examples for how well the system works for those willing to sacrifice and work hard. Yet, in familiar American fashion, genuine white peer acceptance still seems to escape them. And their conservatism still fails to provide this human acceptance. In this way, white racism still operates against them.

Another crucial area related to the eclipse of postwar U.S. hegemony in the world is that of foreign policy. The new black conservatives rightly call attention to the butchery of bureaucratic elites in Africa who rule in the name of a variety of ideologies. Yet they reserve most of their energies to support U.S. intervention in Central America and prevailing U.S. policies toward Israel. Their relative silence regarding the "constructive engagement" U.S. policy with South Africa is revealing. Although most of the press attention they receive has to do with their provocative views on domestic issues, I suggest that their widespread support by Reaganite conservatives and Jewish neoconservatives has to do with their views on U.S. foreign policies.

This is so because an ideological glacier shift is occurring in black America regarding the role of America in the world. An undeniable consequence of the civil rights movement and Black Power ideology in the sixties has been a growing identification of black Americans with other oppressed peoples around the world. This has less to do with skin color and more to do with similar social location, political position, and experiences of oppression by European peoples. Just as many blacks sympathize with Polish workers and Northern Irish Catholics (despite problematic Polish-black and Irish-black relations in Chicago and Boston respectively), so more and more blacks are cognizant of South African oppression of its native peoples, Chilean and South Korean repression of their citizens, and Israeli oppression of Palestinians. This latter identification deeply upsets and worries conservatives in America. In fact, the oppositional potential and radical consequences for domestic issues of this growing black radical international consciousness—usually dubbed anti-Americanism by the vulgar right—frightens the new black conservatives. For they find themselves viewed in many black communities as mere apologists for pernicious U.S. foreign policies.

The second fundamental process in American society that helps us better to understand the new black conservatives is the structural transformation of the U.S. economy. A contracting manufacturing sector and expanding service sector of the labor market yield limited opportunities for semiskilled and unskilled workers. Coupled with this decline of a major source of black employment (i.e., industrial jobs) is the most crucial transformation in the U.S. economy affecting black Americans in the past three decades: the mechanization of southern agriculture. For example, thirty-five years ago 50 percent of all black teenagers worked as agricultural workers, with more than 90 percent of them in the South. As these jobs disappeared, the black unemployment problem in urban centers surfaced. The recent deindustrialization of northeastern and midwestern cities has exacerbated this problem. And with the stiff competition for jobs given the entrance of new immigrants and white women into the labor market, semiskilled and unskilled black workers find it difficult, if not impossible, to find employment. So by 1980, 15 percent of all black men between twenty-five and sixty-four years of age reported to the Census Bureau that they had earned nothing whatsoever the previous year. The only option is often military enlistment (the U.S. Army is almost one-third black).

The new black conservatives rightly perceive that the dominant perspectives of traditional black liberal leadership cannot address these basic structural changes in the American economy. The notion that racial discrimination is the sole cause of the prevailing predicament of the black working poor and underclass is specious. Furthermore, the idea that the courts and government can significantly enhance their plight by enforcing laws already on the books is even more spurious. White racism indeed is pernicious and potent—yet it cannot fully explain the socioeconomic position of the majority of black Americans.

The crisis of black liberalism—liberalism supported by most black elected officials—is the inability to put forward visions, analyses, and programs that can ameliorate the plight of the black working poor and underclass. The new black conservatives highlight this crisis by trying to delegitimate and discredit traditional black liberal leadership. They claim the NAACP, National Urban League, Black Congressional Caucus, and most black mayors are guided by old-fashioned, anachronistic, outdated, and ineffective viewpoints. The overriding aim of the new black conservatives is to undermine this leadership and replace it with black republicans like themselves who downplay governmental regulation and intervention and instead stress market mechanisms and success-oriented values in black communities.

Yet the new black conservatives have been unable to convince black Americans that conservative ideology and Reaganite policies are morally acceptable and politically advantageous. The vast depoliticization and electoral disengagement of blacks already suggest a disenchantment with black liberal leadership and a general distrust of American political processes. And for a downtrodden and degraded people with limited options, any alternative seems to be worth a try. Nonetheless, black Americans systematically reject the arguments of the new black conservatives. This is so neither because blacks are duped by liberal black politicians nor because blacks worship the Democratic party. Rather it is because most blacks conclude that while racial discrimination is not the sole cause of their plight, it certainly is one among various causes of their social location. Most black Americans view the new black conservative assault on traditional black liberal leadership as a step backward rather than forward. Black liberalism indeed is inadequate, but black conservatism is unacceptable. This negative perception partly explains the reluctance of the new black conservatives to engage in rational debates on public forums with black liberals and leftists in the black community and their eagerness to do so in the mass media. A few even go as far as to portray themselves as courageous embattled critics of a black liberal "establishment"—while their salaries, honorariums, and travel expenses are paid by the most well-endowed and conservative foundations and corporations in the country.

The most salutary effect of the new black conservatives on public discourse is to highlight the breakdown of the moral fabric in the country and especially in black working poor and underclass communities. Jesse Jackson's PUSH and other black organizations have focused on the issue in the past. The new black conservatives have made it their obsession and thereby given it national attention. Unfortunately, they view this urgent set of problems in strictly individualistic terms—ignoring the historical background and structural context of the present situation. They claim that the decline of such values as patience, hard work, deferred gratification, and self-reliance have resulted in high rates of crime, increasing early unwed pregnancies and relatively uncompetitive academic performances of black youth. And certainly these sad realities must be candidly confronted.

Nowhere in their writings do the new black conservatives examine the pervasive sexualization and militarization of images promoted in the mass media and deployed by the advertising industry in order to entice and titillate consumers. Since the end of the postwar economic boom, new strategies have been used to stimulate consumption—especially strategies that project sexual activity as instant fulfillment and violence as machismo identity aimed at American youth. This market activity has contributed greatly to the disorientation and confusion of American youth—and those with less education and opportunities bear the brunt of this cultural chaos. Ought we to be surprised that those black youth outside the labor market, devalued by white ideals of beauty of Madison Avenue, marginalized by decrepit urban schools, and targeted by an unprecedented drug invasion (begun during the politically engaging sixties) have high crime and unwed pregnancy rates? My aim here is neither to provide excuses for black behavior nor absolve blacks of personal responsibility. But when the new black conservatives accent black behavior and responsibility in such a way that present-day structural and cultural realities of black people are ignored, they are playing a deceptive and dangerous intellectual game with the lives and fortunes of disadvantaged people.

To hold individual black persons responsible for their actions is imperative; to ignore what these individuals are up against—such as sexualization and militarization of images in the mass media over which they have no control—is invidious. We indeed must criticize and condemn immoral acts of black people but we must do so cognizant of those option-limiting structural features of circumstances in which people are born and under which they live. By overlooking this, the new black conservatives fall into the trap of blaming the bulk of black poor people for their predicament. To make this grand analytical mistake for the polemical purpose of attacking traditional black liberal leadership is to debase intellectual discourse about the disadvantaged in America. Needless to say, the lives of the disadvantaged depend more on the quality of this discourse than on those of us who partake in this discourse.

This polemical purpose guided by ideological blinders is exemplified in the new black conservative attempt to link the moral breakdown of poor black communities to the expansion of the welfare state. For them, the only structural features of the black poor situation are the negative role of the state and the positive role of the market. An appropriate question to these descendants of slaves sold at the auction block is: Can the market do any wrong?

They claim that transfer payments to the black needy engenders a mentality of dependence which undercuts values of self-reliance and that the required living arrangements for these payments undermines the black poor family. They hold that only an unregulated market can support values of independence and a strong family. The new black conservatives fail to see that the welfare state was the historic compromise between progressive forces for broad subsistence rights and conservative forces for unregulated markets. Therefore it should come as no surprise that the welfare state possesses many flaws, shortcomings, and imperfections. I do believe that the reinforcing of "dependent mentalities" and harm done to poor families are two of them. But simply to point out these rather obvious shortcomings does not justify cutbacks in the welfare state. This is so because in the face of high black unemployment, these cutbacks will not promote self-reliance or strong black families but rather produce even more black cultural disorientation and more devastated black households.

The only feasible alternative to the welfare state is more jobs for poor people—and the private sector is simply uninterested and unwilling to provide these jobs. It is simply not in their economic interests to do so, even if they can pay "third world"—i.e., subminimum—wages. Again the political naiveté or unconcern with black enhancement is manifest in the claims of the new black conservatives. Within the practical world of American politics, to attack the welfare state without linking this attack to a credible jobs program (more than likely supported by the public sphere) is to delimit the already limited options black poor people have to survive and live. To go as far as some new black conservatives have done and support the elimination of nearly every federal benefit program for the nonelderly poor (as put forward in Charles Murray's *Losing Ground*) is to serve as ideological accomplices to social policies that have genocidal effects on the black poor. The welfare state has not and cannot win a war on poverty, yet it has and does sustain some boats that would sink given the turbulent condition of unemployment. To cut the lifelines of the latter in order to make an ideological point against black liberal elites is to follow a heartless political perspective that exacerbates an already deplorable situation.

Yet even effective job programs do not fully address the cultural decay and moral disintegration of poor black communities. Like America itself, these communities are in need of cultural revitalization and moral regeneration. There is widespread agreement on this need by all sectors of black leadership. But neither black liberalism nor the new black conservatism adequately speaks to this need. Black liberals and conservatives simply fail to come to terms with the existential meaninglessness and personal despair throughout Afro-America.

Presently, the major institutional bulwarks against such meaninglessness and despair are Christian churches and Moslem mosques. These churches and mosques indeed are fighting an uphill battle and serve as the few spaces of refuge against the terrors of urban ghetto life. Yet even they cannot counter the pervasive influence of sexual and violent images of mass media upon black people, especially black youth. I am convinced that those few prophetic black churches—with rich cultural and moral resources and a progressive political perspective—possess the kind of model it takes to meet the present crisis. That is, they affirm the humanity of black poor people, accent the capacities of black poor people, and keep alive a sense of resistance to the status quo. Unfortunately, there are not enough of these institutions to overcome the crisis.

What then are we to make of the new black conservatives? First, the narrowness of their viewpoints reflects the narrowness of the liberal perspectives with which they are critically obsessed. In other words, their major object of criticism, black liberals, circumscribes their critique. In fact, the relative lack of vision, analyses, and programs—especially the ignoring of crucial structural features of the black poor situation—of both black liberals and conservatives make them mirror-images of each other. The basic narrowness of both groups reveals an internal fight within the black middle-class elite as well as the parochial character of the fight itself—a parochialism inseparable from the highly limited alternatives available in contemporary American politics. Second, the new black conservatives signify a healthy development to the degree to which they call attention to the crisis of black liberalism, thereby encouraging black politicians and activists to entertain more progressive solutions to structural problems of social injustice in American society. Third, the next crucial terrain for black conservative attacks on traditional black liberal leadership will be that of U.S. foreign policy. The visible role of the NAACP and black elected officials in the anti-apartheid movement cannot but come under more ideological assault by the new black conservatives. This assault can only intensify as black liberal leaders find it more and more difficult to pass the conservative litmus tests for pro-Americanism in foreign affairs: uncritical support for U.S. policy toward Israel and U.S. intervention in Central America.

The widening of this split between hegemonic black liberal leaders and black conservative critics may facilitate more principled and passionate political discourse in and about black America. I am confident that if more rational debates are held, with conservative, liberal, and left voices heard, the truth about the predicament of the black poor can be more easily ascertained—with a few valuable insights of the new black conservatives incorporated into a larger progressive perspective which utterly rejects their unwarranted conclusions and repugnant policies. I suspect such a rational dialogue would unmask the new black conservatives to be what they really are: renegades from and critics of black liberalism owing to the limits of this liberalism, yet also highly rewarded and status-hungry ideologues unwilling to interrogate the narrow limits of their own new illiberalism. This parasitic relation with their black liberal foes and patronage relation with their white illiberal friends would be a farce if enacted on stage—but given the actual roles they play in present-day America, there is too much at stake to be simply amused.

On Manning Marable's
How Capitalism Underdeveloped
Black America

Manning Marable is probably the best-known black Marxist in the country. His syndicated column appears in over 140 newspapers. He lectures every year at more than forty colleges as well as at numerous trade union halls and black community centers. And he has played pivotal roles in the formation of the National Black Independent Political Party and, more recently, the Democratic Socialists of America (DSA). Presently, he is a vice-chair of DSA and editor of one of its publications, "Third World Socialists."

Marable first burst onto the intellectual scene with "From The Grassroots: Social and Political Essays Towards Afro-American Liberation" (1980). Here he outlined his "left Black nationalist" position, which combined a Marxist critique of U.S. capitalist society with an appreciation for the distinctiveness and dignity of Afro-American culture. In "Blackwater: Historical Studies in Race, Class Consciousness and Revolution" (1981), Marable put forward a schematic reconstruction of Afro-American history guided by that same perspective. Inspired by the work and style of W. E. B. Du Bois, he intertwined poetic and historical discourses in examining the black radical tradition and in exploring how its subversive elements could be more fully reactivated in our time. Both works were provocative, yet ultimately uneven, owing to Marable's highly ambitious intent and impatient execution.

How Capitalism Underdeveloped Black America is clearly Marable's best work to date. This book overcomes the disjointedness which plagued his earlier works by sustaining a cohesive portrait of Afro-America. It also provides the single most compelling Marxist depiction of the crisis of contemporary black America.

Going beyond the jargon which pervades so much of black Marxist discourse, Marable details the role and predicament of all segments of black society, laying bare its anatomy in a most precise manner.

The book's major strength is its exploration of the depths of political and economic underdevelopment in which black people are submerged

From *The Guardian* (June 27, 1984); review of Manning Marable, *How Capitalism Underdeveloped America* (Boston: South End Press, 1983).

in the U.S. Marable does not simply report the 31 percent unemployment rate of black youth, the recent collapse of black agricultural entrepreneurship, the 42.2 percent poverty rate of young black women householders, the 26.8 percent high-school graduate ratio among the black poor, or the thirty-one thousand black families who have no cash income at all. Rather, he looks at these facts in relation to an overall pattern of underdevelopment which was historically generated and is currently reinforced by an exploitative economy and its racist and sexist outgrowths.

Similarly, Marable does not merely observe that a black man in the U.S. has a six to eight times greater chance of being murdered than a white man, that every year over 8 percent of all Afro-Americans are arrested (representing over 25 percent of all Americans arrested in a given year), or that almost half of all prisoners in the U.S. are black. Again, he places these figures in the context of a historical legacy of crypto-fascist southern terror and racist police violence against Afro-Americans.

Although Marable lauds the efforts of black people to survive against heavy odds, he undermines the fashionable claim that the black middle class—politicians, businesspersons, and preachers—possess significant power. With blacks comprising only 2.3 percent of all construction-firm owners, 0.8 percent of all real estate, insurance, and finance company heads, 0.4 percent of all wholesale trade proprietors, and only a negligible percentage of the management of corporate America, any talk of widespread "black capitalism" is ludicrous indeed.

To put it bluntly, Marable's depiction of the crisis in black America is not only powerful; it is depressing. For, as he suggests, if the processes of underdevelopment are not halted, the logical consequence will be the slow but sure genocide of the majority of Afro-Americans.

But what are the forces of resistance to these destructive processes? It is here that Marable's reliance on dependency theory misguides him. He argues that the black poor, working class, women, and prisoners constitute "the domestic periphery" while black entrepreneurs, politicians, and preachers comprise "the domestic core." Drawing on such theorists as André Frank, Samir Amin, and especially the late Walter Rodney, Marable implies that "the core" lives at the expense of "the periphery" by means of exploitation and oppression—as in the early stages of European colonialism.

Dependency Theory

Yet this analogy surely does not apply to the black middle class who, for the most part, do not live at the expense of the black poor but rather are *parasitic* on the real "domestic core": corporate America and its state apparatus. If Marable does assume such an analogy, he is mistaken. If he does not make this assumption, then his usage of "core-periphery" language is highly misleading. Marable's mistaken application also obscures possible sources of resistance within the black middle class by viewing the black political presence as merely "symbolic."

There surely are no reasons to rest emancipatory hopes on the black petite bourgeoisie, but to abandon it entirely is premature and unwarranted. This is especially so in the face of the current right-wing offensive against an unorganized black underclass and a devastated black working class. Clearly the ultimate aim is to organize and mobilize blacks generally and in the interim the black petite bourgeoisie should not be characterized solely as an enemy—or as a dominating "domestic core."

This shortcoming echoes in the book's silence on the class nature and present role of black Marxist intellectuals. This small though significant portion of primarily the black petite bourgeoisie remains unexamined by Marable. These intellectuals must play a crucial role in the construction of a socialist America—as does Marable himself in his writings and other political activities—but precisely what role is it? How are we to understand this role in relation to other forces of resistance in black America and beyond?

These questions are not, of course, directed solely at Marable's text but at the black left as a whole. The crisis Marable has depicted takes a heavy toll of black lives every day. How can a socialist program speak to it with potency and credibility? Despite the impediments of his interpretation of dependency theory, Marable has attempted to grapple with this crucial query. A more persuasive answer is needed, however, which can lead to an emancipatory black leftist strategy.

The Black Church and
Socialist Politics

Notwithstanding the powerful forces of urbanization and industrialization, the vast majority of Afro-Americans remain religious. Besides the significant though marginal presence of Islam, this religious hold over black people takes the form of an evangelical Protestant Christianity. Like all religious ideologies, this Protestant Christianity is politically ambiguous; that is, it possesses a conservative priestly pole and a progressive prophetic pole. Yet the distinctive feature of Afro-American Christianity has been its capacity to make visible and potent its progressive prophetic pole. Nat Turner, Denmark Vesey, and Gabriel Prosser—Christian preachers who led slave insurrections in the nineteenth century—signify in dramatic fashion the crucial role of the black church in the Afro-American struggle for freedom. In stark contrast with other Africans in the Western hemisphere, black Americans have had relative control over their churches, thereby facilitating a creative fusion of religious transcendence and political opposition, belief in God and liberation themes, faith in the ultimate trustworthiness of human existence and negation of the racism in the prevailing social order. In short, the African appropriation of Christianity under conditions of slavery in the USA, the land of freedom and opportunity in the eyes of many, produces a unique version of Christianity with strong prophetic tendencies.

This Afro-American Christianity serves as the major resource upon which black people draw strength and sustenance in their encounter with the modern American capitalist order—as urban dwellers, industrial workers, bureaucratic employees, and franchised citizens. It is no accident that even this modern status results, in part, from the political struggles waged by the civil rights movement led by the Rev. Martin Luther King, Jr., which drew its cultural potency from the black church. Even the major religious rival of Afro-American Christianity, Islam, was promoted by a former black Christian preacher turned Muslim, the late Honorable Elijah Muhammed, and Malcom X, the son of a black Christian minister.

The prophetic tradition of the black church is worth taking seriously not simply because of its important role in the black freedom movement, but also because it may highlight some of the cultural problems now be-

From *Third World Socialist* (summer 1984).

setting the left in the modern West. The inability of the left, especially in the USA, to deal adequately with the crucial issues of everyday life such as racism, sexism, ecology, sexual orientation, and personal despair may indeed have something to do with its refusal to grapple with the complex role and function of religion. Needless to say, since the majority of American people remain religious in some form or other, the American left (black or white) ignores religious and cultural issues at its own peril.

Yet the question of whether the black church can meet the challenges of the prevailing crisis in black America continues to haunt prophetic black religious leaders. And, despite the expansion of the scope of black elites in the past few decades, black religious leaders remain the most important leaders in black America. Rev. Theodore Jemison's moderate National Baptist Convention, U.S.A., Inc. (the largest black organization among black people in the U.S.), Rev. Benjamin Hooks's liberal National Association for the Advancement of Colored People, Rev. Joseph Lowery's left-liberal Southern Christian Leadership Conference (founded by the late Rev. Martin Luther King, Jr.), Rev. Herbert Daughtry's leftist National Black United Front and African Peoples' Christian Organization, and Rev. Jesse Jackson's People United to Serve Humanity exemplify the religious hegemony of black leadership in the USA.

The crisis in black America is threefold. First, the black community is undergoing a profound economic crisis which most visibly takes the form of unprecedented unemployment, pervasive layoffs, and severe cutbacks. Second, Afro-Americans are facing a political crisis that demands redefining relations to the Democratic party. Third, black people are experiencing a pervasive spiritual crisis as the quotient of black distrust of one another escalates and black suicides and homicides proliferate. In short, black America is at the crossroads.

The economic crisis in black America results primarily from the international crisis of the world capitalist order. The Reagan program of reconstituting global capitalism, supported by repressive cultural sensibilities and antidemocratic restructuring, has one basic domestic thrust: vicious attacks and assaults on the fragile gains of working and poor peoples. These attacks and assaults are disproportionately targeted at peoples of color, especially black women (who head over one-half of black households) and black children. And as deindustrialization proceeds in the Northeast and Midwest, black industrial workers inordinately suffer.

The political crisis in black America is manifest in captivity to the Democratic party. The refusal of most black politicians to explore new forms of political empowerment outside the Democratic party has produced paralysis and powerlessness among actual and potential black voters. The election of Harold Washington as mayor of Chicago revealed the limitations of relying on the Democratic party and the strengths of community mobilizing and organizing; his election is unimaginable without the support of the black churches in Chicago. The candidacy of Rev. Jesse Jackson in presidential primaries may point in a similar direction if he is willing seriously to challenge the Democratic party. With the election of Washington, the campaign of Mel King in Boston, and the vast voter registration drives of Rev. Hooks's NAACP, Rev. Jackson's PUSH, and Rev. Jemison's vast church network, political momentum may be gaining for such a challenge.

The spiritual crisis in black America flows from new class and strata divisions, the impact of mass culture, and the invasion of drugs in the black communities throughout the country. The slow but sure class polarization of the growing black petite bourgeoisie and the increasing black underclass creates immense problems of black communication. These problems have spiritual consequences in that black distrust and disrespect produces widespread frustration and cynicism among black people. The impact of mass culture, especially of radio and television, has diminished the influence of the black church. Among large numbers of black youth, it is black music which serves as the central influence for the shaping of their psyches. Since little of this music is spiritually inspiring, black people have less and less spiritual resources to fall back on in periods of crisis. With the invasion of drugs in the black community—with police indifference and political silence on behalf of the white power structure—a new subculture among black youth has emerged which thrives on criminal behavior and survives on hopelessness. Hence, prison life has become an integral component of black working class and underclass life.

There have been four basic responses to these crises by the black church. First, there is the conservative alternative put forward by entrepreneurial preachers like Rev. Ike who translate vast numbers of peoples' personal despair into self-serving lucrative ends. Second is the politically cautious yet open-ended perspective of moderates like Rev. Jemison and liberals like Rev. Hooks. Third is the prophetically audacious and authentically counterhegemonic praxis of leftists like Rev. Daughtry and left-liberals like Rev. Lowery. And lastly, there is the courageous electoral campaign of Rev. Jesse Jackson.

The central role of the black church in black America ensures its invidious manipulation. Given its relatively loose, uncomplicated requirements for membership and its open and easy access to leadership, the black church is a sitting duck for charismatic con-men. And there is a long tradition of such behavior in Afro-American Christianity. This tradition is captive to American civil religion in that it is usually couched in economic terms: The American Way of Life can be yours if you would only surrender yourself, accept Jesus Christ, and financially support my ministry! The present crises in black America have made this enticing invitation attractive to many black evangelical Christians in deep psychological and pecuniary need. It is this conservative tradition which warrants the vehement and often vociferous criticisms directed at the black church by insiders and outsiders.

Yet this conservative response is not that of the majority of black Christians. Rather the latter is the viewpoint put forward by Revs. Jemison and Hooks. After a long and drawn-out battle over the leadership of the National Baptist Convention, Rev. Jemison was able to defrock the perennial Rev. J. H. Jackson. It was this Rev. Jackson who forced Rev. Martin Luther King, Jr., to break away from the National Baptist Convention in 1961 and form his own Progressive National Baptist Convention, Inc. This rupture not only weakened King's movement; it also left many black Baptists torn between King's social gospel and the old convention's rich heritage. My own beloved grandfather, Rev. Clifton L. West, Sr., who pastored a church in Oklahoma for forty years, struggled with this dual allegiance until his death in 1979. With the replacement of Rev. J. H. Jackson in September 1982, sighs of relief and hopes for reconciliation pervaded many black Baptists across the country. Since Rev. Jesse Jackson's support of Rev. Jemison was crucial for his election, there is a real possibility for a more prophetic outlook on behalf of the leadership of the National Baptist Convention. So far Rev. Jemison is proceeding cautiously, sending out prophetic rhetorical signs yet guarding his priestly organization from discord. For example, the over twenty-year reign of Rev. J. H. Jackson has led him to promote a ten-year limit on the presidency, his friendship with Rev. Jesse Jackson has prompted him to support a vast voter registration drive, and his embarrassment of the convention's treatment of King has resulted in a $100,000 donation to Morehouse College (King's alma mater) to complete its chapel and build a monument honoring King. Rev. Jemison made these proposals—which were ratified by the delegates—in September 1983 at the convention's largest gathering in its history: roughly thirty-five thousand delegates attended its deliberations in Los Angeles. So this religious body is now experiencing new life. Whether it decides to become more openly progressive and prophetic remains an open question.

Needless to say, Rev. Hooks's NAACP is explicitly political, unashamed of its old-style liberalism and reluctant to move toward a more militant progressivism. Echoing the hidden fears and anxieties of the black middle class and stable working class, the NAACP senses that there are new currents on the move in the black community but, in true traditionalist style, it is unwilling to allow itself to be the guinea pig. Given its deep roots in black churches, it is no accident that it applauds the ascendancy of Rev. Jemison while it shares his cautious perspective. In his poignant speech during the recent March on Washington, Rev. Hooks declared war on Reaganism and then proceeded to invoke the Afro-American Christian God of the oppressed and downtrodden. This unusual public display of Christian piety and belief on behalf of a leader of a black secular organization suggests that much is stirring within him. In light of the recent internal turmoil in the NAACP (e.g., his clash with his former chairperson of the board, Margaret Bush Wilson) and the barrage of criticisms from various groups in the black community, Rev. Hooks may indeed be reassessing the direction and vision of the NAACP, the most distinguished black protest organization in Afro-American history. Rev. Hooks certainly possesses the integrity and will to change courses at this crucial historical moment; whether the NAACP has the courage and wherewithal to do so waits to be seen.

The third response to the prevailing crises in black America by Afro-American Christian leftists and left-liberals is salutary yet still marginal. It is salutary in that it speaks to the great issues of our time, e.g., third world struggles against U.S. and/or Soviet domination, maldistribution of wealth in the world, the South African apartheid regime, etc., and links these issues to the Afro-American struggle for freedom. Under the dynamic leadership of Rev. Herbert Daughtry, the National Black United Front (composed of black Christians, Marxists, nationalists, and left-liberals) has established itself as the leading voice of progressive black America. Far beyond liberalism and indifferent to social democracy, this Christian-headed group is staunchly anti-U.S. imperialist and vaguely pro-Socialist with a black nationalist twist. With the founding of the African Peoples' Christian Organization in March 1983, Rev. Daughtry has extended his vision by supplementing the National Black United Front with an exclusively Christian organization, especially for those prophetic black Christians demoralized and debilitated by the secular ideological battles in NBUF: Rev. Daughtry continues to head both organizations. Rev. Lowery's Southern Christian Leadership Conference—much like the Progressive National Baptist Convention, Inc., which still upholds the legacy of King—courageously articulates the needs and interests of the black poor, but with much less ideological fervor and international visibility. Armed with highly talented young leaders, such as Mark Ridley-Thomas in Los Angeles, Rev. Lowery's SCLC sustains the most impressive Christian ecumenical (across black Christian denominations) progressive group in the USA. Yet it still falls short of the comprehensive Christian analysis and vision of Rev. Daughtry's progressive NBUF and prophetic APCO.

Despite their salutary presence and potential growth, these organizations remain marginal to the conscience and praxis of black America. The hegemony of liberal political ideology still holds fast in black America and its Christian churches. Surely the black working poor and underclass sense that liberalism is insufficient, yet this sense is not articulated in political forms. Even Revs. Daughtry and Lowery's groups principally lie outside of the black underclass, with deep roots in regional sections of the country among the working poor and working class. Yet even the marginality of these groups is encouraging, for they constitute an influential marginality which puts necessary pressure on the more visible liberal organizations. They also link the rich tradition of Afro-American Christianity to more sophisticated social analyses, more inclusive moral visions, and more ambitious (though propitious) political praxis.

The last response of the black church to the present-day crises of black America is now a major media event: the candidacy of one of the sons of the black church, Rev. Jesse Jackson. This is an event of utmost importance to black church people. Not since the appearance of King have black Christians had a national figure who commands so much nonblack attention. In a moving interview years ago in *Ebony* magazine (the leading black American magazine), Rev. Jesse Jackson put forward the deep Christian roots of his political practice. This kind of existential candor goes far with the black church. The basic issue is not the extent to which the black church will support Rev. Jackson, but rather the way in which the black church views Rev. Jackson as an extension of itself: what it has produced and given to the nation. Politically, Rev. Jackson remains close to most voting black Americans: liberal on domestic socioeconomic issues, left-liberal on international issues, and ambivalent on cultural issues. Yet he is much more progressive than any of the white candidates vying for the nomination of the Democratic party. His candidacy has already broadened the perimeters of public discourse in American politics, politically enlivened many dormant black voters, and brought together the prophetic forces in the black church; a recent breakfast meeting of local black leaders for Rev. Jackson held in Rev. Daughtry's The House of the Lord church in Brooklyn illustrates this possible unity.

So despite the numerous processes of modernization occurring in black America, the prophetic black church remains the major source for political leadership. But if it is more adequately to meet the present challenges, it must move toward more sophisticated social analyses of the economic depression in black America. Such analyses should highlight the shifting international division of labor and the dominant role of U.S. corporate power. This analysis should be guided by an egalitarian vision which embraces the needs of working class and underclass Hispanics, Asians, women, whites, as well as the concerns of ecologists, feminists, and peace activists. Lastly, this analysis and vision must be coupled with a spiritual awakening which combats the rapacious hedonism and narcissism in late U.S. capitalist culture, thereby enabling a more virtuous and viable left.

Anti-Imperialist Struggle and Black Americans

The anti-imperialist struggle presents a major challenge to the black liberation movement. With the significant exceptions of black Marxists and a few black nationalists, the black liberation movement has failed to take seriously the *international* character and scope of the struggle for human freedom. This is so owing to three basic reasons. First, the historical role of black Americans in the emergence and development of U.S. capitalism has focused black concerns to the national predicament. Second, the difficulties of political alliances across racial lines in the U.S. has rendered many blacks suspicious of such alliances across national lines in the world. Third, those black people who take seriously anti-imperialist struggles tend to focus primarily on the continent of Africa, thereby often downplaying the other continental dimensions of the anti-imperialist struggle.

Following the work of Ernest Mandel, I shall hold that U.S. capitalism has undergone three basic stages: industrial capitalism, monopoly capitalism, and multinational corporate capitalism. It is important to stress that industrial capitalism in the U.S. was built, in large part though indirectly, on the backs of African slaves who labored in a cotton-dominated southern economy. Profits derived from the lucrative cotton production facilitated differentiation of the northern manufacturing economy—not solely in the burgeoning textile industry but also in minimizing British competition with emerging U.S. industries owing to British preoccupation with southern U.S. cotton products.

The consolidation of U.S. industrial capitalism—accomplished by the northern victory in the Civil War—left black people in a precarious situation: allied to a northern industrial ruling class hungry for control of devastated southern land, labor force, and production, and located in a demoralized southern U.S. culture bent on keeping black folk subjugated. The grand yet failed project of northern domination of the South coupled with the granting of political rights to black males—that is, the Reconstruction—revealed the limits of U.S. industrial capitalism. The major limitation consisted of the refusal of northern capitalists and politicians to come to terms with the need for fundamental land reform in

From *LUCHA* (June 1985).

the South, especially for black farmers. Such a land reform would have required the confiscation and distribution of slaveholders' property and thereby violated a sacred principle of U.S. capitalism: the sanctity of private property. After twelve brief years (1865–77) of northern martial law in the South along with black participation in government (which yielded two black U.S. senators, nearly twenty black U.S. congresspersons, and hundreds of black public officials), the Reconstruction was brought to a close. In other words, it became clear that the northern capitalist commitment to private property and profit-maximization was much stronger than commitment to democracy and black political rights. The latter would not be regained until 1965, almost a century later.

As U.S. industrial capitalism strengthened, it extended its imperialist activity against not only Mexican and indigenous peoples on the North American continent, but also against Latin Americans and Asians, including Puerto Ricans, Cubans, and Filipinos. Black presence in such U.S. imperialist armies were quite evident. In fact, to be a soldier in the U.S. (segregated) Army was perceived as a grand achievement for many black Americans at the time. It was one of the few opportunities open to black people for upward social mobility.

With the advent of monopoly capitalism at the end of the nineteenth century and the growth of a small yet significant U.S. empire around the world, black people began to organize for the first time on a national scale—with the founding of the National Organization of Afro-American Women, the National Association for the Advancement of Colored People, and the National Urban League between 1895 and 1910. This political expression of a new engaged black petit bourgeoisie would set the tone of the black liberation movement until the momentous mass movement of Marcus Garvey in the early twenties. The greatness of Garvey's leadership and the significance of his movement was that it injected an international dimension into blacks' perception of their oppression. This internationalism was sometimes tainted by a narrow racialism which hid and concealed class dynamics of worldwide capitalist processes, but it also contained anti-imperialist elements, especially as it related to Africa and blacks in Latin America. In other words, Garveyism, along with the more advanced pan-Africanism of the African Blood Brotherhood, moved the black liberation movement a step closer to full participation in the worldwide anti-imperialist struggle.

As black people underwent urbanization and proletarianization in the twenties and thirties and as monopoly capitalism deepened its crisis into a worldwide depression, anti-imperialist voices spread throughout black America. The strongest voices were those of black Marxists in the Communist Party USA. In this period, black association and/or preoccupation with the USSR enhanced the role of anti-imperialist analysis in the black liberation movement.

World War II was a major setback for anti-imperialist struggles in black America. With the coming of the "American century," as Henry Luce coined it, black political energies almost monolithically turned toward full citizenship status in U.S. capitalist society and against the alleged foes of the U.S. Again, black presence in the Korean War was often viewed as a grand opportunity to support the U.S. cause (and convince the rulers of black loyalty) in its now integrated army. And, of course, the few anti-imperialist black voices in the fifties were systematically repressed by the vicious tide of McCarthyism.

The turning point of the relation of the black liberation movement to anti-imperialist struggle was neither the courageous fight for bourgeois rights in the South led by Martin Luther King, Jr., in the early sixties nor the Black Power movement in the mid-sixties. Rather the turning point was the appropriation of the revolutionary rhetoric of Malcom X by young working class and underclass black youth in the late sixties. Malcom X, murdered in early 1965 (he never witnessed the Watts rebellion), reinjected a version of internationalism which accented anti-imperialism into the black liberation movement. And with the war raging in Vietnam, African countries gaining political independence, and the white new left turning toward Marxist analyses, Malcolm X's rhetoric served as a catalyst for many young black people (including myself—a teenager of fifteen then) to take anti-imperialist struggle seriously. Needless to say, the Black Panther party was the leading exemplar of this anti-imperialist fervor. So, with the solidifying of multinational corporate capitalism aided by the technical innovation in communications information as well as torture techniques, anti-imperialist sensibilities increased among black Americans.

Since the late sixties there has been a permanent black presence in the major anti-imperialist and anti-interventionist efforts in the U.S. This is so, in part, because these efforts are often led by organized U.S. communists and socialists, in which there is a disproportion of blacks (percentage-wise). The turbulent decade of the seventies in the third world—Chile, Angola, Mozambique, South Korea, Philippines, South Africa, Nicaragua, to name a few—witnessed significant participation of black Americans in anti-imperialist activity. Yet problems still persist, problems which primarily have to do with the difficulties of interracial political struggle in racist U.S. society.

There is little doubt that the problems resulting from interracial political struggle in the U.S. have hampered the U.S. role in anti-imperialist struggle in the world. The surface phenomena are well known: white arrogance, sexual jealousy, and Eurocentrism as well as black inferiority anxieties, sexual adventure, and African preoccupations. Yet underlying these phenomena is something more basic: the cultural distance between black and white anti-imperialists. This cultural distance is itself a historical product of racist U.S. society, yet the U.S. left remains, for the most part, unable to overcome it. Hence, U.S. anti-imperialist efforts remain weaker and more fragmented than they should be.

This cultural distance cannot be closed overnight. Yet it can be lessened. For those of us deeply committed to strengthening anti-imperialist activities in the U.S., it is necessary to focus our energies on three fronts. First, we must fight racism (including anti-Semitism) and Eurocentrism within the anti-imperialist movement. This is best done by highlighting the ways in which racism functions in countries buttressed by U.S. imperialism, especially in South Africa, Brazil, Israel, and South Korea. The black liberation movement cannot but take seriously white anti-imperialist activities when such actions perennially line up people alongside black people fighting U.S. imperialism. The crucial though petit bourgeois students' protests against campus investments in South Africa are a grand sign of hope in this regard.

Second, we must practically ground ourselves in particular anti-imperialist struggles in light of theoretical systemic Marxist-like analyses that link anti-imperialist struggles against common capitalist foes. The interplay of particularity and universality is crucial. No narrow particularism nor abstract universalism should be our slogan! In this way, a preoccupation with Central America in no way minimizes the significance of anti-apartheid work—or vice versa. A necessary (though not sufficient) condition for interracial political struggle against international capitalist realities is black and white agreement on common enemies—an agreement that results from Marxist-like analyses of the international capitalist world.

Last, we must strive to bring together black and white anti-imperialist groups for dialogues, discussions, and demonstrations. There can be some degree of political unity only when there is some degree of trust among groups. And such trust comes from common interaction and struggle. New York CIRCUS—the most prominent Christian anti-imperialist group in the country— has, in many ways, been exemplary in this regard. For it is forever seeking interaction with anti-imperialist groups, be they Asian, Latin American, Irish, or African. Needless to say, as a black American Christian I have a special affinity with such a prophetic cloud of witnesses. David Kalke and I have promised each other to more fully deepen the links between New York CIRCUS and the black community, especially black churches. And such matters should be

W. E. B. Du Bois
and the Cold War

W. E. B. Du Bois remains the greatest scholar to emerge from Afro-America. Educated at Fisk University, Harvard University, and the University of Berlin, Du Bois was one of the most knowledgeable persons of his day. Owing to both racist exclusion from the white academy and his deep convictions regarding the practical use of knowledge, Du Bois chose to be an organic intellectual. As a professor at black universities (Wilberforce and Atlanta) and, most importantly, as editor of *The Crisis* (the popular periodical of the NAACP) for over a quarter of a century, Du Bois tried to convey to his fellow citizens an understanding of the deplorable plight of oppressed people in European and American capitalist civilizations. Yet there is not one book that even begins to unravel the complexity of his life, thought, and praxis—only a few mediocre biographies and some hagiographical essays.

Some of the crucial questions that remain unanswered are: Why did Du Bois become in his later years an unrepentant Stalinist? Why did he join the Communist Party USA and immediately leave for Ghana two years before his death? How does one account for his vague pre-Marxist progressive views in the early 1900s, his passionate pan-Africanism thereafter, his preoccupation with Marxist analysis in the thirties, and his communist praxis in the fifties and sixties? Gerald Horne's ambitious book tries to provide some answers to these queries. His basic thesis is that Du Bois's last communist allegiances were a "logical continuation" of his earlier progressive years principally owing to his response to the Cold War in post–World War II USA. Horne argues that Du Bois grasped the profound truth that anti-Red sentiments usually have been linked to antiblack ones in twentieth-century America. Therefore it is no accident that as anticommunist convictions moved most white left intellectuals to the right, Du Bois remained on the left true to his deep anti-racist and anti-imperialist allegiances. Based on impressive research in the recently opened Du Bois papers, Horne concludes that Du Bois was a "tower of strength" in the cause of socialism, peace, and equality during the pervasive repression of the left in mid-century America.

This essay has not been previously published. Review of Gerald Horne, *Black and Red: W. E. Du Bois and the Afro-American Response to the Cold War* (Albany: SUNY Press, 1985).

79

I find Horne's book noteworthy not because it is persuasive but rather owing to its desperate attempt to keep alive the memory of a great and often misunderstood figure. Unfortunately, Horne conceals much of this greatness and contributes to our misunderstanding of Du Bois's ideological development. Horne's own unargued-for pro-Sovietism throughout the book does not lead him to inquire into why Du Bois moved into a pro-Soviet stance. Mere claims about the "ideological consistency" of Du Bois's position won't do. And to invoke such explanations is to write an idealist, un-Marxist history of a major Marxist figure. Furthermore, to suggest that the "core of Du Bois' thought . . . remained immutable" throughout his career is to shun all historical specificity.

Instead, I suggest that Du Bois's greatness lies in his profound grasp and political support of the distinctive historical process of the twentieth century: the decolonization of the third world. He was a pan-Africanist before he was a serious socialist, yet soon concluded that being a socialist was requisite for being a serious pan-Africanist. His initial reactions to the Bolshevik Revolution were predicated principally on the degree to which this first communist nation supported decolonization. The results were mixed—hence his enthusiasm for the USSR ebbed and flowed prior to the Cold War. In fact, his most important Marxist book, *Black Reconstruction* (1935), is pioneering precisely because he locates and situates the struggle over the labor of the ex-slaves in post–Civil War capitalist USA in an international context of labor, racial, and anticolonial struggle.

With the rise of the USA as the world power after World War II, the decolonization process could find substantive support almost solely from the USSR. The intense USA-USSR standoff collapsed political options into crude either/or choices. Since most white left intellectuals were preoccupied with domestic economic issues and relatively uninterested in third world nations, the postwar economic boom gave them little reason to remain on the left. The central concerns became support for American democracy and opposition to Soviet tyranny. In stark contrast, Du Bois's focus was on decolonization around the world and on the black plight in the USA, hence his embracing a pro-Soviet position seemed both unavoidable and desirable. Had not the USSR supported anticolonial struggles more reliably than the USA? Had not the Communist Party USA fought racism more courageously and consistently than any other political organization in America? And was not the paranoid anticommunist rhetoric of the Cold War proof of these crucial roles played by the USSR and Communist Party USA?

Du Bois had to choose, and he simply could not opt for a racist, capitalist West over a communist East that provided support for the de-

colonization of the third world. And given his own historical predicament, we see in retrospect that either choice was a tragic one—especially
for an Afro-American left figure. Yet we must not remain blind of
Du Bois's own blindnesses. Stalinism was Stalinism—and Du Bois's
support for and sentimental attachment to Joseph Stalin cannot be
justified. This also holds for Hungary 1956 and the familiar litany of
Soviet atrocities.

Therefore Du Bois's greatness lies not in the ultimate choices he made
but rather in the profound insights he left us from his passionate
struggles with the major issues he faced. Horne rightly corrects those
who see a fundamental shift from Du Bois's NAACP activism to his later
Marxist praxis, yet by highlighting and supporting Du Bois's Stalinism
Horne unintentionally trivializes his greatness and unwittingly reduces
him to a figure worthy of dismissal. Yet the American left can trivialize
and dismiss Du Bois—be it by means of uncritical praise or vulgar condemnation—only at its own further detriment.

On Stanley Aronowitz's The Crisis in Historical Materialism

Stanley Aronowitz's book is in a class of its own in American Marxism. It is pioneering in its theoretical formulations, penetrating in its philosophical interrogations, powerful in its novel social analysis, and provocative in its prescriptions for political action. No other recent text confronts the major challenges and perplexing problems facing the Marxist tradition with such candor and intelligence.

Critical of both social democratic reformism and dogmatic Leninism, and equipped with an arsenal of insights from sources as different as Georg Lukács and the French poststructuralists, Aronowitz embarks on a quest for that which has perennially eluded Marxism: a theory of the historical specificity of American capitalism. This quest begins with an investigation of Marxism's fundamental theoretical questions and philosophical presuppositions in light of both the failure of proletarian revolution in the West and the rise of cultural movements—various feminisms, nationalisms, religious political formations, and ecological groupings—which appear to circumvent traditional Marxism.

Aronowitz argues that Marxism has not yet adequately come to terms with its basic theoretical notions (such as class), its central philosophical ideas (such as totality), and its pressing practical issues related to various forms of oppression. His detailed treatments of these complex materials are fascinating and often convincing. Yet he goes further by posing a difficult problem only marginally addressed by Marxism: the problem of scientific and technological domination of nature and human nature.

Aronowitz examines the extent to which Marxism remains a captive of scientism and then links this to the subjugation of women and black people in American society. This situation is partly sustained by subsuming women and blacks under the rubric of "otherness" as opposed to white male rationality, discipline, and decorum. For example, women are often associated with the uncontrollability of nature, and black people with sexual eroticism—associations rooted in the repressed, anxiety-

From *The Village Voice* (Jan. 6-12, 1982); review of Stanley Aronowitz, *The Crisis in Historical Materialism: Class Politics and Culture in Marxist Theory* (New York: Praeger, 1981).

ridden white male psyche. His claim is not that patriarchy is identical with racial or caste oppression nor that the origins of each— which predate capitalism—are similar within the evolution of the West. Rather he is saying that a Marxism which does not address the displacement of intraclass rivalries to cultural phenomena (such as sexual jealousy and fear of castration) is a deficient and impotent Marxism.

Aronowitz's cultural leftist perspective prompts a non-Leninist, "beyond reformist" political program. He holds that progressive feminists, black nationalists, ecologists, religionists, and fractions of the working class constitute an emerging anticapitalist and antihierarchical bloc, guided by the vision of a self-managed socialism wherein cultural heterogeneity and democratic processes reign. He develops his unique neo-Marxist viewpoint in a wide range of critical encounters with such ideas as the disaccumulation thesis of James O'Connor and the post-Marxism of Michel Foucault. In short, this book is a tour de force and necessary reading for anyone interested in Marxism, Continental philosophy, or contemporary American life.

On Jon P. Gunnemann's
The Moral Meaning of Revolution

This is a highly ambitious book. Its basic aim is "to clarify the relation-ship between revolutionary practice and moral reasoning" (p. 2). This aim primarily involves presenting a complex argument to show that rev-olution cannot be justified in the usual sense of what it means to justify an act precisely because the ordinary moral courts of appeal are called into question by revolutionaries. This is so because, for Gunnemann, revolution is, fundamentally, a rejection of an existing understanding of the problem of evil and an attempt to put forward a new solution to the problem of evil. Following the pioneering work of Thomas Kuhn in philosophy of science, Gunnemann holds that ordinary moral courts of appeal are rejected by revolutionaries because such courts of appeal "imply residual confidence in the existing theodicy and the revolutionary loses his case merely by submitting to such a process" (p. 43). Hence, revolution is better understood as an apocalyptic event or as a religious conversion than as a moral act. For Gunnemann, conflicting paradigm solutions to the problem of evil—defined by Max Weber as the incon-gruity between destiny and merit—are at the heart of the moral mean-ing of revolution.

Gunnemann's argument is self-consciously limited to certain types of revolutions. He not only distinguishes between a revolt motivated by perceived violations of political principles (rebellion) and a revolt that involves transformation of consciousness (revolution); he also is con-cerned primarily with the consciousness of people involved in revolutions from below, for example, mid-seventeenth-century England, as opposed to revolutions from above, for example, mid-nineteenth-century Japan. This concern leads him to examine the revolutionary du-alistic explanations of evil in society put forward by millenarians (based on the classic works of N. Cohn, Y. Talmon, E. J. Hobsbawm, G. Lewy, and others) and Frantz Fanon. He rightly concludes that these dualistic explanations "simply invert the terms of a theodicy that has been im-posed on them" (p. 91), and, most important, overlook the need for sanctification, the need for disciplined ordering of postrevolutionary life and society. Gunnemann briefly suggests that a more acceptable form of

From *The Journal of Religion* (Apr. 1981); review of Jon P. Gunnemann, *The Moral Meaning of Revolution* (New Haven: Yale University Press, 1979).

dualistic thinking—in the case of renovative violence—is found in Frederick Douglass's account of his famous fight with his master, Mr. Covey.

The chapter entitled "Karl Marx and the End of Theodicy" is the most provocative and controversial section of the book. Gunnemann argues essentially that Marx tries to overcome the need for a theodicy by subsuming all forms of evil under the notion of negative universality which is epitomized by the proletariat in capitalist society. This negative universality is manifest in the proletariat's radical marginality, alienation, and anomie; in short, the proletariat "is not actually included in the theodicy of the larger society" (p. 135). Revolutionary activity by the proletariat can be seen as a move from negative universality to positive universality, from domination to democracy, from an evil world to an emancipated world.

Gunnemann suggests that Marx's argument is insightful yet unsuccessful owing to the incoherence of Marx's understanding of negative universality and his underestimation of the ways in which authentic revolutionary activity by the proletariat can be short-circuited. There are many claims, observations, and interpretations in this rich chapter with which one will disagree, reject, affirm, or question. To put it bluntly, it is well worth reading.

If the Marx chapter is the meat of the book, the last two chapters, though interesting and at times incisive, are the fat of the book. The chapter on Moltmann is a superb critique of Moltmann's political theology. But it is unclear how this critique contributes to the basic aim of the book since Moltmann has so little to say about revolution and, as Gunnemann admits, what Moltmann does have to say about revolution "is in many ways the least satisfactory aspect of this thought" (p. 177).

The last chapter, entitled "Evil, Ethics and Revolution," is disappointing. It is discursive, held together by a string of interesting insights. I expected a more rigorous argumentative treatment bringing together the wealth of sociological, historical, and theological material presented earlier.

The major philosophical shortcoming in Gunnemann's intriguing and intricate argument is his attempt to root his argument in P. Berger's unconvincing claim that theodicy is antecedent to social legitimations, that the experience of evil is "pretheoretical," hence warranting the choice of theodicy as the starting point for understanding revolution. Gunnemann's book certainly reveals the crucial role of theodicy within social legitimations during revolutionary periods, but it does not provide any persuasive reasons as to why we should take seriously Berger's claim—a claim which Gunnemann considers foundational for his own argument.

Where Christian Rhetoric about Love and Moral Arguments about Rights Fall Short— A Systemic Understanding of Torture

Torture is the most direct and unmediated form of dehumanization in our world. It is symptomatic of the widespread institutionalized terrorism found throughout our world. Therefore torture must be understood on a variety of levels—the religious, moral, socioeconomic, and political levels.

Every religion we know places some distinctive value on human creatures. For Christians, this value is bestowed by divine creation and love; that is, all human beings are created in the image of God and are worthy of Jesus Christ giving his life so they may have a more abundant life. This means that all members of the human family possess a certain dignity and deserve a particular treatment which acknowledges their creature-status before God.

All forms of human behavior, social practices, and institutional arrangements which deny this dignity and violate this treatment must be rejected and resisted. The basic biblical criterion for this dignity and treatment is found in the words of Jesus Christ, "Do unto others as you would have others do unto you." This simple yet profound statement provides the ammunition requisite for wholesale and wholehearted Christian opposition to the very existence of torture.

The Christian recognition of the sinful proclivities of human beings makes torture—as it does other forms of dehumanization, comprehensible—yet it never makes it tolerable. Like slavery, racism, sexism, and other gross examples of relegating God's creatures to a position outside the human family, torture is fundamentally un-Christian. In fact a broader Christian consensus exists regarding torture than it does regarding other forms of dehumanization. Yet only recently has torture received the attention it deserves—thereby galvanizing the resistance tor-

---

From *American Christians for the Abolition of Torture* (1984).

ture warrants. But if torture is to be abolished this resistance must intensify.

There is little doubt that torture is an affront to the moral sentiments of people around the world. There simply are no serious arguments which promote and support torture on moral grounds. Powerful moral arguments against torture can easily be based simply on secular Kantian standards—such as treating human beings as ends rather than means—or on utilitarian viewpoints that accent the greatest happiness for the greatest number of people.

The problem in our world regarding torture is not its immorality but rather the cynical amorality generated by paranoid leaders who rule corrupt and unjust power structures and command deferential civil servants to engage in the torture of their fellow human beings.

Torture is an integral component of the repressive apparatus of the modern state. It is a systematic practice employed to secure social order and maintain the status quo. Therefore torture is comprehensible as a sinful proclivity of discrete individuals, but it is to be understood—especially in the specific ways it is in our day employed—as a supportive element in existing systems of power and domination.

First, it is important to note that torture is most widely practiced in countries where a language and heritage of human rights is relatively absent. This does not mean that torture does not exist in countries such as the USA or England. Rather it means that in countries with a tradition of human rights the victims of torture have readily available to them a language and heritage to use against such treatment. Needless to say, those countries may, beyond their borders, support socioeconomic conditions and political regimes which ignore the language and heritage of human rights and flagrantly violate the rights of their citizens. This means we need an understanding of torture which acknowledges the complex international systems of power and domination.

Second, torture is more pervasive in those societies in which the violation of other human rights is widespread. The amount of torture in a society is a good measure of the degree to which dehumanization permeates that society. Therefore torture is best understood as part of a continuum which exemplifies the "quotient of injustice" of a given socioeconomic arrangement.

Third, torture intensifies and expands as the xenophobic and jingoistic perceptions of a nation's leaders grow. Therefore in periods of crisis and unrest, torture is more readily used to control the population and eradicate oppositional groups in the country. In the communist world, this means the control and eradication of dissident ethnic groups, religious communities, and critical intellectuals. In the capitalist world, this means primarily controlling and eradicating communists, socialists, and desperate people of color. And under monarchical or even quasi-feudal rule, this means repressing anyone who threatens prevailing authority.

So the scope and degree of torture can be discerned by these three conjoined conditions: a society's heritage of discourse about human rights, its socioeconomic arrangements, and the repressive apparatus of the state. Therefore the most effective strategy to eliminate torture is neither Christian rhetoric about love nor moral argumentation about rights. Granted, we must engage in such rhetoric and argumentation but we should not expect that such talk will have major impact on cynical, amoral, paranoid leaders (who rule unjust societies in which commands to torture are routine).

If we desire to see torture cease we will best achieve this by applying institutional pressure and exerting social force. Available institutional pressure and social force often reside in the prohetic wing of Christian churches, Jewish synagogues, Muslim mosques, or secular progressive groups. Prestigious watch-groups such as Amnesty International aid in this regard.

Furthermore, in some desperate situations in which it seems possible and credible that violent, fundamental social change will enhance the cries of the citizenry, then—after much prayer—we may decide that tempered support of revolution may be best. Of course, opposition to torture in no way requires support of revolution. But if torture is systemic, then it may not be able to be rooted out without a fundamental change of system.

Since the Christian church is neither solely a social action group nor a revolutionary movement, its role is unique. The church should perennially measure the world in light of the ideal of Christian love, relate this ideal to the prevailing systems of power and control, and commit itself to the struggle for dignity against systems which deny it.

Political struggle for human dignity is not the sole substance of Christian faith, but Christian faith requires that one choose this struggle—one's choice being guided by systemic understandings of power and domination from the victim's vantage point.

Many Christians might argue that the prevailing systems of power and domination—including widespread torture—are imperfect yet desirable over against alternative systems. This argument raises large and complicated issues which often result in agreement concerning the imperfect character of any alternatives and an ideological stand-off regarding the desirability of particular alternatives. Yet we must not permit ourselves while engaging in this broader discussion to lose sight of the undesirability of torture. Regardless of one's commitment to a particular alternative, it is quite possible that one's ideological opponent—both inside and outside the church—would support the elimination of torture. The possibility of common ground on this particular issue transcends ideological conviction. It is the task of prophetic Christians to secure and expand this common ground—cognizant of disagreement at other levels of discussion yet convinced that imperfect betterment is always possible.

On Mark Naison's
Communists in Harlem
during the Depression

Mark Naison's book is a major contribution to our understanding of the complex dynamics of black Harlem's participation in the Communist Party USA from 1928 to 1941. The primary aim of the work is to modify the pervasive view of communist manipulation and betrayal of black American activists and interests put forward by Richard Wright, Ralph Ellison, Harold Cruse, Wilson Record, and others. Naison acknowledges the strong Soviet control of the party, yet he also recognizes that this control, though generally negative for the party, had some positive effects for communist struggles against racism in America. Furthermore, this pervasive control was not exhaustive; rather, some marginal space was created for limited innovative black political activity in the party.

This modest argument has earned the chagrin of the dean of Cold War communist historiography, Theodore Draper. In two blistering articles in *The New York Review of Books* (May 9 and 30), Draper attacked Naison and a host of other leftist historians for waging an "academic campaign for the rehabilitation of American Communism." Yet nothing could be further from the truth in the case of Naison. His aim is to build on the insights of Draper, Cruse, and others, while also critically examining some of their blindnesses—blindnesses that flow from the ideological axes they were out to grind.

The achievements of the party regarding racism in America are well known: the creation of the first interracial space in U.S. political culture, the broad radicalization of a significant segment of the middle-class black intelligentsia, the trade unionization of many skilled and unskilled black workers, and the crucial support of black efforts to make lynching, police brutality, and legal injustice salient issues in U.S. life. These achievements may seem quite small given communist aims of fundamentally transforming U.S. society and thereby eliminating racism. And certainly it was in the interests of a Soviet-controlled U.S. Communist Party to pursue these goals. Yet looking through the lens of black Americans, it is an important fact of U.S. life that the first attempt of a political move-

From *Monthly Review* (Dec. 1985); review of Mark Naison, *Communists in Harlem during the Depression* (New York: Grove Press, 1984).

ment to create and sustain an interracial community (including the touchy personal spheres of sexual and social relations) was undertaken not by Christians, socialists, feminists, liberals, or populists, but by communists. Early communist interracial efforts were expanded and enlarged at the command of Soviet leaders. This command focused on black self-determination of a suppressed "nation" in the South. Yet it resulted in communist participation in crucial black struggles against discrimination and police brutality throughout the country.

And though the first generation of black communists was made up predominantly of West Indians (Cyril Briggs, Richard Moore, Otto Huiswoud) with revolutionary nationalist sentiments, they were soon replaced by upwardly mobile middle-class black Americans (James Ford, Benjamin Davis, Theodore Bassett) eager to use their energies in status positions commensurate with their talents, outraged by their delimited opportunities owing to the rampant racism in U.S. society, and impatient with the parochialism of Afro-American life, especially its churches. The interracialism of the party—much like the left subculture in universities and Bohemian communities today—attracted middle-class black Americans yet kept working-class and poor blacks at a distance.

As Naison rightly points out, this distance was as much cultural as ideological and political. This interracialism, which entailed a willingness to support black struggles, gained the party many black sympathizers, but those who actually joined were primarily middle-class professionals, trade-unionized skilled workers, and marginal plebeian intellectuals, who had mastered the skills of Marxist rhetoric and organizational mobilization. In addition, the black cadre was more male than female—owing, in part, to the fact that black men tend to move to white women more quickly than black women to white men in U.S. interracial practice. In short, the secular Marxist discourse, organizational emphases, and complex exogamous relations were simply too much for the black masses (many of whom were recent rural migrants) to bear.

This middle-class bias is seen most clearly in a major source of the party's attraction to black Americans: the popularization of black cultural productions. Despite the attempts to support and promote black music and theater, the party shunned the culture of the black masses. It excluded musical comedy and vaudeville, remained highly ambiguous in its attitude toward jazz and the blues, and often displayed open contempt toward the playful character and participatory responses of popular black performers and their audiences. In short, the cultural tastes and life of the party simply could not tolerate the everyday life of most black people—though it attracted elements of the black middle class and stable working class.

Black Harlem's activity in the party peaked in 1939, when there were over one thousand members. This peak had much to do with the practical political activity of the party, which focused on particular issues—unemployment, job discrimination, housing, the Scottsboro and Herndon cases—during the popular front period. Yet black suspicion of the party was reinforced by the Italian invasion of Ethiopia (1934-45), during which the Soviet Union refused to halt trade with Mussolini, and by the establishment of the National Negro Congress (1935), which influential black leader A. Philip Randolph denounced as a pernicious communist puppet organization after its third convention in 1940. This suspicion escalated after the party's infamous flip-flop before and after the Nazi-Soviet pact of 1939 and the German invasion of the Soviet Union less than two years later.

By 1941 the party in Harlem was a tolerated yet integral part of the community, with its outstanding members quite visible—including Benjamin Davis, who was twice elected city councilman from the district. But the party was marginal as a political organization. To the degree to which party members functioned as progressive trade unionists, public officials, and activists on local issues, they were welcome; but when they raised the red flag concerning Marxist ideology and Soviet foreign policy, they were ignored.

Regarding black-Jewish relations in the party—an issue highlighted by Cruse and Black Power spokespersons in the 1960s—Naison points out that this issue rarely surfaced during the depression. This was so because Jewish communists, who were highly disproportionate in the party as a whole and were also predominant among whites in the Harlem section, downplayed their ethnic identity in line with the assimilationist ethos of the party. Since black interaction with any whites was so novel, little attention was given to ethnic distinctions among whites. This would change by the late 1930s and 1940s, given the visibility of Father Coughlin's anti-Semitic movement, the revelation of the Holocaust, and the establishment of the State of Israel. Yet it is an important fact of the U.S. left that Jewish communists have remained more universalist, internationalist, and assimilationist than most other American Jews since the Second World War.

What, then, are the pertinent lessons to draw from Naison's impressive study for the present struggle against racism in U.S. society and the U.S. left? First, we must be sensitive to the *cultural expressions of class and strata divisions* among black Americans. Interracial political struggle is more culturally amenable to middle-class and some stable working-class black Americans. This does not mean that exclusivistic nationalist sentiments guide the black working poor and underclass—in fact, Christian and Islamic moral universalism dominate much of their perspectives.

But it does mean that black organizational contexts (outside or within predominantly white leftist groups) attract a larger cross section of black Americans because they feel more free to be themselves and are less intimidated by privileged articulate white leftists.

Second, we must give up the dream that secular sensibilities are requisite for leftist political activity. Those who cling to such a Eurocentric model cannot but be immobilized pessimists of the first order. Rather, we must try to tap those progressive elements in religious symbolism and language, then conjoin these elements with flexible Marxist analyses of liberal capitalist America.

Lastly, we should realize that most black Americans are suspicious of white people, be they radicals, liberals, or conservatives. Yet the trust of black Americans can be won by principled and protracted struggles over issues in which racism plays a role. We are witnessing such a building of trust between black and white radicals in the anti-apartheid movement. As these bonds of trust develop and grow, reciprocal black support in feminist, ecological, and antihomophobic struggles within the context of anticapitalist and anti-imperialist perspectives may result in positive achievements over and beyond those of the gallant efforts of communists in Harlem during the depression.

Race and Class in Afro-American History

The making of the American working class is deeply shaped by the ambiguous relation of blacks to the labor movement in the nineteenth century. As the great black scholar, W. E. B. Du Bois, noted in his monumental study *Black Reconstruction* (1935), the South after the Civil War presented America with the opportunity for a powerful labor movement. Yet, for the most part, organized labor missed this chance principally owing to its captivity to racism. This major Achilles' heel of the American labor movement ought not elide the few glimmers of hope in the past, but it does help us understand the weaknesses of the struggles for workers' power and black freedom in the USA.

Prior to the Civil War, black slaves primarily consisted of an agricultural labor force, with 5 percent of slaves working in industry. The small yet significant number of free blacks in the South—over a quarter of a million in 1850—served as artisans and craftsmen in cities and towns. For example, the majority of artisans in the most developed Southern city in the early nineteenth century—Charleston, South Carolina—were black. In addition, the most famous slave insurrections were led by black artisans or industrial slaves: Gabriel Prosser was a blacksmith, Nat Turner a slave carpenter, and Denmark Vesey a free carpenter.

Free blacks in the North, who numbered slightly less than those in the South, began organizing as artisans as early as 1850. This organizing was motivated not only by labor concerns, but also in response to vicious attacks and exclusionary attitudes of white laborers, especially newly arrived European immigrants. The worst race riots in American history—initiated by Irish workers in reaction to a compulsory military draft to fight for the Union in the Civil War—not only killed over three hundred black people but also culminated in the burning of the headquarters of the American Seamen's Protective Association, which was a black labor organization and the first seamen's grouping of any kind in the country. These infamous draft riots were motivated by anger over unfair exemptions and evasions for the privileged and fear that a Union victory would result in cheap black labor displacement of white laborers.

The widespread white perception of blacks as strikebreakers or "scabs"

From *Le Monde Diplomatique* (Oct. 1984).

regulated most of the responses of organized labor to blacks. And it quickly became a self-fulfilling perception as blacks found themselves caught between exclusionary white trade unions and exploitative white capitalists. And as black "scabbing" increased, as well as white "scabbing" to break black workers' strikes, deep racial cleavages became commonplace in the American working class.

There were gallant attempts to overcome racial cleavages in the early years of organized labor. The National Labor Union, founded in 1866, began with ideals of interracial labor solidarity but soon faltered over political disputes regarding relations with the Republican party. At the time, blacks were reluctant to give up ties to the party of Abraham Lincoln and cast their lot with a new, untried Labor Reform party.

The most significant attempt at black-white labor unity was made by the Knights of Labor, established in 1869. With the majority of ex-slaves caught in the vicious cycle of sharecropping and tenantry, and other blacks on the margin of industrial labor, the Knights' program of land reform, cooperatives, and education was highly appealing to blacks. More important, the strong commitment of the Knights to organizing unskilled workers and to policies of racial equality ensured black support. At the peak of its numerical strength and influence, blacks constituted nearly 20 percent of the organization. On May 1, 1886—the first May Day in labor history—340,000 black and white workers demonstrated together for the eight-hour day. Yet hopes were soon dashed as the Knights' leadership slowly succumbed to segregated locals in order to avoid antagonizing racist white workers. As southern legislatures and peoples exerted force and opinion against the Knights—such as the brutal murders of black and white Knights' recruiters—the leadership put interracial solidarity on the backburner. By 1894, the Knights of Labor officially announced its new policy regarding blacks: federally supported deportation of blacks to Liberia.

Similar patterns of early support of black-white unity and later deference to racist practices can be found in the populist movement and the craft-oriented American Federation of Labor. The famous populist leader Tom Watson first heralded the cause of interracial unity yet ended his career in the Ku Klux Klan. Samuel Gompers, the leader of the AFL from 1881–1924, first refused affiliation with any discriminatory union but soon opened his federation to the most racist unions in the country. And as such racism escalated in organized labor, black people moved toward either independent organizing or paternalistic support from white capitalists.

The Colored Farmers' National Alliance and Cooperative Union was founded in 1891 and quickly acquired 1.2 million members. But it was shortlived due to an unsuccessful cotton pickers' strike which was crushed by the state and the irate opposition of white farmers. Many blacks were lynched in this repressive action. As the strength of white unions pushed black artisans and craftsmen out of jobs and excluded blacks from substantive employment, white paternalism and black self-help became the major alternative to blacks.

The crucial role of black female labor and the dominant leadership of Booker T. Washington is best understood in this context. Working black women—with over 55 percent employed in 1880—were the key to the survival of black people in the late nineteenth century, as the black historian Carter Woodson noted in his poignant account of black washerwomen. Booker T. Washington, once a member of the Knights of Labor, emerged as the most important black leader with his self-help program of agricultural entrepreneurship, technical education, and political complacency supported by white capitalists. At the dawning of the twentieth century, race and class in America was more distant than ever—and would not fuse in a progressive manner until the 1930s and again in the 1960s.

Toward a Socialist Theory
of Racism

What is the relationship between the struggle against racism and socialist theory and practice in the United States? Why should people of color
active in antiracist movements take democratic socialism seriously? And
how can American socialists today learn from inadequate attempts by socialists in the past to understand the complexity of racism? In this chapter I try to address these crucial questions facing the democratic socialist
movement. First, I examine past Marxist efforts to comprehend what
racism is and how it operates in varying contexts. Second, I attempt to
develop a new conception of racism which builds upon, yet goes beyond
the Marxist tradition. Third, I examine how this new conception sheds
light on the roles of racism in the American past and present. Last, I try
to show that the struggle against racism is both morally and politically
necessary for democratic socialists.

Past Marxist Conceptions of Racism

Most socialist theorizing about racism has occurred within a Marxist
framework and has focused on the Afro-American experience. While my
analysis concentrates on people of African descent, particularly Afro-
Americans, it also has important implications for analyzing the racism
that plagues other peoples of color, such as Spanish-speaking Americans
(e.g., Chicanos and Puerto Ricans), Asians, and Native Americans.

There are four basic conceptions of racism in the Marxist tradition.
The first subsumes racism under the general rubric of working-class exploitation. This viewpoint tends to ignore forms of racism not determined by the workplace. At the turn of the century, this position was put
forward by many leading figures in the Socialist party, particularly
Eugene Debs. Debs believed that white racism against peoples of color
was solely a "divide-and-conquer strategy" of the ruling class and that
any attention to its operations "apart from the general labor problem"
would constitute racism in reverse.

My aim is not to castigate the Socialist party or insinuate that Debs

---

Published in pamphlet form by the Institute for Democratic Socialism (1985).

was a racist. The Socialist party had some distinguished black members, and Debs had a long history of fighting racism. But any analysis that confines itself to oppression in the workplace overlooks racism's operation in other spheres of life. For the Socialist party, this yielded a "color-blind" strategy for resisting racism in which all workers were viewed simply as workers with no specific identity or problems. Complex racist practices within and outside the workplace were reduced to mere strategies of the ruling class.

The second conception of racism in the Marxist tradition acknowledges the specific operation of racism within the workplace (e.g., job discrimination and structural inequality of wages) but remains silent about these operations outside the workplace. This viewpoint holds that peoples of color are subjected both to general working-class exploitation and to a specific "super-exploitation" resulting from less access to jobs and lower wages. On the practical plane, this perspective accented a more intense struggle against racism than did Debs's viewpoint, and yet it still limited this struggle to the workplace.

The third conception of racism in the Marxist tradition, the so-called "Black Nation Thesis," has been the most influential among black Marxists. It claims that the operation of racism is best understood as a result of general and specific working-class exploitation *and* national oppression. This viewpoint holds that Afro-Americans constitute, or once constituted, an oppressed nation in the Black Belt South and an oppressed national minority in the rest of American society.

There are numerous versions of the Black Nation Thesis. Its classical form was put forth by the American Communist party in 1928, was then modified in the 1930 resolution, and codified in Harry Haywood's *Negro Liberation* (1948). Some small Leninist organizations still subscribe to the thesis, and its most recent reformulation appeared in James Forman's *Self-Determination and the African-American People* (1981). All of these variants adhere to Stalin's definition of a nation set forth in his *Marxism and the National Question* (1913), which states that "a nation is a historically constituted, stable community of people formed on the basis of a common language, territory, economic life and psychological make-up manifested in a common culture." Despite its brevity and crudity, this formulation incorporates a crucial cultural dimension overlooked by the other two Marxist accounts of racism. Furthermore, linking racist practices to struggles between dominating and dominated nations (or peoples) has been seen as relevant to the plight of Native Americans, Chicanos, and Puerto Ricans who were disinherited and decimated by white colonial settlers. Such models of "internal colonialism" have important implications for organizing strategies because they give particular attention to critical linguistic and cultural forms of oppression. They remind us that much of the American West consists of lands taken from Native Americans and from Mexico.

Since the Garveyite movement of the 1920s, which was the first mass movement among Afro-Americans, the black left has been forced to take seriously the cultural dimension of the black freedom struggle. Marcus Garvey's black nationalism rendered most black Marxists "proto-Gramscians" in at least the limited sense that they took cultural concerns more seriously than many other Marxists. But this concern with cultural life was limited by the Black Nation Thesis itself. Although the theory did inspire many impressive struggles against racism by the predominantly white left, particularly in the 1930s, its ahistorical racial definition of a nation, its purely statistical determination of national boundaries (the South was a black nation because of its then black majority population), and its illusory conception of a distinct black national economy ultimately rendered it an inadequate analysis.

The fourth conception of racism in the Marxist tradition claims that racist practices result not only from general and specific working-class exploitation but also from xenophobic attitudes that are not strictly reducible to class exploitation. From this perspective, racist attitudes have a life and logic of their own, dependent upon psychological factors and cultural practices. This viewpoint was motivated primarily by opposition to the predominant role of the Black Nation Thesis on the American and Afro-American left. Its most prominent exponents were W. E. B. Du Bois and Oliver Cox.

Toward a More Adequate Conception of Racism

This brief examination of past Marxist views leads to one conclusion. Marxist theory is indispensable yet ultimately inadequate for grasping the complexity of racism as a historical phenomenon. Marxism is indispensable because it highlights the relation of racist practices to the capitalist mode of production and recognizes the crucial role racism plays within the capitalist economy. Yet Marxism is inadequate because it fails to probe other spheres of American society where racism plays an integral role—especially the psychological and cultural spheres. Furthermore, Marxist views tend to assume that racism has its roots in the rise of modern capitalism. Yet, it can easily be shown that although racist practices were shaped and appropriated by modern capitalism, racism itself predates capitalism. Its roots lie in the earlier encounters between the civilizations of Europe, Africa, Asia, and Latin America—encounters that occurred long before the rise of modern capitalism.

It indeed is true that the very category of "race"—denoting primarily skin color—was first employed as a means of classifying human bodies by Francois Bernier, a French physician, in 1684. The first authoritative racial division of humankind is found in the influential *Natural System* (1735) of the preeminent naturalist of the eighteenth century, Carolus Linnaeus. Both of these instances reveal European racist practices at the level of intellectual codification since both degrade and devalue non-Europeans. Racist folktales, mythologies, legends, and stories that function in the everyday life of common people predate the seventeenth and eighteenth centuries. For example, Christian anti-Semitism and Euro-Christian antiblackism were rampant throughout the Middle Ages. These false divisions of humankind were carried over to colonized Latin America where anti-Indian racism became a fundamental pillar of colonial society and influenced later *mestizo* national development. Thus racism is as much a product of the interaction of cultural ways of life as it is of modern capitalism. A more adequate conception of racism should reflect this twofold context of cultural and economic realities in which racism has flourished.

A new analysis of racism builds on the best of Marxist theory (particularly Antonio Gramsci's focus on the cultural and ideological spheres), and yet it goes beyond by incorporating three key assumptions:

1. Cultural practices, including racist discourses and actions, have multiple power functions (such as domination over non-Europeans) that are neither reducible to nor intelligible in terms of class exploitation alone. In short, these practices have a reality of their own and cannot simply be reduced to an economic base.

2. Cultural practices are the medium through which selves are produced. We are who and what we are owing primarily to cultural practices. The complex process of people shaping and being shaped by cultural practices involves the use of language, psychological factors, sexual identities, and aesthetic conceptions that cannot be adequately grasped by a social theory primarily focused on modes of production at the macrostructural level.

3. Cultural practices are not simply circumscribed by modes of production; they also are bounded by civilizations. Hence, cultural practices cut across modes of production. (E.g., there are forms of Christianity that exist in both precapitalist and capitalist societies.) An analysis of racist practices in both premodern and modern Western civilization yields both continuity and discontinuity. Even Marxism can be shown to be both critical of and captive to a Eurocentrism that can justify racist practices. Although Marxist

theory remains indispensable, it obscures the manner in which cultural practices, including notions of "scientific" rationality, are linked to particular ways of life.

A common feature of the four Marxist conceptions examined earlier is that their analyses remain on the macrostructural level. They focus on the role and function of racism within and between significant institutions such as the workplace and government. Any adequate conception of racism indeed must include such a macrostructural analysis, one that highlights the changing yet persistent forms of class exploitation and political repression of peoples of color. But a fully adequate analysis of racism also requires an investigation into the genealogy and ideology of racism and a detailed microinstitutional analysis. Such an analysis would encompass the following:

1. A genealogical inquiry into the ideology of racism, focusing on the kinds of metaphors and concepts employed by dominant European (or white) supremacists in various epochs in the West and on ways in which resistance has occurred.

2. A microinstitutional or localized analysis of the mechanisms that sustain white supremacist discourse in the everyday life of non-Europeans (including the ideological production of certain kinds of selves, the means by which alien and degrading normative cultural styles, aesthetic ideals, psychosexual identities, and group perceptions are constituted) and ways in which resistance occurs.

3. A macrostructural approach that emphasizes the class exploitation and political repression of non-European peoples and ways in which resistance is undertaken.

The first line of inquiry aims to examine *modes of European domination* of non-European peoples; the second probes *forms of European subjugation* of non-European peoples; and the third focuses on *types of European exploitation and repression* of non-European peoples. These lines of theoretical inquiry, always traversed by male supremacist and heterosexual supremacist discourses, overlap in complex ways, *and yet each highlights a distinctive dimension of the racist practices of European peoples vis-à-vis non-European peoples.*

This analytical framework should capture the crucial characteristics of European racism anywhere in the world. But the specific character of racist practices in particular times and places can be revealed only by detailed historical analyses that follow these three methodological steps. Admittedly, this analytic approach is an ambitious one, but the complex-

77103

ity of racism as a historical phenomenon demands it. Given limited space, I shall briefly sketch the contours of each step.

For the first step—the genealogical inquiry into predominant European supremacist discourses—there are three basic discursive logics: Judeo-Christian, scientific, and psychosexual discourses. I am not suggesting that these discourses are inherently racist, but rather that they have been employed to justify racist practices. The Judeo-Christian racist logic emanates from the biblical account of Ham looking upon and failing to cover his father Noah's nakedness and thereby receiving divine punishment in the form of the blackening of his progeny. In this highly influential narrative, black skin is a divine curse, punishing disrespect for and rejection of paternal authority.

The scientific logic rests upon a modern philosophical discourse guided by Greek ocular metaphors (e.g., Eye of the Mind) and is undergirded by Cartesian notions of the primacy of the subject (ego, self) and the preeminence of representation. These notions of the self are buttressed by Baconian ideas of observation, evidence, and confirmation which promote the activities of observing, comparing, measuring, and ordering physical characteristics of human bodies: given the renewed appreciation and appropriation of classical antiquity in the eighteenth century, these "scientific" activities of observation were regulated by classical aesthetic and cultural norms (Greek lips, noses, etc.). Within this logic, notions of black ugliness, cultural deficiency, and intellectual inferiority are legitimated by the value-laden yet prestigious authority of "science," especially in the eighteenth and nineteenth centuries. The purposeful distortion of "scientific" procedures to further racist hegemony has an important history of its own. The persistent use of pseudoscientific "research" to buttress racist ideology, even when the intellectual integrity of the "scientific" position has been severely eroded, illustrates how racist ideology can incorporate and use/abuse science.

The psychosexual racist logic arises from the phallic obsessions, Oedipal projections, and anal-sadistic orientations in European cultures which endow non-European (especially African) men and women with sexual prowess; view non-Europeans as either cruel revengeful fathers, frivolous carefree children, or passive long-suffering mothers; and identify non-Europeans (especially black people) with dirt, odious smell, and feces. In short, non-Europeans are associated with acts of bodily defecation, violation, and subordination. Within this logic, non-Europeans are walking abstractions, inanimate objects, or invisible creatures. Within all three white supremacist logics—which operate simultaneously and affect the perceptions of both Europeans and non-Europeans—black, brown, yellow, and red peoples personify Otherness and embody alien Difference.

The aim of this first step is to show how these white supremacist logics are embedded in philosophies of identity that suppress difference, diversity, and heterogeneity. Since such discourses impede the realization of the democratic socialist ideals of genuine individuality and radical democracy, they must be criticized and opposed. But critique and opposition should be based on an understanding of the development and internal workings of these discourses—how they dominate the intellectual life of the modern West and thereby limit the chances for less racist, less ethnocentric discourses to flourish.

The second step—microinstitutional or localized analysis—examines the operation of white supremacist logics within the everyday lives of people in particular historical contexts. In the case of Afro-Americans, this analysis would include the ways in which "colored," "Negro," and "black" identities were created against a background of both fear and terror and a persistent history of resistance that gave rise to open rebellion in the 1960s. Such an analysis must include the extraordinary *and* equivocal role of evangelical Protestant Christianity (which both promoted and helped contain black resistance) and the blend of African and U.S. southern Anglo-Saxon Protestants and French Catholics from which emerged distinctive Afro-American cultural styles, language, and aesthetic values.

The objective of this second step is to show how the various white supremacist discourses shape non-European self-identities, influence psychosexual sensibilities, and help set the context for oppositional (but also co-optable) non-European cultural manners and mores. This analysis also reveals how the oppression and cultural domination of Native Americans, Chicanos, Puerto Ricans, and other colonized people differ significantly (while sharing many common features) from that of Afro-Americans. Analyses of internal colonialism, national oppression, and cultural imperialism have particular significance in explaining the territorial displacement and domination that confront these peoples.

The third step—macrostructural analysis—discloses the role and function of class exploitation and political repression and how racist practices buttress them. This step resembles traditional Marxist theories of racism, which focus primarily on institutions of economic production and secondarily on the state and public and private bureaucracies. But the nature of this focus is modified in that economic production is no longer viewed as the sole or major source of racist practices. Rather it is seen as a crucial source among others. To put it somewhat crudely, the capitalist mode of production constitutes just one of the significant structural constraints determining what forms racism takes in a particular historical period. Other key structural constraints include the state, bureaucratic modes of control, and the cultural practices of ordinary people. The specific forms that racism takes depend on choices people make within these structural constraints. In this regard, history is neither deterministic nor arbitrary; rather it is an open-ended sequence of (progressive or regressive) structured social practices over time and space. Thus the third analytical step, while preserving important structural features of Marxism such as the complex interaction of the economic, political, cultural, and ideological spheres of life, does not privilege *a priori* the economic sphere as a means of explaining other spheres of human experience. But this viewpoint still affirms that class exploitation and state repression do take place, especially in the lives of non-Europeans in modern capitalist societies.

Racism in the American Past and Present

This analytical framework should help explain how racism has operated throughout United States history. It focuses on the predominant form racism takes in the three major historical configurations of modern capitalism: industrial capitalism, monopoly capitalism, and multinational corporate capitalism. It is worth noting that although we have been critical of Marxist explanations of racist practices, Marxist theory remains highly illuminating and provides the best benchmarks for periodizing modern history.

U.S. industrial capitalism was, in part, the fruit of black slavery in America. The lucrative profits from cotton and tobacco production in the slave-ridden U.S. South contributed greatly to the growth of manufacturing (especially textiles) in the U.S. North. The industrial capitalist order in the North not only rested indirectly upon the productive labor of black slaves in the South, it also penetrated the South after the Civil War along with white exploitation and repression of former black slaves. In addition, U.S. industrial capitalism was consolidated only after the military conquest and geographical containment of indigenous and Mexican peoples and the exploitation of Asian contract laborers. On the cultural level, black, brown, yellow, and red identities were reinforced locally, reflecting the defensive and deferential positions of victims who had only limited options for effective resistance. For example, this period is the age of the "colored" identity of Africans in the United States.

The advent of the American empire helped usher in U.S. monopoly capitalism. Given both the absence of a strong centralized state and a relatively unorganized working class, widespread centralization of the capitalist economy occurred principally in the form of monopolies, trusts, and holding companies. As the U.S. took over the last remnants of the Spanish empire (e.g., in Puerto Rico, the Philippines, and Guam) and expanded its economic presence in South America, U.S. racist ideology flourished. Jim Crow laws—consciously adopted models for apartheid in South Africa—were instituted throughout the South. Anti-Asian exclusionary immigration laws—supported by the lily-white American Federation of Labor—were enacted, and reservations ("homelands") were set up for indigenous peoples. Mexican and indigenous peoples were removed from their lands through the use of force and by the courts. A settler colonial regime was established in the Southwest to oversee the extraction of raw materials and to subject the Mexican population. At the same time, America opened its arms to the European "masses yearning to be free," principally because of a labor shortage in the booming urban industrial centers. In this period, a small yet significant black middle class began to set up protest organizations such as the NAACP, National Urban League, and the National Federation of Afro-American Women. Limited patronage networks were established for black middle-class enhancement (e.g., Booker T. Washington's "machine"). This period is the age of the "Negro" identity of Africans in the United States. Some influential blacks were permitted limited opportunities to prosper and thereby serve as models of success for the black masses to emulate. Despite its courageous efforts on behalf of black progress, the NAACP in this period could not help but serve as a vehicle for severely constricted black gains. The NAACP was defiant in rhetoric, liberal in vision, legalistic in practice, and headed by elements of the black middle class which often influenced the interests of the organization.

The emergence of the United States as the preeminent world power after World War II provided the framework for the growth of multinational corporate capitalism. The devastation of Europe (including the weakening of its vast empires), the defeat of Japan, and the tremendous sacrifice of lives and destruction of industry in the Soviet Union facilitated U.S. world hegemony. U.S. corporate penetration into European markets (opened and buttressed by the Marshall Plan), Asian markets, some African markets, and, above all, Latin American markets set the stage for unprecedented U.S. economic prosperity. This global advantage, along with technological innovation, served as the hidden background for the so-called American Way of Life—a life of upward social mobility leading to material comfort and convenience. Only in the postwar era did significant numbers of the U.S. white middle class participate in this dream.

Aware of its image as leader of the "free world" (and given the growing sensitivity to racism in the aftermath of the Holocaust), the U.S. government began to respond cautiously to the antiracist resistance at home. This response culminated in the *Brown v. Board of Education* school desegregation decision (1954) and the Civil Rights and Voting Rights acts of 1964 and 1965 respectively. The ramifications of the court decision and legislation affected all peoples of color (and white women) but had the greatest impact on those able to move up the social ladder primarily by means of education. As a result, the current period of U.S. multinational corporate capitalism has witnessed the growth of a significant middle class of peoples of color. Overt racist language—even under the Reagan administration—has become unfashionable; coded racist language expressing hostility to "affirmative action," "busing," and "special interests" has now replaced overt racist discourse.

As the legal barriers of segregation have been torn down, the underclass of black and brown working and poor people at the margins of society has grown. For the expanding middle class of people of color, political disenfranchisement and job discrimination have been considerably reduced. But, simultaneously, a more insidious form of class and racial stratification intensified—educational inequality. In an increasingly technological society, rural and inner-city schools for people of color and many working class and poor whites serve to reproduce the present racial and class stratified structure of society. Children of the poor, who are disproportionately people of color, are tracked into an impoverished educational system and then face unequal opportunities when they enter the labor force (if steady, meaningful employment is even a possibility).

In the past decade, American multinational corporate capitalism has undergone a deep crisis, owing primarily to increased competition with Japanese, European, and even some third world corporations; a rise in energy costs brought about the OPEC cartel; the precarious structure of international debt owed to American and European banks by third world countries; and victorious anticolonial struggles that limit lucrative capital investments somewhat. The response of the Reagan administration to this crisis has been, in part, to curtail the public sector by cutting back federal transfer payments to the needy, diminishing occupational health and safety and environmental protection, increasing low wage service sector jobs, and granting tax incentives and giveaways to large corporations. Those most adversely affected by these policies have been blue-collar industrial workers and the poor, particularly women and children. Thus Reagan's policies, which are often supported by the coded racist language of the religious right and secular neoconservatives, are racist in consequence. Poor women and children are disproportionately people of color, and jobs in the "rust belt" industries of auto and steel played a major role in black social mobility in the postwar period.

Socialism and Antiracism: Two Inseparable Yet Not Identical Goals

It should be apparent that racist practices directed against black, brown, yellow, and red people are an integral element of U.S. history, including present-day American culture and society. This means not simply that Americans have inherited racist attitudes and prejudices but, more important, that institutional forms of racism are embedded in American society in both visible and invisible ways. These institutional forms exist not only in remnants of *de jure* job, housing, and educational discrimination and political gerrymandering. They also manifest themselves in a *de facto* labor market segmentation, produced by the exclusion of large numbers of peoples of color from the socioeconomic mainstream. (This exclusion results from limited educational opportunities, devastated families, a disproportionate presence in the prison population, and widespread police brutality.)

It also should be evident that past Marxist conceptions of racism have often prevented U.S. socialist movements from engaging in antiracist activity in a serious and consistent manner. In addition, black suspicion of white-dominated political movements (no matter how progressive) as well as the distance between these movements and the daily experiences of peoples of color have made it even more difficult to fight racism effectively. Furthermore, the disproportionate white middle-class composition of contemporary democratic socialist organizations creates *cultural* barriers to the participation by peoples of color. Yet this very participation is a vital precondition for greater white sensitivity to antiracist struggle and to white acknowledgment of just how crucial antiracist struggle is to the U.S. socialist movement. Progressive organizations often find themselves going around in a vicious circle. Even when they have a great interest in antiracist struggle, they are unable to attract a critical mass of people of color because of their current predominantly white racial and cultural composition. These organizations are then stereotyped as lily white, and significant numbers of people of color refuse to join.

The only effective way the contemporary democratic socialist movement can break out of this circle (and it *is* possible because the bulk of democratic socialists are among the least racist of Americans) is to be sensitized to the critical importance of antiracist struggles. This *conscientization* cannot take place either by reinforcing agonized white consciences by means of guilt, nor by presenting another grand theoretical analysis with no practical implications. The former breeds psychological paralysis among white progressives, which is unproductive for all of us;

the latter yields important discussions but often at the expense of concrete political engagement. Rather what is needed is more widespread participation by predominantly white democratic socialist organizations in antiracist struggles—whether those struggles be for the political, economic, and cultural empowerment of Latinos, blacks, Asians, and Native Americans or anti-imperialist struggles against U.S. support for oppressive regimes in South Africa, Chile, the Philippines, and the occupied West Bank.

A major focus on antiracist coalition work will not only lead democratic socialists to act upon their belief in genuine individuality and radical democracy for people around the world; it also will put socialists in daily contact with peoples of color *in common struggle. Bonds of trust can be created only within concrete contexts of struggle.* This interracial interaction guarantees neither love nor friendship. Yet it can yield more understanding and the realization of two overlapping goals—democratic socialism and antiracism. While engaging in antiracist struggles, democratic socialists can also enter into a dialogue on the power relationships and misconceptions that often emerge in multiracial movements for social justice in a racist society. Honest and trusting coalition work can help socialists unlearn Eurocentrism in a self-critical manner and can also demystify the motivations of white progressives in the movement for social justice.

We must frankly acknowledge that a democratic socialist society will not *necessarily* eradicate racism. *Yet a democratic socialist society is the best hope for alleviating and minimizing racism, particularly institutional forms of racism.* This conclusion depends on a candid evaluation that guards against utopian self-deception. But it also acknowledges the deep moral commitment on the part of democratic socialists of all races to the dignity of all individuals and peoples—a commitment that impels us to fight for a more libertarian and egalitarian society. Therefore concrete antiracist struggle is both an ethical imperative and a political necessity for democratic socialists. It is even more urgent as once again racist policies and third world intervention become more acceptable to many Americans. A more effective democratic socialist movement engaged in antiracist and anti-imperialist struggle can help turn the tide. It depends on how well we understand the past and present, how courageously we act, and how true we remain to our democratic socialist ideals of freedom, equality, and democracy.

On Visiting South Africa

In July of 1985 I visited South Africa. Nowhere have I witnessed such breathtaking landscapes. Nor have I ever seen such institutionalized hatred. On a trip sponsored by the United States–South Africa Leadership Exchange Program, James Cone and I spent ten eventful days listening and lecturing, observing and discussing, debating and preaching in Johannesburg, Soweto, Duduza, Pretoria, Durban, Pietermaritzburg, Lamottsville, Capetown, and Crossroads. Needless to say, reading about South Africa is one thing, seeing it is something quite different.

The most striking feature of South Africa is the wealth and comfort of whites alongside the poverty and squalor of blacks. The so-called coloureds, people of mixed race, are hardly well off; yet their middling position accentuates the black/white contrast. The pretty green grass in front of the spacious homes with luxurious swimming pools in the white urban areas appears like a fantasy against the backdrop of dirt and mud surrounding the tiny boxlike houses in the overcrowded black townships. In the cities, small white nuclear families live in two-story homes; in the townships, ten men, women, and children often live in three small rooms. During the day, the cities are bustling with black, brown, and white people on the streets and at work. Yet after 9:00 P.M., no blacks are allowed in the cities unless special permission is given by whites. By 6:00 A.M. the next day black working people have returned.

Black and white South Africans live in two completely different worlds. Unlike the situation in America's Old South, there is virtually no communication and interaction between black and white South Africans outside the boss-employee, master-servant contact. This means not only that there is little, if any, cross-cultural borrowing or overlapping of religious styles. More important, there is little interest in or knowledge of the black predicament among whites. The very possibility of serious and sustained black-white communication hardly exists.

There were many important experiences during my trip—the intense dialogue at the Funda Centre in Soweto, the profound and poignant sermon by the Rev. Allan Boesak at memorial services for the Cradock Four, my own chance to preach at Buitenkant Street Methodist Church in Capetown. But the zenith of my visit was a unique opportunity to address thousands of black South Africans at a funeral in Duduza. With

From *Christianity and Crisis* (Oct. 28, 1985).

109

soldiers and tanks surrounding us and intimidating helicopters hovering overhead, I met Bishop Desmond Tutu for the first time at the makeshift funeral grounds in a hot, dusty football stadium. I also encountered the most inspiring group of young people in my life. They literally ran the funeral—bringing in the corpses, guarding the bodies with extended clenched fists, consoling the heartsick relatives, leading freedom songs, and giving the most powerful speeches. Never have I seen a more politically astute and morally courageous generation of young people. Church leaders indeed were on the speakers' platform, but the real sense of hope and struggle came from the young poets and speakers.

The crucial question in South Africa is: What direction will black subversive energy and utopian desire take? Can the youth sustain the level of protest and make South Africa ungovernable? Or will they only provide more cannon fodder for the repressive South African military? In my view, South Africa today is much like what the United States would have been if it consisted only of the southern Confederate states under conditions of limited industrialization and urbanization. And if this were so, black Americans today more than likely would possess no voting rights or freedom of organization and geographical movement. Both cases require terror and brute force to hold the societies together. Black South African youth have perceived this tragic truth, and still rebel.

Two Strategies

This courageous rebellion destabilizes South Africa, but it alone cannot topple the South African government. In my judgment only two major strategies can bring about fundamental change in South Africa: mass strikes and international financial divestments and trade embargoes. The former requires a developed and supported black trade-union movement; the latter, widespread uncertainty among U.S., European, Japanese, and Israeli banks and governments. Effective mass strikes could literally shut the country down and thereby impel the South African government to negotiate with black leaders. Divestments and embargoes would hit white South Africans where it hurts most—in their incredibly high standards of living. Concerted divestments and embargoes are unlikely, given the deep financial interests of U.S., British, West German, French, Dutch, and Israeli banks and industry in the South African economy. Symbolic gestures are crucial at the moment. Yet it is important that we be realistic about the limits of this popular strategy.

I suggest that the strategy of the mass strike *should* become another major focus of anti-apartheid activity in the future. If the trade-union movement in South Africa can receive a fraction of the international financial and moral support given to the Solidarity movement in Poland, important changes loom large in South Africa. The daily rebellions of heroic young people, coupled with a financially secure and morally supported black trade-union movement able to withhold its labor at will, could spell the end of present-day apartheid in South Africa. Neither the growing Conservative party (attractive to nostalgic and desperate Afrikaners) nor Gatsha Buthelezi's regressive Inkatha group (backed by some loyal Zulus) could secure the status quo under such conditions. And religious leaders and institutions around the world can contribute greatly to this strategy of mass strike.

Is it not ironic that Marx's prediction of the fundamental change in a modern society owing to the actions of an organized working class could for the first time come to pass at the southern tip of the continent of Africa? Of course, the goal is neither the creation of a Soviet-style repressive state nor a new "liberal" South Africa which safeguards the vast economic interests of the white minority. Rather, the aim is precisely what the South African trade-union leaders proclaim: a society of political democracy and a mixed economy in which the rights, liberties, and basic material needs of all South Africans, regardless of race, religion, or sex, are secure. If and when this comes about, I shall fulfill the promise I made to the people of Duduza—I shall return to dance in the streets of a free South Africa.

Critical Theory and Christian Faith

The most salient feature of the global context in which we find ourselves is the extent to which most of the world remains under American, Soviet, and European hegemony. At the beginning of this century, this hegemony took the form of the Europeanization of the world—with a handful of states located between the Atlantic Ocean and the Ural mountains controlling over 87 percent of the land on the globe by 1918. By the middle of this century, this hegemony had been transformed into the Americanization and Sovietization of the world.

In this essay I shall attempt to discern the political task of the Christian church in light of a particular understanding of the institutional forms of evil promoted initially by the Europeanization of the world and reinforced by the Americanization and Sovietization of the world. My strategy shall be as follows. First, I will try to put forward a skeletal analytical framework which highlights the global life-denying institutional forces that victimize people (or lose sight of the God-given dignity and humanity of people) and accent a political perspective that encourages human action, especially collective action, to resist such forces. Second, I will note how these forces deform the public life in the USA and suggest how first world middle-class churches can contribute to these resistance efforts.

My argument assumes that political discernment for Christians in the postmodern world flows from an inescapable and intimate relation between Christian reflection and some form of systemic social analysis. I simply would like to make crystal clear the kind of systemic social analysis I employ and why I employ it.

I understand political discernment to be a specific understanding of and judgment upon the prevailing common good of a set of socio-economic arrangements (be it focused on a society or the world): that is, political discernment makes *descriptive* and *normative* claims about public life within specific human cooperative efforts. I shall suggest that, for Christian thinkers, the descriptive dimension of political discernment rests upon sophisticated systemic social analyses and the normative dimension of political discernment is grounded in an interpretation of the

From *The Witness* (Jan. 1986).

Christian gospel. This is so neither because social analyses are value-free or value-neutral nor because the Christian gospel contains no descriptive powers; but rather because secular systemic social analyses are under-developed in regard to moral vision and rootedness in people's everyday lives, and the Christian gospel is underdeveloped in regard to systemic social analysis.

Any acceptable social analysis employed by Christian thinkers should take seriously the biblical injunction to look at the world both through the eyes of its victims and through the Christocentric perspective which requires Christians to see the world through the lens of the cross. I am not claiming that my skeletal analytical framework is Christian social analysis—for there is no such thing as "Christian" social analysis, just as there is no such thing as Christian mathematics, Christian physics, or Christian economics. Rather I am claiming that there must be political discernment from a Christian perspective and that this discernment should be guided by sophisticated systemic social and historical analyses which highlight and enhance the plight of the disinherited and downtrodden, the exploited and oppressed.

Needless to say, a full-blown Christian perspective should accent our relative victimizing and relative victimization—that is, our various loca-tions on the existential, socioeconomic, cultural, and political scales. Since we all, in some sense, suffer, we all, in some sense, are victims. The Christian tradition, with its many streams and strains, generally holds that we are fellow sufferers who struggle to understand and change our ever-changing historical predicaments, acknowledge our existential fini-tude, and know the subtle difference between the two. This difference is crucial in that for too many Christians the limits of human finitude are identical with the limits of a particular historical moment in the develop-ment of human societies, while for other Christians the recognition of the transient historical limits downplays and ignores our existential fini-tude. My aim is to try to provide a route through the Scylla of a quietis-tic Augustinian Christianity and the Charybdis of a triumphant Prome-thean Christianity while preserving the rich insights of the Augustinian and Promethean traditions in Christian thought and practice.

Hence, though we all suffer, the more multilayered the victimization the more diverse suffering one undergoes. And given the prevailing forms of oppression in our world, the majority of humankind experience *thick* forms of victimization. My own conception of prophetic Christian-ity tries to speak to people undergoing forms of victimization by pro-moting protracted and principled struggles against types of personal despair, intellectual dogmatism, and socioeconomic oppression that foster communities of hope. Such a conception is Promethean in that it makes Pascalian leaps of faith in the capacity of human beings to transform their circumstances, engage in relentless criticism and self-criticism, and project visions, analyses, and practices of social freedom. This conception is Augustinian in that it acknowleges the inability of human beings to conform *fully* to the requirements of the Christian gospel, that is, create selves, communities, societies, and a world which no longer require struggles against despair, dogmatism, and oppression.

I shall begin by making crucial analytical distinctions between exploitation, repression, domination, and subjugation. I will crudely identify each of these forms of oppression with a particular social logic promoted by the Europeanization of the world and deepened by the Americanization and Sovietization of the world. I understand these social logics to be structured social practices over time and space which in effect and consequence dehumanize people. I associate exploitation with the social logic of capital accumulation; repression with the social logic of state augmentation; domination with the social logic of bureaucratic administration; and subjugation with the social logics of white supremacist, male supremacist, and heterosexual supremacist discourses and practices. Building on the seminal work of the late Michel Foucault, I suggest that exploitation and repression are principally extra-discursive affairs in that they result from social formations and institutions such as modes of production and state apparatuses. Domination and subjugation, while linked to social formations and institutions, relate primarily to rhetorics, discourses, and traditions which specialize in shaping and molding, creating and producing identities and subjectivities or self-perceptions and self-understandings of people. Therefore exploitation, repression, domination, and subjugation constitute distinct modes of oppression which we distinguish for analytical purposes while acknowledging that they inseparably relate to each other in complex and concrete ways in specific societies and cultures. In my brief characterizations of these social logics, I shall note both their international scope and their deforming effects on the public life in the USA.

Exploitation and the Social Logic of Capital Accumulation

The emergence and development of the capitalist mode of production is a basic feature of the Europeanization of the world. The operations of this mode of production is dictated by the social logic of capital accumulation. This social logic is driven by profit-maximization. Its aim is not simply the generating of capital but, more importantly, the reproducing of the conditions for generating capital. As Marx noted long ago, capital is neither mere revenue nor money, but rather a social relation between persons within the capitalist mode of production which requires economic exploitation of those who produce or work—that is, those who sell labor power (their time, skills, and energies) to capitalists in order to make a living. The fundamental economic relations are capitalist market relations in that people must sell themselves as commodities on the job market in order to acquire wages requisite to living a decent life. Since the effective ownership of the means of production (land, raw materials, instruments) are held by a small minority of the population, the majority of persons who must sell their labor power to this minority not only are forced to live lives of material insecurity but also lives of economic exploitation. The term "exploitation" is used here not so much as a moral term as an analytically descriptive term which denotes the lack of control of those who work over their conditions of work, the investment decisions of the institutions in which they work, and some say in the use to which their products are put. This powerlessness holds even when relatively high wages obscure such exploitation—high wages are impossible without higher profits in a capitalist mode of production.

The capitalist mode of production is an international economic system which has undergone three basic stages: industrial capitalism, monopoly capitalism, and multinational corporate capitalism. Each stage highlights the dominant institutional form of capital: major owners of distinct industries, large monopolies, and ever-larger multinational oligopolies. The basic effect of this social logic of capital accumulation has been the privatization and centralization of first world economies and the subordination of third world economies to the first world economies. The major blow to these processes has been the rise of the USSR and its satellite countries—yet their centrally planned hierarchical command economies do not provide a preferable and feasible alternative to exploitative capitalist economies.

This is so not only because such command economies are much less efficient—hence unable to yield high levels of productivity—but, more importantly, because the high degrees of centralization and lack of effective democratic mechanisms renders the populace even more powerless than in capitalist societies. In this regard, the social logics of capital accumulation during the Europeanization, Americanization, and Sovietization of the world have resulted in centralized economic power unaccountable to the majority of their populace and usually manipulative and abusive of the neocolonial countries which depend upon them.

In the past decade, the social logic of capital accumulation in the U.S. context has undergone deep crisis principally owing to increased competition with Japanese and European (and even some third world) corporations, energy costs due to third world cartels in oil production, the precarious structure of international debts owed American and

European banks by third world countries, and victorious anticolonial struggles which sometimes delimit lucrative capital investments. The U.S. reponse to this crisis has been, in part, to curtail the public sphere in the forms of cutbacks of federal transfer payments to the needy, diminished public worker protection, erosion of unemployment compensation, diluted environmental protection, enlargement of low wage markets, and incentives and abatements to huge corporations. In short, this response promotes the dissolution of the public sector in the USA.

Repression and the Social Logic of State Augmentation

One of the ironies of the Europeanization, Americanization, and Sovietization of the world is the increasing dissolution of the public sphere occurring alongside the augmentation of the state. This is so primarily because the state is understood more and more to be a channel through which public funds sustain centralized economic power (of multinational corporations in capitalist societies or bureaucratically controlled economic firms in communist societies) as opposed to the public sphere which promotes the common good of these societies. I understand the state to be neither a monolithic institution nor a homogeneous cluster of institutions, but rather a political system of heterogeneous interlocking apparatuses which possess a monopoly on the instruments of legitimate violence and the control of public administration.

There has always been an intimate relationship between capital accumulation and the modern state, but the scope and function of the state has changed radically over time. For example, industrial capitalism neither desired nor sought public regulation—yet it was buttressed by sympathetic courts, supportive military and police, and financially helpful legislatures. Monopoly capitalism openly violated antitrust laws enacted in response to people's movements, but its resiliency and resources—its capacity to insure economic growth—limited an expanding state to the roles of public regulation of monopolies, support for those outside the job market, and legal protection of the marginal. And, of course, multinational corporate capitalism is saddled with a burdensome welfare state whose major recipients are not poor minority female heads of households—as is often believed—but rather corporations *qua* huge contract winners.

The crucial feature of state augmentation since the Americanization and Sovietization of the world is the ever-expanding "disciplinary order," the refinement of modes of surveillance and control over human bodies. These modes—linked to the moral and political technologies informed

116

by the specialized disciplines of knowledge—contribute to increased deployment of mechanisms of repression. Needless to say, the primary function of the state apparatuses in USA and USSR neocolonial countries—from Chile to Cuba, South Korea to Poland—is to control and contain counterinsurgency movements, with brutal techniques often learned from their high-tech patron countries, the USA and USSR.

Increased repression is not identical with the augmentation of the state, but the latter is the precondition of the former. Institutionalized state violence throughout the police and prison systems—especially directed at peoples of color—are but glaring examples of this "disciplinary order." More subtle forms can be seen in the covert operations of the state apparatuses (FBI, CIA) whose expansion threatens personal liberties and whose actions remain beyond public scrutiny and accountability.

The basic difference between the Americanization and the Sovietization of the world is that the USA was born with a precious rhetoric of rights. This tradition of liberalism, though circumscribed by racist, sexist, and class constraints, provides crucial resources for preserving space in the public sphere against the encroachment of repressive state apparatuses. Hence the scope of individual liberties remains broader in the USA than in the USSR—as well as broader in American neocolonial countries than in Soviet neocolonial ones. This rich rhetoric of rights is politically ambiguous in that it can resist both state repression and state support for public life. By confusing state intervention in the economy with state interference in people's lives, healthy libertarian sentiments can lead toward a conservative ideology. Nevertheless, this heritage remains a valuable source for the renewal of public life in countries under the influence of the USA and USSR.

Domination and the Social Logic of Bureaucratic Administration

The social logics of capital accumulation and state augmentation take on institutional forms in bureaucratic organizations. As Max Weber has taught us, these organizations are regulated not only by profit-maximization and/or disciplinary control, but also by efficiency and self-perpetuation. The social logic of bureaucratic administration is guided by impersonal rules and regulations that promote hierarchical subordination and steadfast submission. In fact, the aims of institutional efficiency and organizational self-preservation often enhance profit-maximization and disciplinary control. The intimate relation of capital accumulation, state augmentation, and bureaucratic administration in both capitalist and communist civilizations constitute the three major components of a growing "iron cage" in which human labor power is exploited, human bodies are repressed, and human subjectivities are dominated.

Industrial capitalism, with its nightwatchman state, relied less on bureaucratic administration and more on military-like organization. Monopoly capitalism, with its interventionist state and vast bureaucratic tentacles, deployed administrative techniques and devices throughout society principally owing to the need for managers, professional and skilled workers in corporate bureaucracies, public bureaucracies, universities, mass media, and philanthropic agencies. Multinational corporate capitalism, with its bankrupt and often authoritarian-like state, depends disproportionately on white-collar, college-certified administrators, technocrats, and bureaucrats with highly specialized knowledge and expertise and deep allegiance to the managerial ethos and the ideology of professionalism.

The major responses to bureaucratic administration in the Americanization and Sovietization of the world have been gospels of therapeutic release—preeminently cultural stimulants such as alcoholism, narcotic subcultures, simulated sexuality, cults of sports, and charismatic renewals of religion. These responses are earnest attempts to preserve some vitality and vigor of the self, to overcome the evasive banality of modern administered societies and cultures. In the USA, such responses have often reduced religious rituals to packaged commodities, kerygmatic preaching to dramatic commercials, and protracted struggles of conversion to glib events of sentimental titillation. Rarely, if ever, do these responses result in opposition to capital accumulation and bureaucratic administration. Instead they usually constitute escapist activities that reinforce the status quo. Hence, they leave the public sphere virtually vacuous.

Subjugation and the Social Logics of White, Male, and Heterosexual Supremacist Discourses and Practices

The social logics of capital accumulation, state augmentation, and bureaucratic administration are sedimented with and traversed by the social logics of white, male, and heterosexual supremacist discourses and practices. So the norms of profit-maximization, disciplinary control, efficiency, and organizational self-preservation are contravened by racism, sexism, and homophobia. These supremacist discourses and practices permeate the public and private spheres (including the crucial affairs of everyday life). The effects are that such racist, sexist, and heterosexist practices subjugate black, brown, red, yellow, and gay and lesbian subjects to socially constituted marginal identities, subjectivities, and psycho-sexual anxieties. Hence these social logics transcend class divisions, state apparatuses, and bureaucratic rankings in capitalist and communist civilizations.

Industrial capitalism, with its nightwatchman state and its military-like organizations, boasted of its overt racist practices such as its Jim Crowism against people of African descent in the Diaspora and in Africa, its exclusionary immigration laws against Asians, imperial conquest and geographical containment of Mexican and indigenous peoples; it promoted its cult of domesticity to privatize the role and function of heterosexual women and banish the presence of lesbian women; and it valorized the doctrine of masculinity which degraded "effeminate" heterosexual men and gay men. Monopoly capitalism, with its interventionist state and its bureaucratic administration, tempered its racist practices and refined its racist ideologies against peoples of color—yet nearly committed genocide against Jewish peoples in the midst of "civilized" Europe; celebrated omnifunctional women who worked double loads in the public and private spheres; castigated lesbians and recloseted gay men. Multinational corporate capitalism, with its bankrupt and authoritarian-like state and administrative-intensive work force, turns its principal racist ammunition on the black and brown working poor and underclass; focuses its right wing (or restorative) movements on women's reproductive rights; and often poses lesbians and gays as mere cultural scapegoats. The recent fanning of the social logics of white, male, and heterosexual supremacist discourses and practices in the Americanization and Sovietization of the world further deform and debilitate public life because these logics are attempts to make this sphere the possession of primarily white male heterosexual elites—or those who emulate them, from Margaret Thatcher to Clarence Pendleton, Jr.

On First World Middle-Class Church Resistance

The first task of first world petit bourgeois churches is to engage in a wholesale "self-inventory" (to borrow Antonio Gramsci's term); that is, a critical historical and social situating of one's self and institutions not simply in relation to one's tradition and heritage but also and more importantly in relation to the aforementioned operative social logics which shape this tradition and heritage. In short, contemporary Christian reflection—its ideational forms as well as the institutional matrices which facilitate these forms—is deeply entrenched and ensconced in this prevailing political situation. More specifically our theologies are shot through with the social logics I have briefly and inadequately described.

But can postmodern Christianity, especially its first world middle-class versions, survive such a "self-inventory"? Are there any Christian resources left after one teases out the economic exploitation, state repression, bureaucratic domination, and subjugation of racism, sexism, and homophobia? Does such a candid "self-inventory" yield a post-Christian perspective? I suggest that there are Christian resources left after such intense self-scrutiny but only if we can interpret dramatic Christian narratives (including biblical ones) and accent moral norms which promote the de-Europeanization, de-Americanization, and de-Sovietization of the world. This perspective should not result in a bland and vulgar anti-European, anti-American, and anti-Soviet stance. Rather it yields a position against European hegemony, American hegemony, and Soviet hegemony while building upon the best of the European, American, and Soviet experiments. Furthermore, this viewpoint does not constitute a shift of the church from an alignment with European, American, and Soviet cultures to a "universal," faceless church, but rather from a church caught in European, American, and Soviet captivity to a church more fully grounded in people's basic needs and rooted in people's everyday lives resisting and opposing European, American, and Soviet hegemony. In biblical language, I am promoting a church serious about rooting out its deeply-seeded idolatries.

I understand the distinctive strength of Christianity to be not simply its worldly skepticism and anticipatory triumphalism but especially its promotion of an unstoppable predilection for alternatives grounded in the present. In other words, Christianity, at its best, possesses a unique capacity to highlight critical, historical, and universal consciousness principally owing to its vigilante critical disposition toward existing realities, its processive view of life and history, and its all-inclusive moral outlook. The Christian tradition, despite its vast complicities with the dogmatisms, cynicisms, and status quos of old, contains resources which enable us to build upon and go beyond the present. To put it crudely, these resources are: the indispensable yet never-adequate capacities of human beings to solve problems—hence the deep antidogmatic elements of Christianity which encourage critical consciousness; the good news of Jesus Christ which empowers and links human capacities to the coming of the kingdom—hence the warding off of disenabling despair, dread, cynicism, and death itself; and last, the moral claim to view all human beings as having equal status, as warranting the same dignity, respect, and love, especially those who are denied such dignity, respect, and love by individuals, families, groups, social structures, economic systems, or political regimes—hence the Christian identification and solidarity with the downtrodden and disinherited, with the exploited and oppressed.

For those of us critically aligned with and self-situated in the Christian tradition—those within the hermeneutical circle carrying Christian baggage—there ought to be a deep bias against prevailing forms of dogmatism, despair, and oppression. Yet this bias is followed without making criticism, hope, and liberation a fetish or idol; for such reductions of the Christian gospel result in impotent irony (as with some avant-garde postmodern theologians), shallow self-indulgence (as with many first world churches), or spiritless political struggle (as with some secular political activists).

The second task of first world middle-class churches is to preserve and promote the norms of individuality within community and democratic participation in the decision-making processes of those major institutions which guide and regulate our lives. We arrive at these moral values neither by transcendental reflection upon the nature of morality (as with Kantians) nor by mimicking the prevailing liberal tradition (as with religious and secular neoconservatives). Rather these norms are discerned by interpreting the Christian gospel in light of our present global and local circumstances. This interpretation accents the egalitarian Christian mandate that all human creatures are made in the image of God, thereby endowed with a certain dignity and respect which warrants particular treatments, including a chance to fulfill their capacities and potentialities. This mandate acknowledges the social and communal character of self-realization such that the development of individuality occurs within groups and societies. Furthermore, this interpretation recognizes the depravity of persons in the sense that institutional mechanisms are required which provide checks and balances for various forms of power, wealth, status, and influence. These mechanisms seem to work best in our world when regulated and enforced by democratic convictions. This conception of democracy calls not only for participation within a given set of structures but also for empowerment to change the structures themselves. More importantly, the Christian norms of individuality and democracy are inseparable from systemic social analyses which attempt to keep track of those major social logics which presently undermine these norms. The Christian struggle for freedom is as much a struggle for moral norms and systemic social analyses as it is a struggle against the powers that be precisely because these "powers that be" must be adequately understood if they are to be effectively transformed. In this regard, battles *within* the Christian tradition are often battles over what kind of social analyses Christians ought to employ in understanding our lives, our societies, and our world. I have suggested that Christian thinkers should employ elements of various social analyses of power, wealth, status, and influence that look at the world from the situation of the "least of these," the various kinds of victims in the world. This requirement should not promote an intellectual parochialism regarding social analyses, but rather compel Christian thinkers to justify the kind of social and historical analyses they use. Needless to say, given the complexity and multiplicity of social logics in our world, any acceptable social and historical analytical framework must be both *systemic* and *eclectic*. It should be evident that my own skeletal framework rests upon insights from the traditions of Marxism, anarchism, Weberianism, Garveyism, feminism, womanism, antihomophobism, ecologism, liberalism, and even elements of conservatism. And, of course, this framework is but a rudimentary one which requires vast refinement.

The practical implications of affirming the Christian norms of individuality and democracy is the wholesale rejection of social hierarchies based on class, race, gender, and sexual orientation. Such a rejection would more than likely lead to some form of democratic and libertarian socialism linked to antiracist, antipatriarchal, and antihomophobic ways of life; that is, a socioeconomic arrangement with markets, price mechanisms, an induced (not directed) labor force, a free press, formal political rights, and a constitutionally-based legal order with special protections for people of color, women, gays, lesbians, the elderly, and any other marginalized peoples. This social vision recognizes that centralization, hierarchy, and markets are inescapable realities for modern social existence. The crucial question is how are various forms of centralization, hierarchy, and markets regulated—that is, to what extent can democratic mechanisms yield public accountability of limited centralization, meritorious hierarchy, and a mixture of planned, socialized, and private enterprises in the market along with indispensable democratic political institutions.

In conclusion, the "critical pilgrimage" of the Christian church in our time is first and foremost to bring prophetic judgment to bear upon its own captivity to prevailing American, European, and/or Soviet hegemony. This judgment should be made in light of an interpretation of the Christian gospel which yields the norms of individuality and democracy. These norms are inseparable from a systemic and eclectic social and historical analysis which facilitates protracted and principled struggles against social hierarchies based on class, race, gender, and sexual orientation. Therefore, prophetic Christians must be in the forefront of movements against U.S. and Soviet imperialisms, multicorporate domination of our economy and government, escalating racist, sexist, and heterosexist practices, as well as ecological destruction. The ideals of individuality and democracy are tenuous in our world. Their preservation and extension depends, in large part, upon our understanding of and commitment to a deep sense of justice.

Alasdair MacIntyre, Liberalism, and Socialism: A Christian Perspective

> The burden of our civilization is not merely, as many suppose, that the product of industry is ill-distributed, or its conduct tyrannical, or its operation interrupted by embittered disagreements. It is that industry itself has come to hold a position of exclusive predominance among human interests, which no single interest, and least of all the provision of the material means of existence, is fit to occupy. That obsession by economic issues is as local and transitory as it is repulsive and disturbing. To future generations it will appear as pitiable as the obsession of the seventeenth century by religious quarrels appears today; indeed, it is less rational, since the object with which it is concerned is less important.
>
> R. H. Tawney

> The purpose of studying economics is not to acquire a set of ready-made answers to economic questions, but to learn how to avoid being deceived by economists.
>
> Joan Robinson

In his provocative book, *After Virtue* (Notre Dame, 1981), Alasdair MacIntyre argues that moral discourse in the modern West is in a grave state of disorder. The central terms, privileged notions, and key expressions in Western moral vocabularies constitute fragments of past conceptual schemes, residues of lost theoretical contexts. According to MacIntyre, we are left with the ruins of the West, mere simulacra of morality with no rational standards to adjudicate between conflicting moral theories and perspectives. The dominant moral fictions of our age—rights, utility, and expertise—hide and conceal irrational wills to power, arbitrary expressions of desire.

MacIntyre's creative response to this crisis is to recover and revise Aristotelian ethics. He promotes a virtue-centered moral theory which specifies an essential nature of human beings—a nature that defines their *telos* (or true end understood as a certain kind of life), and a set of moral precepts which enable people to progress toward their *telos*. MacIntyre sug-

From Bruce Grelle and David A. Krueger, eds., *Christianity and Capitalism: Perspectives on Religion, Liberalism, and the Economy* (Chicago: Center for the Scientific Study of Religion, 1985).

gests that only this sophisticated recuperation of an Aristotelian teleological scheme and context can safeguard and sustain us "through the coming ages of barbarism and darkness" (p. 244).

One reason that MacIntyre's understanding of the present crisis in Western morality, culture, and civilization is highly relevant to Christians is that it is rooted in his own personal pilgrimage from Christian to Marxist to neo-Aristotelian. The common denominator of this pilgrimage is the search for the intelligible and rational bases for morality, community, solidarity, and praxis. MacIntyre ultimately concludes that the traditions of Protestant Christianity and Marxism cannot provide such bases.

For MacIntyre, Protestant Christianity fails because of its devaluation of reasons. Luther's characterization of Aristotle as "that buffoon who has misled the church," along with Calvin's severe circumscription of human capacities, both symbolize the Protestant Christian claim that human reason yields no genuine comprehension of the telos of human beings.

Marxism fails owing to its lack of "a morally distinctive standpoint" (p. 243). In situations in which moral responses are required, Marxism tends to resort to Kantianism, as with Eduard Bernstein, Karl Vorlander, and Max Adler; to utilitarianism, as with Lenin and Trotsky; or to Hegel and Spinoza, as with Georg Lukács and Louis Althusser, respectively. In addition, Marxism is excessively optimistic regarding human capacities, especially in the face of the vast moral decline and decay in capitalist societies. MacIntyre succinctly states:

A Marxist who took Trotsky's last writings with great seriousness would be forced into a pessimism quite alien to the Marxist tradition, and in becoming a pessimist he would in an important way have ceased to be a Marxist. For he would now see no tolerable alternative set of political and economic structures which could be brought into place to replace the structures of advanced capitalism. This conclusion agrees of course with my own. For I too not only take it that Marxism is exhausted as a *political* tradition, a claim borne out by the almost indefinitely numerous and conflicting range of political allegiances which now carry Marxist banners— this does not at all imply that Marxism is not still one of the richest sources of ideas about modern society—but I believe that this exhaustion is shared by every other political tradition within our culture (p. 244).

MacIntyre concludes that present projects of political and economic liberation must be abandoned for the more tempered practice of a revised moral Aristotelianism.

What matters at this stage is the construction of local forms of community within which civility and the intellectual and moral life can be sustained through the new Dark Ages which are already upon us. And if the tradition of the virtues was able to survive the horrors of the last Dark Ages, we are not entirely without grounds for hope. This time however the barbarians are not waiting beyond the frontiers; they have already been governing us for quite some time. And it is our lack of consciousness of this that constitutes part of our predicament. We are waiting not for a Godot, but for another—doubtless very different—St. Benedict. (Pp. 244-45)

In what follows I would like to defend Protestant Christianity and the Marxist tradition against MacIntyre's powerful criticisms and against the present challenges of the neoconservative/liberal defenses of "Democratic Capitalism." These two perspectives are the major contenders and alternatives to my own position. My defense shall take the form of putting forward a rudimentary Christian case for democratic socialism. I shall attempt to show that a particular version of Protestant Christianity provides a conception of human nature and morality that requires adopting a social analytical viewpoint deeply influenced by the Marxist tradition. Furthermore, this conception of human nature and morality and this social analytical viewpoint results neither in elitist disengagement from present political and economic struggles and nostalgic yearnings for holistic schema and contexts (as with MacIntyre) nor in ahistorical justifications for the "free enterprise" system. Rather, my view promotes engaged social insurgency—a position tempered by a Christian worldly skepticism, regulated by Christian values of democracy and individuality, and guided by undogmatic Marxist social analysis. I shall begin my defense by critically engaging MacIntyre's argument. I will then try to reveal the empirical vacuity of Robert Benne's liberal defense of capitalist democracies. My own constructive position will emerge in the course of my examination of MacIntyre and Benne.

I find acceptable MacIntyre's claim regarding the interminability of public argument regarding crucial moral issues. This is neither shocking nor surprising in a highly pluralistic culture and heterogeneous society. As MacIntyre notes, the very aim of the secularization of public discourse—the bourgeois liberal effort to establish minimal frameworks of tolerance (a theory of the right) within which differing ways of life (i.e. conceptions of the good) could be aired—presupposed fundamental disagreement regarding the telos, or true end, of human beings. And there is little doubt that any attempt to reestablish a single teleological scheme or context constitutes an authoritarianism rightly abhorred by most moderns, including modern neo-Aristotelians like MacIntyre himself. Aristotelianism, like many other premodern authoritarian moralities, does not take seriously the plurality, heterogeneity, opposition, and conflict inherent in human life and society. Yet such matters are the very motivations for the modern political discourse MacIntyre castigates. Hence, his total rejection of modern politics.

> Modern systematic politics, whether liberal, conservative, radical or socialist, simply has to be rejected from a standpoint that owes genuine allegiance to the tradition of the virtues; for modern politics itself expresses in its institutional forms a systematic rejection of that tradition. (P. 237)

But what does such a rejection amount to if one still believes, as MacIntyre does, that conflict is at the heart of modern society? If, as he states, "Modern politics is civil war carried on by other means" (p. 236), how is such conflict to be dealt with? Is it not preferable over civil war itself? How would a virtue-centered theory of morality come to terms with other conflicting virtue-centered theories of morality? I suggest that MacIntyre's passionate rejection of modern politics is symptomatic of a postmodern weariness of confronting the insoluble problems of social conflict and disorder. He indeed prefers the liberal response to these problems over "the barbarous despotism of the collective Tsardom which reigns in Moscow" (p. 243)—yet his neo-Aristotelianism which builds local communities on the margins of society presupposes the very liberties and protections provided by the liberalism he rejects.

So, despite his castigation of liberal politics, MacIntyre remains, on a practical plane, a liberal; that is, the *praxis* of his viewpoint assumes and affirms liberalism. On a deeper level, MacIntyre's neo-Aristotelianism bears the indelible stamp of the liberal Enlightenment—no matter how persuasive his claim regarding its failure. This stamp can be seen in his discarding of three basic features of past forms of Aristotelianism, namely, the acceptance of fixed inherited social roles, the naturalization of cultural ways of life, and the promotion of exclusivism in societal relations.[1] Once one has been bitten by the Enlightenment bugs of critical consciousness, historical consciousness, and universal consciousness, a wholesome rejection of liberalism is impossible. The only credible alternative is to build upon and go beyond it. What is needed is a thoroughgoing critique of liberalism's own uncritically accepted assumptions. The tradition of Protestant Christianity provides many of the resources needed for just such a critique.

The distinctive strength of Protestant Christianity is neither its worldly skepticism (for this can be found in pagan cynicism or secular poststructuralism) nor its anticipatory triumphalism (for this can be found in non-Christian forms of apocalypticism and millenarianism). Rather, this strength resides in its recognition of the interplay between fallible finitude and the demand for engaged praxis, between acknowledged fallenness and received empowerment. This interplay incorporates worldly skepticism and sustains anticipatory triumphalism thereby precluding ill-founded optimism and paralyzing pessimism. More importantly, it promotes and encourages an unstoppable predilection for alternatives grounded in the present. In other words, Protestant Christianity—at its best—possesses a unique capacity to highlight critical, historical, and universal consciousness.

This capacity owes principally to its realistic assessment of human proclivities, its processive view of life and history, and its all-inclusive moral outlook. The Protestant Christian tradition—especially as developed by American thinkers from Jonathan Edwards and William James to Reinhold Niebuhr and Martin Luther King, Jr.—views *history* as a battlefield upon which to fuse with comrades in a struggle against evil, and *nature* as a realm of reality with which one communes and in which one delights. These viewpoints provide resources and riches which aid in the effort to go beyond modern liberal bourgeois society. Put simply, these resources are as follows. First, there is a recognition of the indispensable yet inadequate capacities of human beings to solve problems—hence the deep antidogmatic thrust of Protestant Christianity which fans and fuels critical consciousness. Second, there is the good news of Jesus Christ which empowers and links human capacities to the coming of the kingdom—hence the spiritual resources necessary for coping with despair, dread, disappointment, and death itself. And finally, there is an acceptance of and an insistence upon the moral obligation to view all human beings as having equal status, as warranting the same dignity, respect, and love, especially those who are denied such dignity, respect, and love by individuals, families, groups, social structures or political regimes— hence the Christian identification and solidarity with the downtrodden and disinherited, with the exploited and oppressed.

The systematic ecclesiastical interpretations of these crucial resources and riches of Protestant Christianity remain the province of Protestant theologians. And this activity should persist. But what is most interesting about our present postmodern moment is that there is a consensus among many contemporary Christians regarding the need to struggle against forms of dogmatism, despair, and oppression. Furthermore, there is widespread agreement that the preferable rhetoric of Christian ethics should be that of freedom and democracy, self-determination and control over one's destiny. No longer are Christians seduced by pagan venerations of the power and benevolence of reason nor by secular projections of a "new humanity" or an "unselfish, altruistic species" rising upon the advent of the good society in history. The moral debates in modern society among intellectuals in general and among Christian thinkers in particular are lively and intense—but assumptions against dogmatism, despair, and oppression as well as preferences for rhetorics of freedom and democracy are widely shared by most interlocutors.

This situation forces us to amend MacIntyre's characterization of public moral discourse as conceptual fragmentation. This fragmentation surely exists when the situation is viewed diachronically (in relation to the past); but when viewed synchronically (in relation to its internal character and structure) public moral discourse contains a consensus of assumptions and agreement on rhetorics. A genuinely creative response to the present crisis in ethics cannot consist simply in a historical reconstruction that accounts for conceptual fragmentation. Rather, what is needed is a theoretical and methodological reflection on the *social analytical* presuppositions of the varying moral positions which share common assumptions and rhetorics. MacIntyre hints at these crucial strategies when he states that "Philosophical analysis will not help us" and, more importantly, that any moral philosophy "characteristically presupposes a sociology" (pp. 2, 22). Yet he does not pursue the latter strategy in regard to his own neo-Aristotelianism.

I suggest that the major terrain of contestation in moral discourse for Christians and non-Christians alike is no longer over the degree of mutability and plasticity of human nature or philosophical attempts to provide ahistorical grounds for standards and criteria for principles and judgments. Rather the major terrain is that of contesting social analytical understandings of forms of power, wealth, status, oppression, freedom, and democracy in modern societies. For these understandings are what deeply shape one's conception of human nature as well as one's formulation of ethical standards and criteria. The starting point of one's ethical reflections is always already sedimented and permeated with presuppositions of social theory, cultural perceptions, and personal socialization. This acknowledgment leads neither to a vulgar sociology of knowledge in which persons are locked into social boxes unable to change or be changed nor to crude amoralism in which morality is rejected owing to its impurity or lack of full-fledged autonomy. Instead, a proper historicizing of ethics results in a more self-conscious theoretical and methodological articulation of the relations between social theory, hermeneutics, and ethical reflection, including such crucial variables as the role of tradition, authority, critique, and resistance.

For those of us critically aligned with and self-situated in the Christian tradition there ought to be a deep bias against prevailing forms of dogmatism, despair, and oppression. Yet this bias should be followed without making criticism, mental health, or liberation a fetish or idol; for such reductions of the Christian gospel result in impotent irony, shallow self-indulgence, and superficial justice, respectively. Contrary to

MacIntyre's interpretation of Protestant Christianity, reason, like life itself, ought to be viewed as a divine gift wrought with contradictions owing to its various forms, styles, and uses. We must continually reflect upon the limits of reason, while perennially problematizing the status of our perception of those limits, if we are to remain true to the insights of Protestant Christianity.

I suggest that Christian ethical reflection upon political, cultural, and socioeconomic arrangements yields two fundamental norms: individuality within community and democratic participation in the decision-making process of those major institutions which guide and regulate our lives. We arrive at these norms neither by transcendental reflection on the nature of morality nor by historical mimicking of the liberal tradition but rather by interpreting the Christian faith in light of our present circumstances. This interpretation accents the egalitarian Christian mandate that all human creatures are made in the image of God and are thereby endowed with a certain dignity and respect which warrants a particular treatment, including a chance to fulfill their capacities and potentialities. This mandate acknowledges the social and communal character of self-fulfillment such that the development of individuality occurs within collectivities, groups, and societies. Furthermore, this interpretation of the Christian faith recognizes the depravity of persons thereby requiring institutional mechanisms which check and balance various forms of power, wealth, status, and influence. These mechanisms seem to work best in our world when regulated by the ideal of democracy. This ideal of democracy highlights not simply participation within a given set of structures, *but also empowerment to change the structures themselves.*

The important contribution of neo-Marxist social analysis to Christian ethical reflection is that it puts forward a social analytical viewpoint from the vantage point of those victimized by existing structures of oppression and promotes a postliberal conception of democracy. For the Christian, neo-Marxist social analyses and moral visions are to be judged in light of the interpretation of Christian faith in our time, including the norms of individuality and democracy. To the degree to which such social analyses and visions promote these norms, Marxism is indispensable for Christian ethical practice. To the degree to which they violate these norms, neo-Marxist analyses warrant rejection. Like MacIntyre, I suggest that Marxist social analyses remain important sources of insight and illumination regarding the operations of power in modern societies; unlike MacIntyre, I will argue that Marxism is not *completely* exhausted as a political tradition—though, like Christianity, most of its visible manifestations should be severely criticized and transformed.

This point is best seen in the case of present-day liberal and neoconservative discourses regarding modern capitalist countries, especially the USA. I have in mind here the writings of such figures as Robert Benne, Michael Novak, Richard Neuhaus, and Peter Berger. There is no doubt that the advent of capitalist modes of production—with their distinctive types of markets, opportunities, and motivations for technological innovation and efficiency as well as class exploitation, domination of foreign territories and reappropriation of patriarchal and racist structures—diffused feudal forms of centralized power. This occurred principally by undercutting medieval and mercantilist regulations and controls over the market. There also should be little doubt—given the glaring economic failures and political despotisms in the command economies of market-less communist regimes—that market activities of some sort, with price mechanisms that balance supply and demand and reflect cost and use-value, are the only modern alternative to large, powerful, unaccountable bureaucratic hierarchies of full-fledged central planning. On this point, the powerful insights of major conservative thinkers such as Ludwig von Mises (1951), Friedrich Hayek (1961), and Milton Friedman (1962) should not be overlooked—though we must reject their morally repugnant laissez-faire conclusions. The central problems of liberal and neo-conservative thinkers regarding modern capitalist societies is that their claims about prevailing distinctions between economic and political power and the decentralization of power are theoretically naive and empirically weak. It is this naiveté and weakness which leads many of their critics to view their claims are mere vulgar ideology deployed to buttress the status quo.

Robert Benne's book, *The Ethic of Democratic Capitalism: A Moral Reassessment* (Fortress, 1981), is an exemplary defense of capitalist democracy. It is informed, urbane, liberal, Christian—yet theoretically naive and empirically weak. Benne brings together a version of Niebuhr's heuristic mythological interpretation of Christianity with Rawls's revisionist liberal conception of justice in a creative way. Yet his Achilles' heel is his third pillar: the refined neoclassical economics of Paul Samuelson.

For example, in defense of his claim regarding the decentralization of economic power in the USA, Benne argues that from 1899 to 1959 the national income gained by monopolistic enterprises has decreased from 17.4 percent to 11.5 percent. Relying heavily on the Warren G. Nutter and Henry Einhorn study (1969), Benne suggests that the clout of monopolies is far less than Marxist thinkers claim it to be. In response to this suggestion, I would note first, and Benne acknowledges this, that any such picture can look quite differently depending on one's definition of monopoly. Second, and more importantly, the crucial index is not earnings but holdings, not income but wealth—especially given escalating income taxes in the period studied. And when we turn to wealth and holdings, empirical studies done from various ideological persuasions concur that 0.5 percent of the population own 22 percent of the wealth, 1.0 percent own 30 percent of the wealth, including 50 percent of all corporate stock and 52 percent of the bonds.[2] These figures have remained roughly unchanged since 1945. Furthermore, as long ago as 1971, Harvard Professor William Hueller reported before the U.S. Senate Select Committee on Small Business that 111 industrial corporations with assets of a billion dollars or more had more than half of all assets employed in manufacturing and received more than half of the earnings on more than half of the sales. So much for the decentralization thesis.

Benne goes on to argue that effective, fair, and robust competition exists in the corporate sector of the American economy (no one doubts this is so in the entrepreneurial sector). His aim is to controvert the claim concerning the domination and price-setting role of oligopolies and monopolies put forward by socialists like John Kenneth Galbraith or Marxists like Paul Sweezy. He defends this claim by invoking the neoclassical fiction—promoted by M. A. Adelman and others—that there is no necessary relation between firm size and market power—as if large corporations are not relatively large in their markets principally owing to the advantages of their size and their capacity to disproportionately influence the market.

The major empirical gap in liberal and neoconservative analyses of modern capitalist societies is found in the central power dynamics of these societies: the well-documented realities of corporate influence in the political and governmental processes, especially the intimate behind-the-scenes relations between the public bureaucracies of the government and major corporations.[3] Such relations can be seen between the Department of Agriculture and agribusiness, the Department of Transportation and the automobile industries, the Federal Communications Commission and television and broadcasting networks, the Interstate Commerce Commission and the trucking industry, the Atomic Energy Commission and its supplying industries and, most notoriously, between the Department of Defense and weapons firms. These relations, often cozy ones, do not simply raise crucial questions regarding the scope and intensity of competition; they also require serious scrutiny of their relative lack of public accountability. This is so because when we closely examine the special-interest process in American government—especially the money committees of Congress such as the Senate Banking, Housing and Urban Affairs Committee, the House Banking, Finance and Urban Affairs Committee as well as the advisory committees to both the congressional committees and public bureaucracies—we find overwhelming evidence for far-reaching corporate influence. Examples of the vast impact of oil executives on the National Petroleum Council or that of corporate polluters on the National Industrial Pollution Control Council are well known.

Even a self-proclaimed liberal political scientist such as Grant McConnell sadly concludes that the decentralization thesis of fellow liberals (and neoconservatives) is not simply problematic, but more pointedly, faulty. He then tries to show that the collapse of the decentralization thesis does not entail that there is a ruling class in America. Instead he holds that there is a small corporate elite that influences and controls a substantial part of the U.S. government but that it does not have full control owing to the nature and character of the presidency and Supreme Court. It is no accident that when liberals and neoconservatives defend the autonomy of American politics from corporate influence they often invoke presidential elections. Yet rarely do they engage in serious empirical scrutiny of the candidate-selection process. Not only does such scrutiny reveal vast corporate influence in both parties (often the same corporation in both parties!) but also surreptitious efforts to discourage sustained policy discussion, serious political education, and even sometimes voter registration. Furthermore, similar empirical studies would have to be done regarding the hidden policy-formation process—the institutional mechanisms which develop and implement general policies—that includes such powerful formations as the Council on Foreign Relations, Committee for Economic Development, Business Roundtable, Business Council, the American Assembly, and the Conference Board. Attention also should be given to the crucial ideological process, especially the role of mass-media, schools, and churches in the formation and dissemination of beliefs, sentiments, and viewpoints throughout the general populace.

If the decentralization thesis is false, then liberal and neoconservative defenses of capitalist societies in the name of democracy rest upon shaky ground. And if this is so, then their arguments must justify anti-democratic capitalist social relations and corporate domination of the economy and government on other grounds—such as efficiency, high productivity, and increased standards of living. Such arguments contain a moral dimension yet lack serious moral substance; they remain within the limits of technological rationality, instrumental reason, and cost-benefit analysis.

The typical strategy employed by liberals and neoconservatives against the democratic socialist claim that workers should have some say in the decisions made at the workplace that shape their destinies is that workers' control over the productive process is not required by a substantive ideal of democracy. As Benne notes, "a person can be paid for specific services in a complex process without having a claim to control over the process" (p. 223).

It is difficult not to view this strategy as a justification not simply for class subordination (or lack of democracy in the workplace), but also, by implication, as an argument against democratic participation *per se*. My concern here is not that workers should have "full control" over the process of production. Such claims about "full control" are undesirable in a fully democratic order, because nonworkers should also have a say in such decisions. Rather, my point here is that the liberal and neoconservative strategy against democratic mechanisms in the economic sphere can serve as well against democratic mechanisms in the political sphere. Such mechanisms must indeed be coordinated with considerations of efficiency, demographic difficulties, and technological innovation; but they surely ought not to be prematurely precluded from the economic sphere on dogmatic ideological ground. If so, this constitutes a blow against the ideal of democracy. Furthermore, it reveals just how deep one's commitment to the ideal of democracy really is.

For the Christian thinker, the basic problem of liberal and neoconservative arguments supporting modern capitalist societies is that their social analytical presuppositions and economic theoretical assumptions are antithetical to the Christian mandate for peoples' participation and empowerment in regard to fulfilling their unique capacities and potentialities. This mandate can be best enacted when one adopts social analyses of power, wealth, status, and influence and economic theories of production, distribution, and consumption that look at the world from the situation of the "least of these"—the victims—in existing societies. Neo-Marxist analyses and theories presently are the most developed perspectives which adopt such a victim's viewpoint.

Just as I believe that the Christian faith in the modern world—given its allegiance to democracy and individuality—requires resistance to race-based and gender-based social hierarchies, so I believe that it demands opposition to class-based social hierarchies. These hierarchies undermine the God-given dignity and violate the respect due to each of God's creatures. Wholesome Christian rejection of such hierarchies must lead to some form of democratic and libertarian socialism—a socio-economic arrangement with markets, price mechanisms, and induced (not directed) labor force, a free press, formal political rights, and a constitutionally based legal order with special protections of the marginalized. Such an arrangement would consist of five major sectors: First, state-owned industries of basic producer goods, such as electricity networks, steel, oil, petrochemical, and financial institutions whose macroplans must be approved by an elected democratic assembly. Second, independent self-managed socialized enterprises which operate on a local scale. Third, cooperative enterprises that control their own property. Fourth, small private businesses run by self-employed entrepreneurs. And last, a large number of self-employed individuals, e.g., artists, freelance writers, plumbers, farmers.

This version of democratic and libertarian socialism—similar to those defended by distinguished economists such as Ota Sik (1976), Branko Horvat (1982), Wlodimierz Brus (1972; 1980), John Kenneth Galbraith (1973) and especially Alec Nove (1983)—is well aware of the dangers of the centralization of power and management in multileveled, hierarchically organized, plan bureaucracies found in marketless communist command economies. Yet this view also recognizes existing forms of centralization in capitalist democracies—including vast corporate influence in the economy and government. It attempts to make such centralization publicly accountable, while preserving the separations of powers, countervailing forces, and checks and balances against abuses of publicly controlled centralization. This is why the fusion of limited centralized planning, socialized and private enterprises in the market with democratic political institutions is so important.

Centralization, hierarchy, and markets are inescapable economic realities for modern social existence. The crucial question is how various forms of centralization, hierarchy, and markets are to be understood, conceived and judged in light of Christian commitments to democracy and individuality. And given the threat to the biosphere, nonhuman organisms, and the planet itself, it is clear that we must rethink whether industrial modes and expansionist policies are desirable. For Christians, the desirable and feasible society—both here and abroad—should consist of a distinctive version of democratic and libertarian socialism which encourages nonracist nonhomophobic and nonsexist cultural ways of life and which incorporates ecological consciousness in its future outlook. In this way, the riches of Protestant Christianity are conjoined with the best of neo-Marxist, feminist, ecological, antihomophobic, and antiracist perspectives.

The ideals of democracy and individuality are tenuous in our world. They are associated with risky social experiments that have a short history and heritage. The crucial issue of our time is whether this history and heritage can be extended and strengthened—can the vast human misery and suffering be lessened by democratic empowerment and libertarian constraints within societal institutions? MacIntyre says "no," weeps bitterly, and retreats into his intellectual monastery. Liberals and neoconservatives say "yes," enshrine the limited success of the American experiment, and shun additional innovation and transformation, here and abroad. Democratic socialists say "maybe," but only if our understanding of and commitment to democracy and individuality are deep-

Left Strategies Today

The major task of the American left in this period is to gain a foothold in the public discourse of the nation in order to articulate both a moral vision and an economic program. Such a project must offer a vision of common good that appeals to and expands the latent popular support for many of the New Deal and Great Society government services. This task requires that the left engage in a more explicit *class politics*. The present class offensive by the business community must be met by a counter-offensive by the organized victims of pro-business policies. Class politics must be the prism through which black politics are elaborated.

This strategic perspective will make three basic assumptions. First, it will assume that the major culprit is not Reaganism per se but rather the effective politicization of the business community. Second, it will presuppose that the left is too weak to lead a popular-front-like strategy against the business assault. Third, it will hold out the possibility that the ideological, political, and racial polarization in the country may open new discursive space into which the left can enter.

The first assumption delivers us from a seductive yet deceptive preoccupation with who wins the next presidential election. The crucial issue is the scope and influence that business will have in the long run within both the Republican and Democratic parties—not simply whether pro-business neoliberals will replace even more probusiness conservatives in the White House in 1988. Of course, the former is preferable, but this has little to do with the larger political battles with which the left must be concerned. We must remember that the business assault began in 1978 under President Jimmy Carter and there is little reason to think that a neoliberal administration will counter this assault. In fact, given the budgetary constraints of the Gramm-Rudman Bill, it may benefit the right for neoliberals to be forced to do the "dirty work"; for example, cut back even more on social programs. So regardless of the 1988 scenario, the left must focus its attacks on the consolidation of business interests in both parties and thereby transcend the obsession against mere Reaganism.

The second assumption reminds us that the left has neither the depth nor strength to play a major unifying role in a counteroffensive against the business assault. Yet this does not mean that the left should jump on

From *Socialist Review* (Mar.-Apr. 1986).

the neoliberal bandwagon or that the left should disengage from the arena of practical politics (on the national, state, or local levels). Rather it means that the left should more eagerly put forward its socialist, feminist, antiracist, antihomophobic, and anti-imperialist views and programs such that the larger questions of the distribution of wealth and income between groups and the erosion of power of the lower middle class, working class, and poor gain visibility in public discourse.

The distinctive contribution of the U.S. left has never been and is not now its ability to mobilize or organize the populace. Rather it is the substance of its moral vision and the relevance of its economic programs for the common good of the nation. When there have been liberals in power who appropriated certain aspects of these visions and programs, U.S. mainstream politics has been at its best. I remain unconvinced that neoliberals would act accordingly when in power. Hence, the need to refine our vision, sharpen our ideas about postindustrial economic programs, and not lose sight of those state and local struggles in which we might make a practical difference.

The third assumption concerns the particular progressive campaigns or movements that the left can support in order to make our visions and programs more visible to the American people. The conventional wisdom was once that the Democratic party, and especially its liberal wing, should be the privileged arena in which left practical politics could be conducted. But the weakness of the labor movement (principally owing to declining workforce representation, increasing hostility from management and structural changes in the workplace which send jobs to low-wage, third-world nations) has undermined the stability of the liberal wing of the Democratic party. In addition, political issues about U.S. foreign policy, abortion, and affirmative action have further fragmented the liberal coalition of the Democratic party. The conventional left wisdom, therefore, no longer holds.

If the left is to benefit from the ideological, political, and racial polarization in the country, it must attempt to work closely and in a principled manner with those progressive forces that are themselves on the margins of the Democratic party. The Democratic presidential candidate will more than likely be some neoliberal scrambling for the center of the U.S. electorate. Our aim must be to unleash new possibilities among socialists, progressives, and whatever new social forces may in the near future constitute a class counteroffensive against the business assault.

And who are the major progressive forces on the margins of the Democratic party? First and foremost, Afro-Americans. Then, the elderly, Jews, women, Hispanics, small farmers, trade unionists, Arabs, displaced industrial workers, and crucial slices of the educated white middle class, for example peace and ecological activists. This may sound like a mere laundry list but it does constitute a majority of Americans. Depoliticization as well as internal conflicts prohibits this majority from becoming a major political force. I put Afro-Americans at the top of this "list" because they have proven to be the most reliable group—and therefore are the key to—resisting the business assault. They have most consistently supported candidates critical of the business assault, and have shown a willingness to launch a counteroffensive as enacted in the Jackson campaign of 1984, which became the major recent progressive upsurge against business conservatism.

Yet this high political reliability of Afro-Americans does not entail the desirability of a racial (or, even worse, race-first) political strategy. In fact, the effectiveness of a black counteroffensive depends on its ability to adopt a transracial political strategy and thereby promote a broad class counteroffensive to the business assault. Jesse Jackson's Rainbow Coalition, and his presidential campaign in 1988, remain the most promising progressive possibility on the national scene, yet its social base must extend beyond the black community. Of course, Jackson's moral vision and political rhetoric go far beyond this narrow approach, but both the practice and the popular perception of the Rainbow Coalition often remain within it. This discrepancy reflects the cultural and existential distance between black and nonblack progressives, the influential portrayal of Jackson as a "black candidate" by the mass media and the delicate issue of Jackson's principled though controversial views on U.S. foreign policy. Yet some of the discrepancy between Jackson's vision and the practices of his organization has to do with a narrow black nationalism still incipient in both elements of the Rainbow Coalition and the black community.

This narrow black nationalism—often more reflective of the anxieties and interests of marginal black intellectuals, status-hungry black preachers, and power-seeking black politicians and businessmen than of the needs and sentiments of the black community—is understandable, but in no way justifiable. It is understandable because racial polarization in America invariably produces deep black distrust and suspicion of coalitions and alliances with others. Ironically, the business community has itself adopted a stance that supports black business nationalism as a strategy for black enhancement. Wrongly dubbed "black capitalism," these conservative business efforts to increase black entrepreneurial activity only reinforce black self-perceptions of social, political, and economic encapsulation.

A symbolic figure like Louis Farrakhan emerges because he articulates a bold rhetoric of black defiance and black dignity in the face of the *material* effects of the business assault and the *existential* effects of the black encapsulation. Needless to say, this rhetoric is shot through with antiwhite, anti-Jewish, and homophobic xenophobia as well as support for a feeble black business nationalist strategy for black betterment. Yet it does reveal just how far removed white America, both left and right, is from black realities and sentiments when most believe that what attracts a cross section of black America to Farrakhan's speeches is his anti-Semitism. Are we to suggest, as does Irving Kristol, that the Moral Majority are more reliable allies than black Americans in a fight against anti-Semitism? Has the litmus test for enrollment in the fight against anti-Semitism degenerated into a mere uncritical support for the policies of the state of Israel? Concrete response to these questions must take the form of linking struggles against anti-Semitism to principled criticisms of the Israeli (and other Middle East) governments.

Narrow black nationalism is unjustifiable, simply because it cannot deliver what it promises to achieve: black enhancement, especially of the black working poor and underclass. The black community does not possess the necessary wealth and power—nor will it possess them in the future—to alleviate the deplorable plight of the black working poor and underclass. Indeed, black America can do much better with its economic and cultural resources than it presently is doing. But the notion that the destiny of black America can be set right by means of black economic development (as argued by black conservatives) or racial political strategies (as argued by black liberals) can only lead black people into a political cul-de-sac. As the great Martin Luther King, Jr., repeatedly noted, the destiny of black America is inextricably bound with that of America. In fact, to reject this claim is to reinforce the very aims of the right: to enshrine the operations of private business, to racially polarize the political process, and to block transracial strategic alliances that challenge the prevailing business assault.

If Jackson's Rainbow Coalition can develop a transracial political strategy commensurate with his moral vision and his soon-to-be-revealed social-democratic economic program, there will be new discursive space in the public conversation in which left perspectives can be aired. This is so, not because Jackson is a socialist or running as a socialist candidate. Rather it is because the kind of issues Jackson raises opens the populace to taking seriously socialist perspectives. In other words, Jackson occupies social-democratic space—the most progressive space in national political discourse—which presents unprecedented opportunities for the socialist left to make a contribution to this discourse. And without participation in the public discourse, there can be no possibility of a concerted class counteroffensive against the business assault.

Jackson's moral vision and political rhetoric during his 1984 campaign embraced the interests and needs of Afro-Americans, the elderly, women, Hispanics, indigenous peoples, small farmers, Arabs, displaced industrial workers, trade unionists, gays and lesbians, Jews, and peace activists more than the other Democratic party candidates. His major problem has been and remains convincing three major liberal constituencies—labor, feminists, and Jews—that he is serious about his vision and rhetoric. And it is here that the left can contribute greatly to Jackson's efforts. The issue is not whether one "likes" Jackson or whether one fully agrees with his views. Rather it is whether labor, feminists, and Jews can better pursue their interests and be true to their values in a period of business assault *without* a Rainbow Coalition. To this question we can say only a resounding *no!* The exigencies of our historical situation require that the issues such as regulation of management, women's access to reproductive rights, and commitments to fairly distributed government services will surface most tellingly in public discourse *owing to* a Jackson campaign. This may not have been so with Walter Mondale in 1984 or Ted Kennedy in 1988. But neither of them—nor any such traditional liberal candidate—will be available in 1988. Despite Mario Cuomo's deceptive gestures, traditional liberalism has no future in the Democratic party. The choice is now between neoliberals of various stripes and social-democrats such as Jesse Jackson. The former represent an attenuated version of the business assault; the latter, a weak countervailing force against the business assault.

If the left is to pursue its own task, it must struggle within traditional liberal groups, especially labor, feminists, and Jewish circles, in order to lessen the ill-founded dispositions toward the major social-democratic force linked to the Democratic party, namely, Jackson's Rainbow Coalition and 1988 campaign. Like any new political development this social-democratic force is far from perfect, but it is the only available stepping-stone towards a class counteroffensive against the business assault.

Whatever tension existed in the past must be confronted, but with the knowledge that the limited options of the present require that either public discourse be expanded or we be doomed to a rather shallow debate between Republican conservatism and Democratic neoliberalism. In desperate times like these, even former hostilities must be superseded by common interests and values against business-class assaults. Not since the 1920s have we seen such assaults, but resistance movements of the 1930s must never be dislodged from our memories.

The major issues impeding this possible progressive effort (even at the level of the primaries) are those of U.S. foreign policy. Although there is widespread agreement on attitudes toward the Soviet Union, China, Poland, Afghanistan, and Cuba, there is much controversy regarding developments in Central America, the Philippines, South Korea, and maybe even South Africa. There indeed are basic differences on these matters among the left and progressives, yet tendentious ideologues on the right and center and biased misinformation offered by the mass media often distort perceptions of the various positions. The first step toward grappling with this matter should be the airing of differences, both behind closed doors and in open conferences. Much encouraging dialogue in this regard has been initiated within the labor movement. Much more is needed between people of color and feminists and Afro-Americans and Arab-Americans and Jewish-Americans. The basic aim should be not to reach some impossible consensus, but rather to put forward the rational bases and moral grounds for various positions such that mutual understanding, respect, and trust may result. And since foreign policy issues are rarely the major factor motivating domestic political behavior, for example, voting, this understanding, respect, and trust is required if victims of the business assault and their supporters are to work together.

What are the common grounds for the left and progressives on the margins of the Democratic party besides vague notions of justice, freedom, and peace? What are the specific issues that can gain the attention of the U.S. populace and thereby expose them to left and progressive viewpoints? I suggest that four major issues—issues visibly associated with the common good and public interest—should play a central role in our efforts to initiate a class counteroffensive to the business assault: jobs, national health care, the unjust distributive effects of prevailing taxation, and the deplorable plight of homeless people and poor women and children.

The old issues of underemployment and unemployment must remain at the core of a class counteroffensive. We must try to shift public attention, as did Jackson in his 1984 campaign, to the personal devastation caused by the sudden loss of a job and to the grinding drudgery of boring jobs. Our focus on jobs should be not simply a quantitative one that highlights the kind of lives people should be able to enjoy. In short, the quality of people's lives is not reducible to their standards of living.

There is already a growing interest in the country about escalating health costs. And the privatization of health services is causing even some state legislatures (such as Texas) to act in order to prevent inhumane treatment of patients that results from cost-calculating behavior of hospital administrators. The left and progressives—through a Jackson campaign—can seize the initiative and make national health care a bone of contention in the public discourse. We can put conservatives and the business community on the defensive by rightly associating them with mean-spirited hospital officials who refuse to care for patients from different races and ages. We can highlight the fact that the USA claims to be a moral leader in the world, but every other industrial nation, including the communist ones, takes better care of its citizens than we do.

Third, we must make more visible to the American people the gross maldistribution of wealth and income in the country. Now that taxation is a hot issue, we must try to make it clear that the abstract debate about equity vs. efficiency is really about the scope of the power of the business community and about "who gets what from government." For example, the left and progressives, especially Jackson's public voice, must drive home the points that income from stock-market speculation (of which most Americans know little yet surmise that some people are getting rich and richer—easy!) is taxed much more lightly than income derived from the sweat of their brow, that corporations hardly pay taxes, and that high levels of productivity can go along with much higher degrees of equality than we have now.

Last, we must attempt to persuade the American people that the impoverished lives of homeless people and poor women and children are *moral symbols* of the present socioeconomic arrangement accentuated by the business class assault. Local movements for the homeless are growing and the issues of the feminization and childrenization of poverty—who are disproportionately but not exclusively people of color—are becoming more visible. Again, we must try to make these issues part of the national political debate. The right is already in the hot seat on some of them, given their dishonest attempts to justify the business assault on many Great Society programs by invoking a few welfare cheats. In short, we must identify the business community and its assault with the escalation of social misery. We must find ways to appeal to the moral sense of Americans.

Each one of these four issues accents what the left and progressives need: concrete issues that permit us to channel moral outrage through social perceptions and analyses that lead people to conclude that effective forms of public services are possible and necessary. This outrage presupposes moral sentiments aroused by the articulation of a moral vision; the analyses assume feasible programs that result from serious intellectual work. Needless to say, we need more moral vision and intellectual work on the left. Yet the vision and work remain academic without political entrée to the public discourse. Jackson's Rainbow Coalition and campaign in 1988, as it adopts and practices a transracial political strategy, will be the major vehicle for progressive national political entrée in the immediate future. In this way, black politics and class politics are inseparable for left strategies in present-day capitalist America.

Christian Realism as Religious Insights and Europeanist Ideology: Niebuhr and the Third World

The battle raging over the legacy of Reinhold Niebuhr looms large in our day. Leftists, liberals, neoconservatives, and old-style conservatives can find bits of textual evidence in Niebuhr's wide-ranging corpus to make their case. Yet in regard to international affairs and U.S. foreign policy, there should be little doubt that the Christian realism of Niebuhr led him to adopt an exemplary cold war liberal perspective in the post–World War II period. His particular interpretation of notions such as moral ambiguity, situational complexity, and historical irony were skillfully deployed in the service of an Europeanist ideology that promoted U.S. hegemony in the world.

In this paper, I shall attempt to demystify Niebuhr's realist version of Europeanist ideology; that is, I will try to disclose the ways in which his rhetorical strategies and argumentative claims undercut outdated liberal idealist and isolationist forms of Europeanist ideology in U.S. foreign policy and replaced them with a more acceptable and attractive realist version. This demystification shall proceed on three levels. First, I will put forward a brief genealogy of the emergence of Christian realist discourse in international studies and U.S. diplomatic discourse. The aim of this genealogy is to show how liberal American thought met the new challenges and problems of living in a period of profound realignment and repositioning of world powers. Second, I shall pursue an immanent critique of the major motifs of Christian realism regarding international affairs—balance of power, national interest, strategic and tactical thinking, the wise statesman as vigilant civil servant—and reveal the degree to which the vagueness and indeterminacy implied by these motifs are shaped and contained by means of ideological fiat, that is, by unquestioned and unargued for biases, prejudices, and presuppositions. Last, I shall suggest that Niebuhr's reflections and judgments regarding the third world—of which the Middle East shall serve as the paradigmatic case—best exemplify the insights and blindnesses—and role and function—of Christian realism as a liberal form of Europeanist ideology best

---

An address delivered at a Niebuhr symposium at Union Theological Seminary, Sept. 1987.

suited in "the American century" (1945–73) to further U.S. hegemony for an influential group of American political elites.

A Brief Genealogy of Christian Realism

F. O. Matthiessen once quipped that the USA was the only nation to move from innocence to corruption without a mediating stage of maturity. Yet the emergence of Christian realism as a source for guiding and regulating U.S. foreign policy subverts such a flippant claim. This emergence signified the maturation of American liberalism after the eclipse of the European domination of the world. The end of the European age (1492–1945) produced a profound and persuasive realignment of powers such that the burden of responsibility for the world order—especially in the military, economic, and geopolitical spheres—rests with the USA. This "first new nation" born liberal and modern had edged its way toward economic world status by the end of the First World War. After rapid geopolitical expansion (by means of displacement of indigenous peoples and dispossession of lands) and national consolidation (resulting from a bloody Civil War), the USA enjoyed a favorable isolation from great power invasion or attack and a proximity to militarily vulnerable and economically valuable regions, such as Latin America, rich in resources and labor.

This American economic expansion was accelerated by a vigorous protectionist policy after the First World War—a policy promoted by domestic agricultural and manufacturing firms fearful of revamped farms and rebuilt industries of Europe and legitimated by strong economic nationalism in Europe. This tremendous U.S. economic growth—along with a feeble state, weak trade-union movement, and ever-growing population imported primarily from impoverished sections of Europe—served as a material condition for an influential Wilsonian idealism in international affairs. This idealism rests upon liberal Christian ideas about the inevitability of progress, the unilinearity of historical direction, and the possibility of a peace without incessant strife and conflict.

By the 1920s, the import protectionist and export expansionist policies of the USA had shifted international capital flow from London to New York City—though France possessed the most formidable land army and air force in the world. The First World War indeed shook the foundations of liberal idealism—yet it invested some of its romantic hopes in the new social experiment in Russia. In fact, the first rudimentary formulations of Niebuhr's Christian realism in its left-liberal form

145

attempted to reconcile the quest for justice by means of socialist arrangements with sobering acknowledgment of the ineluctability of conflict and strife.

The 1930s is the watershed period. With the consolidation of Stalinism in the USSR—and the slow but sure recognition of failed hopes for justice and progress in Europe—as well as the rise of Nazism in Germany, liberal idealism became a less attractive and available option in American political life. Furthermore, the collapse of the world economic order—signified not by the decline of the price of securities on the New York Stock Exchange in October of 1929 but rather by the repudiation by Great Britain of the gold standard in September of 1931— prompted economic recovery by means of rearmament in an unprecedented manner throughout Europe and, in some degree, the USA. In this sense, Hitler's military buildup was but one kind of response to international economic anarchy.

A second-generation German immigrant in search of a secure American identity—and bitten by the bug of Anglophilism—Niebuhr held fast to his rudimentary version of Christian realism in the thirties. This version consisted of profound religious insights regarding the tragic character of human life and history, a distrust of all forms of moral absolutism and political perfectionism, and a radical historicist sensibility about the complexity and ambiguity in human affairs. This version resulted in a defense of democratic socialism that opposed Stalinism, fascism, and a corporate-dominated U.S. capitalism; it also supported anti-colonial struggles—India, for example— in the third world. Niebuhr's texts in this period—from his classic work, *Moral Man and Immoral Society* (1932) to *Beyond Tragedy* (1937)—articulate this powerful and insightful Christian realist perspective.

The battle for Britain was the turning point for Niebuhr. This battle forced him to reformulate his Christian realist position in terms of the flawed yet defensible liberal heritage of the West (represented by Britain) against the ferocious aggression of a barbaric Nazism. This shift marked the explicit articulation of a Europeanist element in his Christian realism—a Europeanist element that pitted Western civilization against totalitarianism. The defense of Britain symbolized the defense of the West. The fact that his wife was a British citizen with relatives in England indeed deepened this stance—yet it was fueled principally by his conviction that to save Britain was to save Europe, the bastion of modern civilization. His 1940 resignation from the Socialist party and his 1940 founding of *Christianity and Crisis* were both prompted and propelled by his belief that the USA must enter the war to liberate Europe from Nazi oppression. Furthermore, his founding of the Union for Democratic Action (UDA) in 1941 and his new position as a contributing editor of the *Nation* in September 1941 gave him more organizational and intellectual space to air his interventionist views.

This transitional episode is crucial for understanding the beginning of Niebuhr's more influential and "mature" version of Christian realism for three reasons. First, it situates the well-known Christian realist opposition between realism and ideology. Realism is constructed in this discourse as a militant, no-nonsense defense of Western civilization (located in selective European ways of life) that lies outside of ideology. Ideology is viewed as a remnant of utopian idealism that refuses to come to terms with the problem of evil—especially the evils threatening European civilization, such as Nazism in the 1940s, Stalinism in the 1950s, student radicalism in the 1960s, etc. Note that in Niebuhr's rudimentary version of Christian realism, "realism" was conceived as a sober critique of the evils of American civilization—a critique that purged liberal idealism of its utopian illusions yet preserved its quest for justice against oppression within capitalist societies. Niebuhr rightly viewed this "realism" as shot through with ideology. Yet it was a self-critical and self-correcting ideology owing to its recognition of limits and its commitment to substantive democracy and freedom. In his new version of Christian realism—under different historical circumstances—realism stands over against ideology owing principally to Niebuhr's Europeanist bias—or his idea that the value of European civilization is so far beyond questioning (as he has construed it) that to be isolationist and pacifist is to be a nonrealist, that is, an ideologue.

Even at this stage in the emergence of the influential form of Christian realism, one could be a realist and a socialist. The litmus test of a realist was defense of the Allies against Nazism. I am not suggesting that Niebuhr was wrong in taking this particular stance nor that certain ideals concocted in the modern West are not worth fighting and dying for. Rather I am trying to show how Niebuhr's readjustment of the meaning of "realism" and "ideology" to justify his particular stance fundamentally shaped the trajectory of Christian realist discourse in American life.

The second reason this transitional episode is noteworthy lies in the contextualizing of the opposition between moral rhetoric and prudential judgment. This central opposition in Christian realist discourse is often associated with the opposition between ideology and realism. Yet again, one can easily reject crude utopian forms of moral rhetoric in the name of a particular kind of prudential judgment and still draw different conclusions that those Christian realists often make. In this way, the self-description of "realistic" and "prudential" are rhetorical strategies that attempt to hide and conceal the degree to which Christian realist discourses are permeated with ideology and moral rhetoric—the very blinding features they accuse their opponents of having.

My point is not simply that ideology and moral rhetoric are inexpungible elements of any formulation of foreign policy. It also is that it makes little sense to accuse one's opponents of being wrong by appealing to the existence of ideology and moral rhetoric in their views. Such a gesture precludes rational exchange and becomes mere political posturing and bullying that depends ultimately on finger-pointing, name-calling, and vitriolic vituperation. In this regard, the self-conscious Christian realist makes explicit the ideological assumptions and moral convictions that guide social and historical readings of a specific situation without appeals to the vulgar oppositions of ideology vs. realism, rhetoric vs. judgment.

The last reason it is important to highlight Niebuhr's shift is that it contains the seeds of Europeanist sentiments that soon sprout in diverse and ultimately objectionable ways. By the mid-1940s, America replaces Britain as the major protectorate of European civilization. Niebuhr indeed continued to look inward with a critical eye—more so than many of his fellow Christian realists. Yet his critique became far less substantive and structural. Furthermore, when he looks outward to non-European areas of the world, he sees principally a battle between European civilization, that is, American or European influence, and barbarism, that is, totalitarian influence. This Manichean perspective couched in the rhetoric of complexity, ambiguity, and irony denies the relative autonomy—and ultimately the humanity—of third world peoples, cultures, and countries.

With the end of the Second World War and the emergence of the USA as the world power, Niebuhr's verison of Christian realism—along with George Kennan's more aestheticizing (with its stress on diplomatic style) and anti-urban version—became the basis of Cold War liberal U.S. foreign policy. The transformation of the Union of Democratic Action (UDA) into the Americans for Democratic Action (ADA) in 1947, the elevation of Niebuhr to the status of "the official establishment theologian" on the cover of *Time* magazine's twenty-fifth anniversary issue (March 8, 1948), and his membership in the Council on Foreign Relations—all intimately linked with Niebuhr's exemplary fusion of fervent anticommunism with New Deal liberalism—signified Niebuhr's Christian realism as the dominant form of Europeanist ideology that promoted and legitimated U.S. hegemony in the world.

An Immanent Critique of Christian Realism

The extent to which Christian realism in its influential form served as a set of rhetorical strategies to promote and encourage U.S. hegemony in the world is best seen in a close scrutiny of the basic "realist" notions of balance of power, national interest, the primacy of strategy and tactics, and the wise statesman as vigilant civil servant. These central motifs can have a variety of meanings and can be used in many different ways. I shall argue that the particular interpretations of these notions put forward by Christian realists like Niebuhr and Kennan are guided by Europeanist biases and Amerocentric aims. I will try to show that Christian realist formulations fall short of the very criteria they claim to satisfy.

The most fundamental idea in Christian realist reflections about international affairs is balance of power. This idea is deployed in an attempt to understand the dynamics of interaction between discrete nation-states involved in military, economic, ideological, and geopolitical competition. The phrase had two essential meanings for Christian realists. Its negative meaning was the prevention of a hostile hegemonic presence on the Eurasian terrain; its positive meaning was the preservation of U.S. world power and its expansion if circumstances permitted.

The notion of balance of power—a phrase that evokes the nineteenth-century diplomatic discourses of equilibrium— presupposes power centers around the world in need of balancing. Furthermore, it assumes that there is some way of ascertaining the weight of these power centers such that some comparable judgments can be make regarding a desirable equilibrium. Lastly, and, most importantly, the idea of balance of power takes for granted that all power centers had the same motivations and goals and, thus, could be viewed as playing the same games.

The fact that the notion of balance of power became central to a discourse put forward by elites struggling to come up with a conception of the scope of U.S. responsibility in the postwar world means that it concretely assumes some form of U.S. dominance. Christian realists indeed were not mere ideological zealots trying to remake each and every corner of the world in their own image—for they were much concerned with the limits of U.S. power. Yet they could easily justify quick and often brutal U.S. military intervention in order to insure the appropriate balance of power. In this way, the notion connotes less a relatively decentralized set of power centers of equal weight and more a hierarchical ranking of nation-states in which the "natural" dominance of some over others was justified. The post–World War II circumstances set the context for dominating powers, and Europeanist cultural biases dictated the political potential of most of the dominated peoples.

The concomitant idea of national interest in the Christian realist discourse of balance of power was highly problematic. This discourse not only assumed that the "nation" was itself a self-evident notion, but also that something called "the national interest" could be objectively discerned. Given the historical consciousness promoted by Christian realists, it is not surprising that attempts to find foundations for the idea of "national interest" outside, beneath, or among the plurality and relativity of concrete aims of people proved difficult. Yet to concede this quest for foundations would be to admit that national interest was an ideological construct—a mere value-laden descriptive term whose content rests upon what a particular national leadership defined and determined it to be in its operations of rhetoric and power. Both Niebuhr and Kennan opted for an ingenious alternative: the national interest could be ascertained by examining the very structure of the government propagating it. Such a definition distinguished U.S. foreign policy from Soviet foreign policy owing to the vastly different governments, yet it remained empirically open-ended enough and theoretically vacuous enough to conclude that actual national leadership was the linchpin for foreign policy.

In fact, much of the Christian realist veneration of wisdom and prudence, strategic and tactical thinking, and the statesman-like civil servant was a critique of certain kinds of national leadership—namely, those of the liberal idealist and conservative crusader. Its latent antifoundationalism regarding "national interests" forced Christian realists to conceive of and push for a new type of national leadership—that is, an elite corp of civil servants with historical sensibilities, concrete orientations, sober expectations, and Europeanist/Amerocentric biases. For example, Kennan's preoccupation with establishing a foreign service school similar to West Point—but a place for broad humanistic study and back-breaking labor in agriculture—was his attempt to infuse wisdom into U.S. foreign policy by means of the *Paideia* of elite civil servants. Needless to say, Niebuhr embodied such a figure, though linked to public service through private efforts, to the Christian realists.

In this way, the notions of balance of power and national interest and the stress on strategic and tactical thinking by historically informed statesman-like diplomats constitute the pillars of an emergent ideology among liberal political and intellectual elites in post–World War II America.

Niebuhr and the Third World

It is no accident that the major critics of Christian realism—from William Appleton Williams to Latin American liberation theologians—often focus their critiques on the impact of U.S. foreign policy on third world peoples. I have tried to show that Christian realist discourse emerged, in part, as an effort to come to terms with Europe-U.S. relations. Even its strong anticommunist sentiments were initially directed toward the situation in Europe. Christian realists tended to assume U.S. economic domination of Latin America, European colonial control of Africa, and cultural stagnation in Asia. I also have attempted to disclose the ways in which the central notions of Christian realism were regulated, in part, by Europeanist bias and Amerocentric prejudice. In this last section, I shall examine a particular instance in which these biases and prejudices are at work: the case of Niebuhr on the Middle East, and particularly his reflections on the founding of the state of Israel.

Niebuhr's defense of the establishment of the state of Israel was passionate and candid. His passion was motivated by a profound and admirable sense of moral outrage at the Holocaust. His candor flowed from his struggle to reconcile his democratic sentiments with Europeanist bias and political realism. Yet this attempt at reconciliation ends in truncating his commitment to nonracial democracy and thereby degrading his political realism to ethnocentric expediency.

For example, in his major reflections on the state of Israel Niebuhr displays exemplary features of Christian realist discourse on the third world: relative ignorance and racist sentiment. In his support of a 1947 (November 21) letter in defense of the idea of partitioning Palestine, he rightly criticized the suppression of the Christian majority by the Arab League in Lebanon yet defended the subordination of the Palestinian majority by the Jewish population in Palestine. In an influential article in 1946, Niebuhr argued that Palestinian Arab opinion was of little weight owing to the failure of a middle class and a "technical and dynamic civilization." This failure justified a Jewish imposition upon such backward peoples in order to further modernization. Similarly, in a renowned 1942 piece in *The Nation,* Niebuhr claimed—uncharacteristic of a liberal—that Jews as a people (not individuals) had rights which entitled them to the land of Palestinian Arabs. Unlike many crude Zionists, Niebuhr did believe that the issue of the interests of Palestinian Arabs warranted attention. Yet in typical Europeanist fashion, he held that these interests were best served by Westernized Jewish rule over Palestinian Arabs. He candidly characterized his position as "imperialistic realism"—a good label for Europeanist paternalist policy toward third world peoples. In fairness to Niebuhr, it should be pointed out that his attitude toward non-European Jews—the growing majority in present-day Israel—seemed to be one of suspicion and distrust.

In short, Niebuhr's conception of a crucial third world region like the Middle East tended to overlook the claims of self-determination of peoples of color and colonized peoples. His views on Asia—a region that lacks "historical dynamism"—and Latin America bear out this fear of third world self-assertion. The third world was conceived not as diverse places in which peoples attempt to resist and overcome centuries of feudal oppression and years of Western colonialism in a way more radical than that of Western patterns of development, but rather a region for the struggle of U.S. containment of Soviet aggression and influence. It is no accident that the first major critique of Christian realism came from Latin American liberation theologians who stressed this "dark" side of Niebuhr's Europeanist bias.

Since I believe that the religious insights of Christian realism—its sense of the tragic, rejection of perfectionism, and sober historicist orientation—are valuable and indispensable, I locate the blindness of Niebuhr and other Christian realists in two matters: Europeanist bias and skewed social analysis. This Europeanist bias is acceptable to the degree to which it promotes a *genuine* commitment to modern forms of democracy and critical consciousness; it is objectionable in that it limits such commitments when reflecting on the third world. The skewed social analysis is a more serious and contentious matter owing to my fundamental differences in the assessments of the positive and negative consequences of U.S. hegemony in the world. My aim here is not to defend a particular kind of social analysis over against that of Niebuhr; rather it is to call attention to the way in which Europeanist bias reflects Niebuhr's views toward the third world.

In conclusion, Niebuhr's exemplary Christian realism emerged, in part, as a liberal response to the new realignment of international powers after the Second World War. Christian realism was forward looking in that it provided a sober and tempered reading of the scope of possibilities and weight of responsibilities of the USA in relation to new European realities. Christian realism was backward looking in its notions of discrete national entities constituting preferable power centers in a balanced manner. The relative eclipse of Christian realism in the late sixties and early seventies resulted partly from the new utopian energies from oppressed peoples around the world and the decline of U.S. hegemony in the world. The current resurgence of Christian realism is a desperate effort of a largely discredited liberalism to highlight the limits of U.S. power or a robust endeavor of an aggressive neoconservatism to promote U.S. hegemony in the world. As a Christian leftist who harkens back to the religious viewpoints and political judgments of Niebuhr's rudimentary version of Christian realism, the contemporary struggle over the legacy of Niebuhr is noteworthy. Yet, more importantly, the insights of Niebuhr's work can be empowering to present-day thinkers when his blindnesses are acknowledged and assessed in regard to U.S. foreign policy in the third world. This acknowledgment and assessment is a matter of life and death for many of the wretched of this earth.

PART TWO
Religion and Culture

Sex and Suicide

The body may be a poor vessel for transcendence, yet it now is the last such vessel for many. This is especially so for teenagers in our culture—though it also holds for large numbers of adults. How does one account for the privileged role of sexual activity in our society? What is its significance for Christians?

This past week I lectured at a high school in Brooklyn and received a rude awakening: I discovered that suicide, not sex, was the major issue on the minds of a majority of the students I encountered. The reasons had little to do with an impending nuclear holocaust or the brutalities in South Africa, Poland, and Chile. Rather, the motivations for suicide the students saw as cogent were more traditional ones: the sheer meaninglessness of human existence, the limited options (especially personal) in the future, and the inability to feel "alive." For these students, the materialistic rat race of getting and spending, consuming and posturing, yields banal and empty lives.

As I drove home to New Haven, I pondered this situation—in fear and trembling. I asked myself whether our cultural and religious resources were no longer adequate to sustain the younger generation; whether we Christian adults were merely enacting a holding operation which simply conceals (mainly from ourselves) the explosive nihilism harbored by our young people; and last, whether commercialized sexuality—the stimulation of sexual appetites for pecuniary and personal aims—was but a strategy of power elites in the mass media aimed at keeping a lid on such potential nihilistic explosions.

Back home, I discovered what may be a clue to these questions as I listened to Prince's albums *Purple Rain* and *Around the World in a Day*. These recordings by one of the leading contemporary pop artists articulate the deep conflicts and contradictions experienced by young people today. Their major theme is sexual liberation, but within the framework of a narrow version of apocalyptic Christianity. Although the Christian quest for transcendent meaning in life and history is rejected in Prince's lyrics, the idea of divine intervention in the form of eschatological catastrophic presence is preserved. In the interim, life is a party, a sustained effort to stay alive by feeling "alive," keeping the adrenalin flowing for the purpose of frequent climax. This viewpoint, reflected and

From *Christianity and Crisis* (June 10, 1985).

155

condensed by Prince in his music and his performance style, promotes and encourages an orgiastic way of life in which sex is an opiate of the people. The major alternatives are drugs and suicide—both strongly rejected by Prince.

This response to the spiritual sterility and wasted energies of modern life was neither initiated by young people nor created by Prince. We can find it in James Joyce's literary obsessions with bodily stimulation or Charlie Parker's musical expressions of orgasmic peaks. Unlike Joyce and Parker, Prince and his generation no longer view transcendence as embodied in a religion of art which focuses on sexual activity. Rather, transcendence itself is incarnate in the lived experience of sexual stimulation. There is no longer any critical distance between reality and reflection, experience and expression. It is no accident that much of young people's music involves enactments of sexual activity. Nor is there any longer a distinction between the act and its meaning, intercourse and its significance. Instead, we are impelled into a pulsating world of surfaces, seeking to secure some vitality and vigor for our desperate selves.

These postmodern sensibilities of narcissistic play and hedonistic indulgence present enormous challenges to all sectors of the Christian church. For priestly Christians, they preclude institutional integrity and continuity; for prophetic Christians, they prevent moral commitment and political struggle; and for avant-garde Christians, they relegate their actions to the mainstream. To put it bluntly, the moral decay and deterioration of personal relations in our culture are radically prohibiting the mission of the church.

There seems to be no serious response to these challenges forthcoming from church or society, only glib conservative calls to return to the "golden age" of sexual chastity and repression. In the meantime, our youth continue to float on clouds of anxiety and meaninglessness; our priests still remain encapsulated within institutions whose death knell sounds daily; our prophets invoke values and judgments that fail to inspire and ignite; and our rulers try to downplay our decadence with patriotic rhetorics of self-congratulation and self-celebration. Needless to say, refined forms of pessimism and paralyzing cynicism are but symptoms of the situation rather than enabling responses to it. And since we all are so deeply shaped by the decay, it would be dishonest to overlook its effects upon us. But the crucial question still haunts us: Can the abundant life provided and promised by Jesus Christ break through the predominant sexual forms of negative transcendence in our contemporary culture? If so, how? Through our youth, a dark, anarchic future presses for an answer.

Violence in America

The most striking feature of contemporary American society is its sheer violence and brutality. Civic terrorism pervades the streets of our cities. Sexual violation and abuse are commonplace in our personal relationships. And many of our urban schools have become policed combat zones. By the year 2000, much of America may become uninhabitable—that is, it may be impossible to live here without daily fear for one's life.

Such perceived decay in the moral and social fabric of our communities sits at the center of the rage and despair displayed in the recent controversy over the case of Bernhard Goetz in New York City. Yet it is important to remember the context. America has always been a relatively violent country. Race riots are frequent occurrences in our history. Lynching is a unique American institution, literally invented here. We have the bloodiest history of capital-labor relations in the modern industrial world. Vigilante activity has often gained legitimacy among significant segments of the populace. And, of course, the making of America consisted, in part, of imperial military conquest of indigenous and Mexican peoples.

We are the only modern peoples who regard a gun culture as a precondition of liberty. The classic Whig notion that an armed populace is necessary for self-government still has deep roots in the American psyche. Since there is no insurrectionary tradition of any substance (a tradition of armed attacks on the seats of power), the violence of the gun culture is directed at fellow citizens. And as the victims begin to include more and more white middle-class persons (as well as more and more peoples of color), rage and despair escalate.

Progressive and prophetic people rarely address the pressing issues in the everyday lives of ordinary people—to our own detriment. And our relative silence on the increasing fear generated by pervasive violence can only produce more negative results. We must acknowledge that people have a right to feel outraged by the rampant violence in our society—just as we have a right to oppose the U.S.-supported violence in Central America and South Africa.

The crucial issues are, first, how such outrage can be channeled against the right targets: the established authorities who tolerate the desperate circumstances that facilitate violent acts; and, second, how we instill

From *Christianity and Crisis* (Apr. 1, 1985).

values, discipline, and order in the lives of those who perpetrate such violent acts. The first issue is principally a pedagogical and political challenge. Our voices must be sympathetic to victims of violence while providing convincing accounts of how certain economic and political policies promote and encourage the hopelessness upon which much of present-day violence feeds.

The second issue is a moral challenge. We must acknowledge and attack the cold cruel amorality that permeates American society, including the communities of poor people. This can be done best by attempting to resurrect and reconstruct moralities that give people reasons to strive for dignity and excellence. Such moralities are requisite for any form of political struggle. Without them, we have merely analyses of problems and no potential agents for change. Needless to say, such a situation can lead only to our own coffins, be it caused by young hoodlums with misdirected energies or the ruling barbarians with destructive policies.

Not-Always-Perfidious Albion

I have never understood why I am an Anglophile. I abhor the haughtiness of the British ruling class. I dislike the deferential dispositions of the middle class. And I find the cockneyish language of the working class too alien to appreciate. Yet something about the British attracts me. During my recent nine-day stay in England, I discovered the source of this attraction: the British take engaged argument seriously. The implications of this seemingly minor trait for British culture, including the British church, are large.

This premium on argument encourages a thriving public sphere; that is, an open arena in which journalists, publicists, politicians, and even professors put forward rational defenses of various positions that focus on the common good of the country. This public sphere not only provides the occasion for a wide variety of voices to be heard: it also permits the nation to interrogate itself in a wholesale manner. Liberals, conservatives, socialists, Irish nationalists, and black progressives hear one another's substantive arguments and reply in kind, not simply with slogans and shibboleths.

A vital public sphere tempts intellectuals to intervene and devalues bureaucratic modes of problem solving. It is no accident that ivory-tower Oxford linguistic philosophers run for Parliament (A. J. Ayer) and head anti-apartheid commissions (Michael Dummett). Or that the House of Commons, with its late medieval trappings and chivalric protocol, is the last legislative body in the modern West where actual dialogue and discussion—not mere speech making and filibustering—take place.

The best examples of the British public sphere are neither its first-rate journalism nor its superb BBC. Rather, they are the institutions of local authority and of the left intelligentsia. The Greater London Council (GLC) best exemplifies the former; and the incredible production of the most sophisticated intellectual work in contemporary historiography, social theory, and black critical thought epitomizes the latter.

The GLC is the most impressive popular institution in Britain. Led by the dynamic Ken Livingstone—whose socialist, feminist, antiracist, and antihomophobic credentials are impeccable—this body has played a political and pedagogical role unprecedented in any other modern West-

From *Christianity and Crisis* (Feb. 4, 1985).

ern urban center. For example, the GLC declared 1984 "Antiracist Year." Supported with millions of pounds from public funds and administered by an ethnic minorities unit under the guidance of the able Paul Boateng, this GLC program is transforming London's housing, schools, and jobs in light of antiracist mandates. These mandates not only include enhancing the plight of Afro-Caribbeans, Africans, Asians, and the Irish but also promoting public awareness of apartheid in South Africa and of racist violence in the U.S. Prophetic white and black Christian ministers—such as the Rev. Hewlette Andrews and the Rev. David Haslam of the Methodist church—play important roles in this antiracist campaign. Though linked to the crippled Labor party, the GLC has an autonomous constituency. Its greatest support is found in those groups alienated from the political process, namely blacks, feminists, gays, lesbians, and independent Marxists. The response of the Thatcher government is to attempt to abolish the GLC (and elected local government in general), an event that will more than likely occur next year.

The work of a cluster of left thinkers—among them E. P. Thompson, Christopher Hill, and Sheila Rowbotham in history, Raymond Williams and Terry Eagleton in cultural criticism, and Anthony Giddens and Bob Jessop in social theory—puts Britain at the center of progressive intellectual work. In addition, the pioneering writings of Stuart Hall, Darcus Howe, and A. Sivanandan—along with solid journals such as *Race Today* and *Race and Class*—serve as a contemporary standard for black critical thought. In short, the performance of the British left intellectuals far outshines the work of their American counterparts.

Only in regard to prophetic Christian thought do the British fall short. This is so, in part, because of the peculiar and delimited role of religion in British life. Yet federations such as the Christian Organization for Social, Political, and Economic Change (composed of twenty-six groups) have a disproportionate effect on British society. And the development of an independent black church tradition with a progressive political dimension among the recent Afro-Caribbean immigrants—led by Pentecostal pastors like the Rev. Io Smith—will contribute even more to this Christian influence. If there is a choice between liberation theology in the academy or prophetic Christian praxis from the pew, let us hope that in Britain the latter prevails.

Subversive Joy and Revolutionary Patience in Black Christianity

Profound preoccupation with the Christian gospel is a distinctive feature of Afro-American culture. This near obsession with the "good news" proclaimed by Jesus of Nazareth is rooted in the unique Afro-American encounter with the modern world. And like every understanding of the gospel, the black Christian perspective is shaped by a particular history and culture.

The trauma of the slave voyage from Africa to the New World and the Euro-American attempt systematically to strip Africans of their languages, cultures, and religions produced a black experience of the absurd. This state of "natal alienation"—in which Africans had no right to their past or progeny—prevented widespread transmittance of tradition to American-born Africans. Such alienation was more pervasive in the USA than in other parts of the New World principally because of a low ratio of blacks to whites which facilitated more frequent and intense black-white interaction. Only 4.5 percent of all Africans imported to the New World came to North America, though an incredibly high rate of slave reproduction (or induced breeding) soon quadrupled this percentage figure. Therefore second- and third-generation Africans in the USA made sense of and gave meaning to their predicament without an immediate relation to African worldviews and customs.

With the slow but sure "death of the African gods," many blacks creatively appropriated the Christian gospel peddled by religious dissenters in American life, that is, by Methodists and Baptists. The evangelical outlook of these denominations stressed the conversion experience, equality of all people before God, and institutional autonomy. The conversion experience often resembled African novitiate rites in which intense emotional investment and ecstatic bodily behavior signified vital faith. This experience equalized the status of all before God, thereby giving the slaves a special self-identity and self-esteem in stark contrast with the inferior roles imposed upon them in American society. Institutional autonomy insured black control over the central organization in the Afro-American community—a crucial characteristic which sets

From *Le Monde Diplomatique* (Oct. 1984).

blacks in the USA apart from other New World Africans in Catholic Latin America and Anglican Caribbean.

The black interpretation of the Christian gospel accented the tragedy in the struggle for freedom and the freedom in a tragic predicament. The African slaves' search for collective identity could find historical purpose in the exodus of Israel out of slavery and personal meaning in the bold identification of Jesus Christ with the lowly. Furthermore, the slaves empathized with the senseless persecution of Job and the deep despair of Ecclesiastes. Afro-American Christianity is Christocentric to the core: yet Jesus Christ is not simply understood as an agent of deliverance, but also a human exemplar of pain and agony. The crucified Christ looms as large as the risen Christ.

The conception of freedom prevalent in Afro-American Christianity possesses three dimensions: the existential, the social, and the eschatological. Existential freedom is a mode of being-in-the-world which resists dread and despair. It embodies an ecstatic celebration of human existence without affirming prevailing reality. Like many pagan religions, this celebration consists of a rejoicing in the mere fact of being alive; yet like Christianity, it contains a critical disposition toward the way the world is.

Existential freedom in black Christianity flows from the kinetic orality and affective physicality inherited from West African cultures and religions. This full-fledged acceptance of the body deems human existence a source of joy and gaiety. Physical participation and bodily involvement in religious rituals epitomizes this kind of freedom. In short, black Christianity has a strong Dionysian element.

The tension and anxiety produced by the harsh conditions of oppression accentuates this Dionysian aspect. Rhythmic singing, swaying, dancing, preaching, talking, and walking—all features of black life—are weapons of struggle and survival. They not only release pressures and desperation, they also constitute bonds of solidarity and sources for individuality. For example, the famous loud "cry" of black religious and secular singers or the guttural "shout" of preachers are simultaneously groans of hurt, acts of communal catharsis, and stylizations of unique vocal techniques. The heartfelt groans acknowledge the deplorable plight of a downtrodden people. The cathartic acts provide emotional and physical relief from the daily scars of humiliation and degradation. The individual stylistic vocals assert the sense of "somebodiness" in a situation which denies one's humanity.

The first artistic gift of Afro-Americans to the world—the spirituals—exemplify existential freedom in action. At the level of form, these "sorrow songs" contain subtle rhythmic elements alongside brooding melodies. They invoke deep passions not of self-pity or self-hatred but of lament and hope. The spirituals give artistic form to the frustrations and aspirations of a battered people constantly under siege with few human allies. The lyrical focus is often the liberating power of God, but the stylistic forms stress the self-invested moan, the risky falsetto, and the nuanced syncopation. Often confused with mere circumlocution and repetition, the lyrics and styles of the spirituals directly confront existential dread and despair with the armor of vocal virtuosity, rhythmic facility, and faith in God. Subsequent developments such as the blues, jazz, and gospel music may reject or revise the Christian commitment, vocalize instruments, and add more complex rhythms, but the cultural crucible of such developments rests in the distinct musical articulation of Afro-American Christianity.

Religion, rhythm, and rhetoric have been the three spheres in which Afro-American existential freedom have taken root. Oppression excluded other areas. Black preaching of the gospel is rhythmic, cathartic, and full of moans and groans. Black rhythm is rooted in religiosity, liminality, and full of call and response. And the gospel is understood in terms of existential self-involvement, moral flexibility, and political improvisation.

The social dimension of the freedom predominant in black Christianity does not primarily concern political struggle but rather cultural solidarity. The politics of the black church is highly ambiguous, with a track record of widespread opportunism. Yet the cultural practices of the black church embody a basic reality: sustained black solidarity in the midst of a hostile society. Black Christianity is not merely a reaction to white exclusion; rather it is a distinct culture which revels in its own uniqueness. This uniqueness—displayed in black existential freedom—is the mark of black identity and a guide for future black church development. Black people do not attend churches, for the most part, to find God, but rather to share and expand together the rich heritage they have inherited. This heritage, sustained by close familial relationships and friendships, evolves around a personal dependence on God which facilitates a communal fellowship. The common black argument for belief in God is not that it is logical or reasonable to do so, but rather that such belief is requisite for one's sanity and for entrée to the most uplifting sociality available in the black community.

The eschatological aspect of freedom in black Christianity is the most difficult to grasp. It is neither a glib hope for a pie-in-the-sky heaven nor an apocalyptic aspiration which awaits world destruction. Rather, it is a hope-laden articulation of the tragic quality of everyday life of a culturally degraded, politically oppressed, and racially coerced labor force. Black Christian eschatology is anchored in the tragic realism of the Old Testament wisdom literature and the proclamation of a coming kingdom by Jesus Christ. Anthropologists have observed that there is a relative absence of tragic themes in the ancient oral narratives of West Africa. Is it no accident that the black understanding of the gospel stresses this novel motif, the utterly tragic character of life and history?

Yet the black Christian conception differs from more traditional tragic perspectives. It promotes a tragic sense of life which affirms the workings of evil forces beyond human control while promoting struggle against particular forms of evil in the world. In sharp contrast to notions of tragedy that yield conservative politics, the black Christian tragic sense of life focuses on resistance and opposition in the here and now against overwhelming odds. The regulative ideal for such resistance is a kingdom beyond history, but this kingdom is ultimately brought about by divine intervention. So this tragic sense of life, with deferred triumph, vastly differs from either Greek conceptions of tragedy or modern notions of the tragic vision.

Tragedy is, of course, a literary form inherited from the Greeks. It usually entails an initial act of shame or horror which violates the moral order. This act results in conscious and intense suffering that yields some transcendent knowledge of what it is to be human. This knowledge—often an affirmation of the ultimate worthwhileness of life and a perception of the objective character of the moral order—is the only saving grace for the hero who is crushed by the intractable limits of his or her situation. The basic assumptions are that there is a moral order, that suffering is meaningful, and that heroic effort is noble. For black Christianity, this perspective is unacceptable because its mode of closure elevates Fate and its positive form of knowledge remains contemplative.

The modern tragic vision is a truncated version of Greek tragedy. The purpose of suffering is rendered problematic and the knowledge which results from suffering is suspect. The very notion of a moral order is called into question and displaced by a preoccupation with the consciousness occupying the suffering, the details of the context in which the suffering occurs, and the ways in which suffering is evaded or tolerated. This viewpoint has little persuasive power for black Christianity in that its rejection of any end or aim of human existence discourages purposeful struggle, especially communal and collective struggle. Such a viewpoint tends to presuppose luxury in that it may stimulate the ironic consciousness of a declining petit bourgeoisie, but it spells suicide for the downtrodden. Like Greek tragedy, it may generate profound insights, but it is disenabling for degraded and oppressed peoples.

The tragic sense of life in black Christian eschatology views suffering as a stepping-stone to liberation. Yet liberation does not eradicate the suffering in itself. Therefore suffering is understood only as a reality to resist, an actuality to oppose. It can neither be submitted to in order to gain contemplative knowledge nor reified into an object of ironic attention. Rather, it is a concrete state of affairs which produces discernible hurt and pain, hence requiring action of some sort. Black Christian eschatology focuses on praxis against suffering, not reflection upon it; personal and collective resistance to suffering, not a distancing from it. And ultimately, with the aid of divine intervention, suffering is overcome.

The radically comic character of Afro-American life—the pervasive sense of play, laughter, and ingenious humor of blacks—flows primarily from the profound Afro-American Christian preoccupation with the tragedy in the struggle for freedom and the freedom in a tragic predicament. This comic release is the black groan made gay. Yet this release is neither escapist nor quietistic. Rather, it is *engaged gaiety, subversive joy,* and *revolutionary patience* which works for and looks to the kingdom to come. It is utopian in that it breeds a defiant dissatisfaction with the present and encourages action. It is tragic in that it tempers exorbitant expectations. This perspective precludes political disillusionment and its product, misanthropic nihilism.

The gospel in Afro-America lauds Calvinistic calls to transform the world yet shuns puritanical repression. It promotes the Pascalian wager yet transcends Jansenist self-obsession. Life is viewed as both a carnival to enjoy and a battlefield on which to fight. Afro-American Christianity promotes a gospel which empowers black people to survive and struggle in a God-forsaken world.

On Louis Dupré's
Marx's Social Critique of Culture

Despite the proliferation of fine works on Marx, Dupré's learned text deserves attention. This is so because it provides a superb critical exposition of the complex development of Marx's social vision and theory as well as a provocative organicist critique of cultural disintegration in the modern West. In his close readings of Marx's works—from the doctoral dissertation to the third volume of *Capital*—Dupré displays an intellectual patience, historical sensitivity, and philosophical acumen rarely found in scholarly treatments of Marx. By refusing to succumb to either uncritical presentation or tendentious dismissal, he provides one of the most reliable, succinct, and engaging interpretations we have of Marx's own writings.

Yet Dupré's ambitions go far beyond mere critical exposition of Marx. He also intends to treat Marx as the first major social critic of modern European cultural disintegration. For Dupré, Marx's notions of social coherence, organic wholeness, and mutual determination—though often misunderstood by his followers—provided the sources for a profound understanding and critique of modern society and culture. Marx stands above other nineteenth-century critics and theorists in that he shuns "the subjectivism of the modern epoch and reintroduces an ideal of integral harmony" (p. 278).

This ideal is neither a naive return to nature nor an idealist flight into a fanciful future. Rather, it is a recognition of the social relatedness at the center of consciousness, an acknowledgment of the dialectical interaction between human beings and nature, and the projection of individuality in light of technological possibilities and, most important, of democracy and freedom. Marx's attempt to recover the sense of social holism of the Greek polis under modern conditions gains Dupré's tempered, though genuine, praise.

Dupré's own critique of Marx is put forward in the name of a more wholesale organism. Marx's subtle quest for a new social totality puts him above his peers, yet he remains "partly within the ideological horizons of the modern age" (p. 13) in respect to one fundamental assumption: the priority of economic production. Following the pioneering

From *The Journal of Religion* (Jan. 1986); review of Louis Dupré, *Marx's Social Critique of Culture* (New Haven: Yale University Press, 1983).

work of R. H. Tawney, Hannah Arendt, and Jürgen Habermas, Dupré accuses Marx of ultimately subscribing to two modern tendencies: the instrumentalization of the world and the economization of the political realm. This does not mean, as Dupré rightly points out, that Marx promoted a crude economic determinism or a vulgar social productivism. Rather, it means that Marx's vision of "a dialectical, all-integrating view of man's social existence" (p. 278) conflicts with his stress on the primacy of economic activity. And as Jean Baudrillard, Marshall Sahlins, and Anthony Giddens have pointed out, this stress not only valorizes productivity, it also "naturalizes" earlier societies by reading back into them the mode of production as the essential form that distinguishes them. This Marxist version of essentialism flies in the face of the Marxist principle of historical specificity, which highlights "the radical historicity of all social structures" (p. 103).

A plausible objection to Dupré's treatment of Marx is that it accents the richness of Marx's social vision at the expense of Marx's social theory. We are left with a Marx who provides a profound perspective regarding the need for social reintegration alongside poverty-ridden social explanations regarding the role of power, wealth, and status in modern capitalist societies. And, to put it bluntly, Dupré's reiteration of the various critiques of Marx's explanatory concepts, such as the dialectic, surplus value, and ideology, leaves Marxist social theory in shambles. Marx's insights remain powerful, but the theoretical framework is found wanting.

Are we to think of Marx in company with Thomas Carlyle, John Ruskin, and William Morris rather than with Max Weber, Émile Durkheim, and Georg Simmel? Is Marx more a visionary and cultural critic than a theorist and social scientist? Dupré's picture of Marx implicitly answers these queries in the affirmative. I believe that Marx belongs in both camps: that of cultural critics as well as social scientists. Therefore, Marx's social critique of culture is, as Dupré's interpretation implies, a greater achievement than most others and an intellectual blinder for those caught within it. Unfortunately, Dupré does not end his excellent book pointing to those organicist thinkers who have worked through the Marxist critique yet are not blinded by it—as enacted in the cultural Marxist writings of the distinguished British critic Raymond Williams. Nonetheless, this book is a good read.

Postmodernity and Afro-America

A distinctive feature of postmodern artistic practices is that they are American in origin. The historical conjuncture of the rise of the USA as the world power in the mid-forties with the American reception of high modernist art produced a paradoxical phenomenon: the incorporation of iconoclastic modernist art within Establishment institutions. This peculiar situation prevented a whole generation of Americans from acknowledging and accentuating the subversive and transgressive dimensions of modernist masters such as Joyce, Kafka, and Brecht in literature or Mies, Gropius, and Le Corbusier in architecture. Only in America was modernism diluted and domesticated into an artistic armpiece of the "vital center," that is, postwar liberalism and, as Andreas Huyssen has noted, "a propaganda weapon in the cultural-political arsenal of cold war anti-communism."

With the expansion on an unprecedented scale of a middle class accompanied by its mass consumer culture in the fifties, and the transformation of modernist art into an aspect of affirmative high art in opposition to mass culture, the historical stage was set for the emergence of postmodernism. Although first articulated in architectural practices, postmodernism was the unique American version of avant-gardist revolt against Establishment high art (i.e., modernism) in the name of subversion, transgression, rupture, discontinuity, and, above all, freedom from political, social, and cultural hierarchical traditions. Like the historical European avant-garde, especially Dada and surrealism, this American postmodern revolt highlighted the redemptive function of art, called for the integration of art into everyday life, and attacked the institutional forms that preserved the autonomy of art. As Peter Berger has shown, the avant-garde regarded ideologies of autonomy as modes of legitimizing the cultural hegemony of Establishment high art. The enmeshing of art into everyday life called into question this hegemony and revived the emancipatory potential of art. American postmodern practices—such as Jencks and Johnson in architecture and Barth, Pynchon, and Reed in literature—reenacted this avant-gardist gesture; more importantly, it did so within an American context in which black art—that is, jazz, blues, rhythm-and-blues—deeply influenced its mass consumer culture and in

---

From *Art Papers* (Jan.-Feb. 1986).

which black people were exemplary embodiments of otherness, difference, and transgression.

In the contemporary debate on postmodernism, the historical role and function of black artistic practices and the rhetorical figure of "Afro-America" has been, for the most part, overlooked. Yet, on the historical plane, anti-Establishment activity was initiated in the McCarthyite fifties by the black freedom movement (which set in motion similar activity by women, Hispanics, gays, and lesbians); and, on the cultural front, black artists in the forties and fifties, especially black musicians, contested the tradition of high art under the banner of artistic eclecticism, play, and performance—the central motifs of postmodernism. While the black political struggle fought for integration into American society, black cultural producers created art within the context of Afro-American everyday life.

My claim is neither that Afro-American artists were the "first postmodernists" nor that Afro-American art prefigures American postmodernism. Rather, I am suggesting that a thorough investigation into the content and character of postmodernism which takes seriously the role and function of black political and cultural practices will shed new light on the contemporary debate, revealing its blindnesses and silences. For example, the conservative position of Hilton Kramer that trashes postmodernism and upholds the seriousness of high modernism becomes a nostalgic attempt to recover American hegemony in the world (much like that of the mid-forties) and resituates high art as a legitimizing agent in this hegemony. The liberal view of the late Lionel Trilling that confuses the postmodern revolt with "modernism in the streets" bespeaks a fear of anarchic energies (already let loose in modernist texts!) in response to the collapse of liberal consensus and retreats into the private sphere of domestic tranquility, for example, his praise of Jane Austen's novels in the seventies.

The social democratic perspective of Jürgen Habermas that exalts Enlightenment reason in the face of the "irrationality" of postmodernism discloses a deep German horror of political unreason, for example, charismatic and chiliastic movements which bring back memories of Nazism. Last, the Marxist view of Fred Jameson that sees postmodernism as primarily the flat, lifeless surfaces of the commodified and commercialized culture of late capitalism relies upon a utopian past when art and politics worked together for emancipatory ends. Each of these positions tends to focus attention away from the artistic and political practices of marginal peoples, especially Afro-Americans.

This is seen most clearly in the professional renegades from the literary critical Establishment who borrow from French poststructuralist discourses about otherness, difference, and transgression to articulate their anti-authority sensibilities inherited from the sixties. This borrowing indeed has emancipated them from the theoretical parochialism of New Criticism and the mythic structuralism of Northrop Frye, yet it still restricts them to highbrow French academic language and blinds them to the realities of black (and female, Hispanic, gay, and lesbian) otherness, difference, and transgression occurring beneath their very noses in America.

I do believe that Derrida, Deleuze, Barthes, Foucault, Althusser, Kristeva, and others have had a salutary effect on American intellectual and cultural life. Yet the politics of "traveling theories" must be confronted. The prevailing left discourses of the seventies in America—vulgar Marxisms, rudimentary feminisms, and crude black nationalisms—understandably impelled young oppositional intellectuals comfortably nested in the Academy to look elsewhere. Yet this search has now reached a dead end. And, as John Dewey noted long ago and Richard Rorty now echoes, ontology must give way to "our" histories, epistemology to "our" practices, transcendentalism to "our" politics. French poststructuralist discourses indeed lead to these conclusions, but only "we Americans" can make them historically specific, socially pertinent, and politically relevant for "us." Is it not ironic and a bit embarrassing that the recent American preoccupation with the French recuperation of the textually playful and politically transgressive side of high modernism should lead us back to our own racially heterogeneous postmodernism? And cannot the French learn much from our situation as racism escalates in France?

To take seriously "Afro-America" as a political reality in process and a rhetorical figure in textual motion does not mean that we shun European critical discourses, especially those of the Frankfurters (Adorno, Marcuse) and French fries (Derrida, Foucault). Rather, it requires that we delve more deeply into them with a sense of our own historical past and political present. I am simply suggesting that black political and cultural practices—especially the black freedom movement and black musical production—are appropriate points of entry that may provide illumination heretofore overlooked in the contemporay debate about postmodernity.

On Black-Jewish Relations

The state of black-Jewish relations in this country is worthy of serious scrutiny. These relations are complex and delicate, and at present they are deteriorating. Those concerned about the evil power of racism and anti-Semitism need to address this situation with candor, bringing to it their powers of rational assessment and moral judgment.

Black-Jewish relations in the United States have not always been as problematic as they are now. The xenophobic sentiments in nineteenth-century American society facilitated early alliances between Afro-Americans and Jewish Americans. With the influx of large numbers of Jewish immigrants into primarily urban northeastern centers at the turn of the century, the first stage of black-Jewish relations crystallized.

Fortunately, this stage was, in many ways, a salutary one. The black struggle for freedom fused with a strong egalitarian and progressive tradition among European Jews to create a solid and mutually beneficial alliance. Major Jewish leaders publicly spoke out against racial injustice; major black leaders publicly condemned anti-Semitic practices. On the international front, black American leaders denounced German Nazism—and Jesse Owens became a major symbol of the revolt against the insidious doctrine of Aryan supremacy. Yet, the indescribably evil Holocaust that European Jews underwent during Hitler's tyrannical reign introduced fundamentally new factors into black-Jewish relations: first, a post-Holocaust consciousness among Jews that engendered a deep sense of group identity and fostered distrust of non-Jewish would-be allies; second, the creation of Israel, a Jewish nation-state with—to say the least—hostile neighbors.

Initially, these new realities did not alter the relatively positive and congenial relations between the two groups. As the black freedom struggle reemerged in the form of the civil rights movement, Jewish support was significant, widespread, and quite visible. But the rise of black nationalism in the late 1960s proved troubling to black-Jewish relations. This was so for three basic reasons.

First, the call for black power implied black control over black communities where some Jewish shopkeepers and entrepreneurs were located. Second, the centrality of racial identity raised questions of group affiliation already fermenting within the post-Holocaust consciousness

---

From *Christianity and Crisis* (Apr. 30, 1984).

of many Jewish Americans. Third, early forms of black nationalism—though never dominant in the black community—were, in part, xenophobic, especially antiwhite and, at times, anti-Semitic. So by the early seventies, the second stage of black-Jewish relations ended with both groups still supportive of liberal politics—witness their allegiance to George McGovern in 1972—but headed toward conflict.

The third stage of black-Jewish relations commenced with the Yom Kippur War of 1973—an invasion of Israel that renewed Jewish-American memories of the Holocaust by raising the possibility of a new one. On the domestic front, Jewish-American upward social mobility flourished, with an astonishing presence in elite universities and such professions as law, medicine, and journalism. Meantime, principally owing to the black freedom struggle, unprecedented numbers of black people entered middle-class status, hence occupying similar places, slots, and jobs as their Jewish counterparts in American society. The clash over the validity and feasibility of quotas to ensure equality of opportunity was occasioned, in part, by the simultaneous entrance of large numbers of Jewish Americans and moderate numbers of black Americans into the middle class. Yet this conflict was but a portent of what was to come.

The Palestinian Issue

As the plight of Palestinian people became more visible, American foreign policy more insistently pro-Israel, and South African–Israeli relations less belligerent, many black Americans began to think more critically about the difficult predicament of Israel—questioning not their support of Israel, but rather Israel's treatment of its Arab inhabitants and the drift toward the right within Israeli politics.

Contrary to widespread misperceptions, major black American leaders have never supported, or called for support of, the Palestinian Liberation Organization. But, like many Americans and some Israelis, some black figures have encouraged various voices of the Palestinian people to be heard. And to the degree to which these voices are those of the PLO, some black leaders have tried to listen—but never uncritically. The terrible assaults of the PLO on the Israeli people are well known and deplorable, just as the Israeli dispossession of Palestinian lands and treatment of Arabs in Israel, though less well known, are deplorable. This tragic deadlock continues, with little sign of change, and, just as in South Africa, the Philippines, Central America, and Poland, violence, suffering, and fear prevail.

In the meantime, many Jewish Americans accuse black Americans of betrayal, of a failure to grasp the Israeli plight of living under the threat of national death, and of supporting quotas for their own group gain. And many black leaders accuse Jewish Americans of retreat, of giving uncritical support to conservative Israeli policies, and of opposing quotas for their group gain. These accusations—quite rational ones, worthy of serious dialogue—often degenerate into charges of anti-Semitism and racism. We know perfectly well that criticism of Israeli policies is not necessarily anti-Semitic and rejection of quotas is not inherently racist. But with the erosion of trust and respect, such criticisms and rejections rouse suspicion. As we reach the end of the third stage of black-Jewish relations, we seem to have reached their nadir.

Yet a fourth stage looms in the present. It can begin—in earnest—when a candid and rational dialogue between black and Jewish people replaces calculated misunderstandings and petty name-calling. The importance of this dialogue is not only the possible resolution and reconciliation of disagreement—for some of the disagreements may be genuinely irreconcilable—but also the restoration of civility and respect for one another as interlocutors in a dialogue. Afro-Americans and Jewish Americans still have much to learn from one another and still have to face the common enemy of American xenophobia, especially racism and anti-Semitism. Let us hope that in the last decades of this century we will witness a renewal of honest and rational dialogue which characterized the first decades of the century. But this will be so only if we make it so.

In Memory of Marvin Gaye

Much of the significant truth about the career of the Afro-American singer Marvin Gaye may be obscured by the problems of his later life and the manner of his dying (he was shot to death by his father April 1, 1984, in a tragic, and as yet unexplained, incident).

First and foremost, Gaye was a Christian artist. He was also one of the most gifted performers produced by the Afro-American religious experience. Raised in his father's Pentecostal church, located in the East Capitol projects in Washington, D.C., Gaye was imbued with a deep spiritual sensitivity anchored in a Christ-centered ethic of love. Initially this sensitivity was expressed in his instrumental virtuosity—especially on the organ, piano, and drums. Although Gaye sang in the church choir, his vocal talent did not surface until he filled the first-tenor slot of Harvey Fuqua's Moonglows, a smooth harmony rhythm and blues group. When Gaye's silky and soulful voice caught the attention of Berry Gordy, Jr.—the founder of Motown Recording Company—in a Detroit nightclub in 1961, he was immediately offered a contract. The public career of Marvin Gaye had begun.

Motown was the Jackie Robinson of black popular music: after crossing the color line in its field, it went on to excel and to win the hearts of vast numbers of nonblack Americans. As with other Motown stars— Diana Ross, Lionel Richie, and Michael Jackson—Gaye's relationship with Motown enabled his talent to become visible to the world. Unlike these other artists, Gaye's musical and philosophical roots remained in the Afro-American Christian tradition. His first classic recordings were neither adolescent, rhythmic dance records (as with the Supremes and the Jackson Five) nor funky rock renderings (as with Lionel Richie's Commodores). Rather, Gaye's great early achievements—sung with the incomparable Tammi Terrell—were poignant and powerful love songs, written by the team of Nickolas Ashford and Valerie Simpson of White Rock Baptist Church in New York City. These classics—such as "Your Precious Love," "Ain't Nothing Like the Real Thing," "You're All I Need to Get By," and "Ain't No Mountain High Enough"—were the pivotal songs that directed the Christian religiosity of black church music into the secular spirituality of Afro-American popular music. For the first time in American history, the musical depth of the black church was let

---

From *Christianity and Crisis* (June 11, 1984).

loose into the mainstream of American society. And American popular music would never again be the same.

Upon the tragic death of Tammi Terrell, who collapsed in Gaye's arms during a performance in 1967, Gaye went into hiding. Despite his success as a solo performer ("I'll Be Doggone," "Ain't That Peculiar," and "I Heard It through the Grapevine" all reached the Top Ten), Gaye became reclusive, melancholic, and deeply dissatisfied with his music. He would not perform publicly for five years.

"What's Going On"

Yet Gaye's tortuous struggle with the sudden death of Tammi Terrell, his younger brother Frankie's firsthand accounts of atrocities in Vietnam, the escalation of the civil rights movement into black power advocacy, the widespread invasion of drugs among unemployed black youth, and the rise of ecological consciousness produced the greatest album in Afro-American popular music: *What's Going On* (1971). This ground-breaking album was not only the first conceived and enacted by the artist (as opposed to studio staffers) but also the first concept album that hung together by means of a set of themes—themes concerned with socio-economic critique and Christian outlook.

Gaye's critique of American society was explicit. "Rockets, moon shots," he wrote in "Inner City Blues," "Spend it on the have nots." With "radiation underground and in the sky," he saw birds and animals dying in "Mercy, Mercy Me (The Ecology)." Instead of brutality, he asked attention: "Talk to me, so you can see" ("What's Going On"). And in such songs as "Save the Children," "God Is Love," and "Wholly Holy," he explicitly evoked the love ethic of Jesus Christ as the basis for negating and transforming the world: If we learn from the book Jesus left us, we can rock the world, we can "holler love across the nation."

What's Going On was not only the best-selling album in Motown history at the time; it also set standards of Afro-American popular music that remain unequaled. Only Gaye's marvelously gifted pupil, Stevie Wonder, has attempted to exceed such standards by fusing the spiritual richness of Afro-American music, the sense of social engagement, and the love ethic of Jesus Christ.

What's Going On was the peak of Gaye's career. He continued to produce popular albums and hits. Yet, principally owing to two painful divorces, Oedipal obsessions, paranoiac fits, and suicidal impulses, Gaye became captive to a form of bondage he admonished others to avoid: drugs. His songs still portrayed a longing for transcendence, but instead

of the agapic praxis of communities he highlighted erotic communion—
as in his albums *Let's Get It On* (1973) and *I Want You* (1976) and his
Grammy Award single "Sexual Healing" (1982).

In his last years, Gaye oscillated from earthly pessimism to eschatological hope: from the notion that nuclear holocaust was imminent to a
faith that only Jesus can save us. During his sporadic bouts with suicide,
Gaye is reported to have viewed Jesus and sins that would never be for-
given as the primary motivations to live. And, at the height of this turmoil, the last words he wrote for his last album, *Midnight Love* (1982),
were "I still love Jesus, all praises to the Heavenly Father." May this
troubled musical genius, deeply immersed in the Afro-American religious experience and genuinely sensitive to the harsh realities of American society, rest in peace. And may his artistic Christian witness live
forever.

On Afro-American Popular Music: From Bebop to Rap

The salient feature of popular music in first-world capitalist and third-world neocolonialist societies is the appropriation and imitation of Afro-American musical forms and styles. The Afro-American spiritual-blues impulse—of polyphonic, rhythmic effects and antiphonal vocal techniques, of kinetic orality and affective physicality—serve as major sources for popular music in the West. This complex phenomenon, the Afro-Americanization of popular music, prevails owing to three basic reasons. First, the rise of the USA as a world power focused international attention more pointedly to native U.S. cultural forms and styles. Second, vast technological innovations in mass media and communications facilitated immediate and massive influence of certain forms and styles upon others. Third, and most important, Afro-American music is first and foremost, though not exclusively or universally, a countercultural practice with deep roots in modes of religious transcendence and political opposition. Therefore it is seductive to rootless and alienated young people disenchanted with existential meaninglessness, disgusted with flaccid bodies, and dissatisfied with the status quo.

Afro-American popular music constitutes a crucial dimension of the background practices—the ways of life and struggle—of Afro-American culture. By taking seriously Afro-American popular music, one can dip into the multileveled life-worlds of black people. As Ralph Ellison has suggested, Afro-Americans have had rhythmic freedom in place of social freedom, linguistic wealth instead of pecuniary wealth. I make no attempt here to come to terms with the complexity of the evolving forms and content of Afro-American popular music. Rather I simply try to provide a cognitive mapping of the major breaks and ruptures in Afro-American popular music in light of their changing socioeconomic and political contexts from bebop to rap, from Charlie Parker to the Sugar-hill Gang.

Our starting point is the grand break with American mainstream music, especially imitated and co-opted Afro-American popular music, by the so-called bebop jazz musicians—Charlie Parker, Theolonius Monk, Dizzy Gillespie, and others. Their particular way of Africanizing Afro-American jazz—with the accent on contrasting polyrhythms, the

From *Le Monde Diplomatique* (Nov. 1983).

deemphasis of melody, and the increased vocalization of the saxophone—was not only a reaction to the white-dominated, melody-obsessed "swing jazz"; it also was a creative musical response to the major shift in sensibilities and moods in Afro-America after World War II. Through their technical facility and musical virtuosity, bebop jazz musicians expressed the heightened tensions, frustrated aspirations, and repressed emotions of an aggressive yet apprehensive Afro-America. Unlike the jazz of our day, bebop jazz was a popular music, hummed on the streets, whistled by shoeshine boys, and even danced to in the house parties in urban black communities.

Yet the bebop musicians, like Thomas Pynchon in our time, shunned publicity and eschewed visibility. Their radical nonconformist stance—often misunderstood as a repetition of the avant-garde attitude of the *fin de siècle* artists—is reflected in their famous words "We don't care if you listen to our music or not." Their implicit assumption was that, given the roots of their music, black folk could not *not* listen to it and others had to struggle to do so. Yet as the ferment of the short-lived "bebop era" subsided into the "cool" style of the early fifties, it was clear that bebop had left an indelible stamp on Afro-American popular music. Despite the brief ascendancy of black "cool" artists such as (the early) Miles Davis and John Lewis and white "cool" musicians like Chet Baker and David Brubeck, the Afro-American spiritual-blues impulse (always alive and well in Count Basie's perennial band) surfaced quickly in the sounds of Charles Mingus, Ray Charles, and Art Blakey's hard bebop Jazz Messengers who all paved the way to the era of soul and funk.

Needless to say, most black folk in the fifties listened weekly to spiritual and gospel music in black churches—sung by young choir members such as Sam Cooke, Dionne Warwicke, Aretha Franklin, Gladys Knight, and Lou Rawls. With increased strata and class differentiation in the ever-blackening urban centers throughout the USA, secular attitudes proliferated and financial rewards for nonreligious and nonjazz black popular music escalated. On the one hand, jazz—under the influence of John Coltrane, Miles Davis, Ornette Coleman, and others—became more and more a kind of highbrow, "classical" avant-garde music its originators and innovators abhorred. On the other hand, black churches turned their theological guns on "the devil's music" (traditionally pointed at the blues) resulting in more and more marginality for black religious music. So the stage was set for a black popular music which was neither jazz nor gospel: soul music.

Soul music is more than either secularized gospel or funkified jazz. Rather, it is a particular Africanization of Afro-American music with intent to appeal to the black masses, especially geared to the black ritual of attending parties and dances. Soul music is the populist application of bebop's aim: racial self-conscious assertion among black people in light of their rich musical heritage. The two major artists of soul music—James Brown and Aretha Franklin—bridge the major poles in the Afro-American experience by appealing to agrarian and urban black folk, the underclass and working class, religious and secular men and women. Only the black upper middle class of long standing—and most of white USA—initially rejected them. Ironically, though unsurprisingly, none of James Brown's and few of Aretha Franklin's gold records were or are played by nonblack-oriented radio stations. Yet their influence, including white appropriations and imitations, flourished.

As the black baby boom catapulted and black entrepreneurial activity in mass communications expanded, it became apparent that a youthful black market could support a black recording industry. In the South, Otis Redding, the great soul singer, had moved far along on this road, yet white power stubbornly resisted. So when in 1958 Berry Gordy, a black industrial worker in one of Detroit's Ford plants, decided to establish Motown, black popular music took a tremendous leap forward. Far ahead of black literary artists and scholars in this regard, major black popular musicians, writers, singers, and producers could now work in a production unit owned by and geared toward black people.

Motown was the center of Afro-American popular music in the sixties and early seventies—with the phenomenal success of over 75 percent of its records reaching the Top Ten rhythm and blues tune charts in the mid-sixties. The musical genius of Stevie Wonder, Michael Jackson, and Lionel Richie; the writing talents of Smokey Robinson, Nicholas Ashford, Valerie Simpson, Norman Whitfield, Barrett Strong, Eddie and Brian Holland, Lamont Dozier, and Marvin Gaye; and the captivating performances of the Temptations, the Miracles, the Supremes, the Four Tops, Gladys Knight and the Pips, the Jackson Five and the Commodores set Motown far above any other recording company producing Afro-American popular music.

Motown was the Jackie Robinson of black popular music: it crossed the color line for the first time, then proceeded to excel and thereby win the hearts and souls of vast numbers of nonblack folk. The most successful Motown figures—Diana Ross, Stevie Wonder, Michael Jackson, and Lionel Richie—now have secure status in mainstream American popular music. And outside of Motown, the only black singers or groups to achieve such transracial acceptance are Nat King Cole, Louis Armstrong, Johnny Mathis, Dionne Warwicke, Jimi Hendrix, Sly and the Family Stone, Lou Rawls, and Earth, Wind and Fire.

Like Jackie Robinson, Motown reflected the then stable, persevering, upwardly mobile working class in Afro-America. At its height, Motown produced smooth, syncopated rhythms, not funky polyrhythms (like

James Brown or the Watts 103rd Street Rhythm Band); restrained call-and-response forms, not antinomian antiphonal styles (as with Aretha Franklin or the late Donny Hathaway); and love-centered romantic lyrics, not racially oriented social protest music (like Gil-Scott Heron or Archie Shepp). Yet Motown delicately and wisely remained anchored in the Afro-American spiritual-blues impulse.

There is little doubt that Motown produced some of the great classics in Afro-American and American popular music. The Temptations' "My Girl," "Since I Lost My Baby," "You're My Everything"; the Miracles' "OOO Baby Baby," "Choosey Beggar," "Here I Go Again"; Marvin Gaye and Tammi Terrell's "Your Precious Love," "If This World Were Mine," "Ain't Nothing Like the Real Thing"; Stevie Wonder's "For Once in My Life," "My Cherie Amour," "You Are The Sunshine of My Life"; and Gladys Knight and the Pips' "Neither One of Us" will stand the test of time.

As Motown became more commercially successful with the larger white American audience, it began to lose ground in Afro-America. On two musical fronts—fast funk and mellow soul—Motown faced a serious challenge. On the first front, Motown had never surpassed James Brown. Yet Motown had produced music for Afro-America to dance—to twist, jerk, boogaloo, philly dog, and skate. With the appearance of George Clinton's innovative Funkadelic and Parliament, a new wave of funk appeared: technofunk. Never before had black folk heard such deliberately distorted voice and contrapuntal rhythmic effects filtered through electronic instrumentalities. Building principally on James Brown, the Funkadelic's "I Wanna Know If It's Good to You," "Loose Booty," and "Standing on the Verge of Getting It On" sounded musically revolutionary to the ears of the masses of black folk. Motown quickly moved into technofunk with the Temptations' successful "Cloud Nine," "I Can't Get Next To You," and "Psychedelic Shack," but it was clear that the change of image (and personnel) could not give Motown hegemonic status on fast funk.

On the second front—that of mellow soul—Motown had no peer until the rise—precipitated by the roaring success of the Delfonics—of the Philly Sound at Sigma Sound Studio in Philadelphia. The poignant music and lyrics of Kenneth Gamble and Leon Huff, Thom Bell and Linda Creed, Joseph Jefferson, Bruce Hawes and Yvette Davis, Norman Harris, and Allen Felder surfaced in the late sixties and early seventies with force and potency, as witnessed by the popular songs sung by the O'Jays, the Spinners, Harold Melvin and the Blue Notes, Blue Magic, Teddy Pendergrass, Major Harris, the Jones Girls, Lou Rawls, and even Johnny Mathis. Furthermore, the noteworthy presence of Harlem's Main Ingredient, Chicago's Chi-Lites, Detroit's (non-Motown) Dramatics, Jersey City's Manhattans, and Los Angeles's Whispers on this front yielded a more diverse situation.

The early seventies witnessed slightly more political overtones in Afro-American popular music. Surprisingly, the political ferment of the late sixties did not invoke memorable musical responses on behalf of popular Afro-American musicians, with the exception of James Brown's "Say It Loud I'm Black and I'm Proud." The youthful black market thrived on music for dance and romance; and such music was the mainstay of the late sixties. As the Vietnam War intensified (with over 22 percent of its U.S. victims being black), the drug culture spread, and black elected officials emerged, recordings such as the Temptations' "Ball of Confusion," the Chi-Lites' "Give More Power to the People," James Brown's "Funky President (People, It's Bad)," and the Isley Brothers' "Fight the Power" revealed more explicit concern with the public life and political welfare of Afro-America. Ironically, this concern was exemplified most clearly in the greatest album produced by Motown: Marvin Gaye's *What's Going On*. True to their religious roots, Afro-American popular musicians and writers couched their concerns in highly moralistic language, devoid of the concrete political realities of conflict and struggle. Marvin Gaye's classical recording openly evoked Christian apocalyptic images and the love ethic of Jesus Christ.

The watershed year in Afro-American popular music in this period was 1975. For the first time in Afro-American history, fast funk music seized center stage from mellow soul music. In the past, it was inconceivable that a black rhythm and blues group or figure—no matter how funk-oriented—not possess a serious repertoire of slow mellow, often ballad, music. It is important to remember that James Brown's early hits were mellow soul, such as "Please, Please, Please," "Bewildered," "It's a Man's World." Given the demand for nonstop dance music in discotheques in the early seventies and the concomitant decline of slow dancing and need for mellow soul, black dance music became dominant in Afro-American popular music. Barry White's sensual upbeat tunes, Brass Construction's repetitive syncopations, Kool and the Gang's distinctive Jersey funk, and Nile Rogers and Bernard Edwards's classy chic are exemplary responses to the disco scene. Yet the most important Afro-American response to this scene occurred in 1975 when George Clinton and William "Bootsy" Collins released two albums: Parliament's *Chocolate City* and *Mothership Connection*.

By building directly upon Clinton's Funkadelic, such as deploying the same musicians, Parliament ushered forth the era of black technofunk—the creative encounter of the Afro-American spiritual-blues impulse with highly sophisticated technological instruments, strategies, and effects. Parliament invited its listeners, especially the dwellers of "Chocolate cities" and to a lesser extent those in the "Vanilla suburbs," to enter the "Fourth World," the world of black funk and star wars, of black orality, bodily sensuality, technical virtuosity, and electronic adroitness. The cover of the first Parliament album, *Chocolate City,* portrayed Washington, D.C.'s Lincoln Memorial, Washington Memorial, Capitol Building, and White House melting presumably under the heat of black techno-funk and the increasing "chocolate" character of the nation's capital. The album contained only one mellow soul song ("I Misjudged You"), a mere ritualistic gesture to the mellow pole of Afro-American popular music. The second album, *Mothership Connection*—now joined with the leading saxophonists of James Brown's band, Maceo Parker and Fred Wesley—literally announced the planetary departure to the "Fourth World" on the mothership, with not one earthbound mellow love song.

The emergence of technofunk is not simply a repetition of black escapism nor an adolescent obsession with "Star Trek." In addition to being a product of the genius of George Clinton, technofunk constitutes the second grand break of Afro-American musicians from American mainstream music, especially imitated and co-opted Afro-American popular music. Like Charlie Parker's bebop, George Clinton's techno-funk both Africanizes and technologizes Afro-American popular music—with polyrhythms on polyrhythms, less melody, and freaky electronically distorted vocals. Similar to bebop, technofunk unabashedly exacerbates and accentuates the "blackness" of black music, the "Afro-Americanness" of Afro-American music—its irreducibility, inimitability, and uniqueness. Funkadelic and Parliament defy nonblack emulation; they assert their distinctiveness—and the distinctiveness of "funk" in Afro-America. This funk is neither a skill nor an idea, not a worldview or a stance. Rather, it is an existential capacity to get in touch with forms of kinetic orality and affective physicality acquired by deep entrenchment in—or achieved by pretheoretical styles owing to socialization in—the patterns of Afro-American ways of life and struggle.

Technofunk is a distinctive expression of postmodern black popular music; it constitutes a potent form of the Afro-American spiritual-blues impulse in the pervasive computer phase and hedonistic stage of late capitalist U.S. society. Ironically, the appeal of black technofunk was not a class-specific phenomena. Technofunk invigorated the "new" politicized black middle class undergoing deep identity-crisis, the stable black working class fresh out of the blues-ridden ghettos, the poor black working class hungry for escapist modes of transcendence, and the hustling black underclass permeated by the drug culture. Black technofunk articulated black middle-class anxieties toward yet fascination with U.S. "hi-tech" capitalist society; black working-class frustration of marginal inclusion within and ineffective protest against this society, and black underclass self-destructive dispositions owing to outright exclusion from this society. For black technofunk, in a period of increasing black strata and class divisions, there are no fundamental cleavages in Afro-America, only the black nation. The cover of George Clinton's 1978 Funkadelic album, *One Nation under a Groove,* portrays black folk from all walks of life hoisting up Marcus Garvey's Afro-American liberation flag (of red, black, and green stripes) with "R & B" printed on it—the initials not for rhythm and blues but rhythm and business. In vintage black nationalist patriarchal fashion, the inside of the album contains a beautiful naked black woman lying on her back, signifying the biological source and social "backbone" of the black nation.

Again like bebop, technofunk's breakthrough was brief. Its intensely Africanizing and technologizing thrust was quickly diluted and brought more and more into contact with other nonblack musical currents, as witnessed in Prince's creative Minneapolis sound and Midnight Star's "freakazoid funk." Since 1975, four noteworthy trends have surfaced: the invasion of Afro-American popular music by ex–avant-garde jazz musicians, the meteoric rise of Michael Jackson (aided by Rod Temperton and especially Quincy Jones) as a solo performer, the refreshing return of gospel music, and the exuberant emergence of black rap music. Miles Davis's canonical album, *Bitches Brew,* in 1970 already displayed the influence of soul music on jazz; his admiration of the California funk of Sly and the Family Stone is well known. Yet by the late seventies the influx of bonafide jazz musicians—most notably George Benson, Quincy Jones, Herbie Hancock, and Donald Byrd—into Afro-American popular music (rhythm and blues) was phenomenal. The motivation was not simply financial; it also was symptomatic of perceived sources of vitality and vigor in black music in late capitalist U.S. society and culture. In avant-garde jazz, Ornette Coleman's and John Coltrane's free jazz—like Arnold Schonberg's atonal music in the Western classical tradition—symbolized both grand achievements and dead ends. For example, Pharaoh Sanders, who briefly upheld the rich legacy of Coltrane's "new wave" jazz, was soon recording with B. B. King, the great blues singer and musician, at the Fillmore East. In short, jazz musicians were not only making a monetary bid for musical popularity; more important, they were acknowledging the legitimacy of the music of the black masses. In short, they were reaffirming the original vision of the great revolutionary figure in jazz, Louis Amstrong. White middlebrow audiences and black old-timers continued to support the great jazz singers—such as Ella Fitzgerald, Sarah Vaughan, Carmen McRae, Billy Eckstine, and Joe Williams—but jazz instrumentalists could hardly make it. In many ways, this continues to be so, though the youthful genius of Wynton Marsalis may rearrange the terrain of jazz itself. Notwithstanding the present predicament of jazz musicians, George Benson, a superb jazz guitarist, acquired immediate fame as a Motown-like smooth, mellow soul singer; Herbie Hancock, a "cool" jazz pianist with the early Miles Davis, moved into his own brand of technofunk; and the Van Gelder studio group—Bob James, Grover Washington, Eric Gale, and others—produced an ingenious "pop jazz," often based on rhythm and blues tunes. The most successful jazz musician turned rhythm and blues producer, Quincy Jones, joined his immense talent with that of the leader of the most beloved of black singing groups—Michael Jackson of the Jackson Five.

The distinctive talent of Michael Jackson is that he combines the performative showmanship of James Brown (whom he imitated in his first 1968 exhibition to gain a contract with Motown), the lyrical emotional intensity of Smokey Robinson, the transracial appeal of Dionne Warwicke, and the aggressive though attenuated technofunk of the Isley Brothers. In this regard, Michael Jackson stands shoulders above his contemporaries. He is the musical dynamo of his generation. This became quite clear with his highly acclaimed 1979 *Off the Wall* album and further confirmed by his record-setting 1982 *Thriller* album. The point here is not simply that the albums sell millions of copies and stay on top of the tune charts for several months. Rather, the point is that Michael Jackson is the product of the Afro-American spiritual-blues impulse which now has tremendous international influence, thereby serving as a major model for popular music in the world, especially first-world capitalist and third-world neocolonialist countries. Like Muhammed Ali—and unlike most of his musical contemporaries—Michael Jackson is an international star of grand proportions, the most prominent world-historical emblem of the Afro-American spiritual-blues impulse.

Ironically, and unlike the only other comparable figure, Louis Armstrong, Michael Jackson is not a musical revolutionary within Afro-American history. Rather, he is a funnel through which flows many of the diverse streams and currents of the Afro-American musical tradition. It is precisely his versatility and diversity—from old funk, technofunk, and mellow soul to ballads with the ex-Beatle, Paul McCartney—which marks his protean musical identity. The only contemporary figure comparable to Michael Jackson is Stevie Wonder and though Stevie Wonder is more musically talented and daring (as well as more politically engaged), Jackson possesses a more magnetic magic on stage and in the studio. Yet neither Wonder nor Jackson explore the musical genre which exploded on the scene in the late seventies and early eighties: gospel music.

The black church, black-owned and black-run Christian congregations, is the fountainhead of the Afro-American spiritual-blues impulse.

Without the black church, with its African roots and Christian context, Afro-American culture—in fact, Afro-America itself—is unimaginable. Yet, as should be apparent, the black church has suffered tremendous "artistic drainage." The giant talents of Mahalia Jackson, James Cleveland, and Clara Ward prove that the black church can keep some of its sons and daughters in the artistic fold, but for every one who stayed with the gospels, there have been four who went to rhythm and blues. In the late sixties Edwin Hawkins's "Oh Happy Day" received national visibility, but the gospel explosion—partly spawned by the Pentecostal thrust in the black religious community—did not take off until the reunion of James Cleveland and Aretha Franklin in their historic 1972 double album set *Amazing Grace*. The towering success of this live concert at the New Temple Missionary Baptist Church in Los Angeles convinced many reluctant recording companies that gospel music was marketable. And soon superb albums such as Andraé Crouch's *Take Me Back,* Walter Hawkins's (Edwin's brother) *Love Alive* and *Love Alive II* proved them correct. Although gospel music remains primarily a black affair—written and performed by and for black people—the recent Christian conversions of the popular Deneice Williams and disco queen Donna Summers may broaden the scope.

The most important development in Afro-American popular music since 1979 is black rap music. This music has been performed on ghetto streets and between stage acts during black concerts for many years. In 1979, Sylvia Robinson, the major songwriter for the mellow soul group *The Moments* (recently renamed Ray, Goodman and Brown), decided to record and release "Rapper's Delight" by Harlem's Sugarhill Gang. Within months, black rap records were filling record shops around the country. Most of the first black rap records were musically derived from big hits already released and lyrically related to adolescent love affairs. Yet as more sophisticated rap performers, such as Kurtis Blow and Grandmaster Flash and the Furious Five, emerged, the music became more original and the lyrics more graphic of life in the black ghetto. Kurtis Blow's "The Breaks" and "125th Street" and Grandmaster Flash and the Furious Five's "The Message" and "New York, New York" are exemplary in this regard.

Black rap music is more important than the crossover of jazz musicians to rhythm and blues, the rise of the "older" Michael Jackson, and the return of gospel music because, similar to bebop and technofunk, black rap music is emblematically symptomatic of a shift in sensibilities and moods in Afro-America. Black rap music indeed Africanizes Afro-American popular music—accenting syncopated polyrhythms, kinetic orality, and sensual energy in a refined form of raw expressiveness—while its virtuosity lies not in technical facility but rather street-talk quickness and linguistic versatility. In short, black rap music recuperates and revises elements of black rhetorical styles—some from our preaching—within black musical and rhythmic production. Black rap music recovers and revises elements of black rhetorical styles—some from black preaching—and black rhythmic drumming. In short, it combines the two major organic artistic traditions in black America—black rhetoric and black music. In this sense, like bebop and technofunk, black rap music resists nonblack reproduction, though such imitations and emulations proliferate. Yet unlike bebop and technofunk—and this is a crucial break—black rap music is primarily the musical expression of the paradoxical cry of desperation and celebration of the black underclass and poor working class, a cry which openly acknowledges and confronts the wave of personal cold-heartedness, criminal cruelty, and existential hopelessness in the black ghettos of Afro-America. In stark contrast to bebop and technofunk, black rap music is principally a class-specific form of the Afro-American spiritual-blues impulse which mutes, and often eliminates, the utopian dimension of this impulse. The major predecessor of black rap music was the political raps of Gil-Scott Heron and the powerful musical poems of the Last Poets over a decade ago; their content was angry, funky, and hopeful. Black rap music is surely grounded in the Afro-American spiritual-blues impulse, but certain versions of this music radically call into question the roots of this impulse, the roots of transcendence and opposition. Without a utopian dimension—without transcendence from or opposition to evil—there can be no struggle, no hope, no meaning. Needless to say, the celebratory form of black rap music, especially its upbeat African rhythms, contains utopian aspirations. But this form is often violently juxtaposed with lyrical hopelessness of the oppressed poor people of Afro-America. My hunch is that the form (the funky rhythms) have basically a ritualistic function: music for cathartic release at the black rituals of parties and dances. In short, even the rhythms conceal the unprecedented phenomena in Afro-American life; the slow but seemingly sure genocidal effects upon the black underclass and poor working class in late capitalist U.S. society and the inability of poor black folk to muster spiritual, let alone political and economic, resources to survive. This is especially so for young black people. The black suicide rate among 18–30 year olds has quadrupled in the past two decades; black homicide is the leading cause of death among young black men; over 50 percent of black households are headed by abandoned and abused young black women; black prison population has doubled since the 1960s; and black churches, led by either rip-off artists like Rev. Ike, devout denominational leaders such as Rev. Jemison of the National Baptist Convention, or dedicated prophets like Rev. Daughtry of the National Black United Front—do not reach the vast majority of young black people.

Black rap music is the last form of transcendence available to young black ghetto dwellers, yet it, tellingly, is often employed to subvert, undermine, and parody transcendence itself. Such artistic strategies—such as play, silence, and performance—are typical postmodern ones in which petit bourgeois artists, philosophers, and critics wallow. Yet the indigenous proliferation of these strategies among the (once most religious) now most degraded and oppressed people in the urban centers of the richest country in the history of humankind signifies a crisis of enormous proportions for Afro-America.

It is ironic that the Afro-Americanization of popular music around the world occurs at the time that the transcendent and oppositional roots of the Afro-American spiritual-blues impulse is radically challenged from within the Afro-American musical tradition. This challenge occurs not simply because of lack of will or loss of nerve but primarily because of treacherous ruling-class policies, contemptuous black middle-class attitudes, and the loss of existential moorings due to the relative collapse of family structures and supportive networks. To put it bluntly, the roots of the Afro-American spiritual-blues impulse are based on the opposition that somebody—God, Mom, or neighbors—cares. Some expressions of black rap music challenge this supposition. The future of the Afro-American spiritual-blues impulse may well hang on the quality of the response to this challenge. In this sense, the vitality and vigor of Afro-American popular music depends not only on the talents of Afro-American musicians, but also on the moral visions, social analyses, and political strategies which highlight personal dignity, provide political promise, and give existential hope to the underclass and poor working class in Afro-America.

On Fox and Lears's
The Culture of Consumption

Since its revolutionary inception, America has baffled those preoccupied with its fundamental transformation. Despite its beginnings in anti-imperialist warfare, this country has persistently resisted efforts at structural social change. This stubbornness—often dubbed American exceptionalism—has left many progressive and prophetic persons shipwrecked, afloat in the sea of pragmatic liberalism.

The essays brought together by Richard Wightman Fox and T. J. Jackson Lears in *The Culture of Consumption* do not exactly provide a way out of the dilemma, but they do offer some valuable insights regarding the extent of our political problem. This collection is a kind of manifesto of a new generation of revisionist historians (trained or teaching primarily at Yale) who attempt to bring together Marxist analysis, neo-Freudian psychology, and Weberian theories of action. Following Lears's *No Place of Grace,* they focus solely on the reactions and responses of the northeastern Protestant upper bourgeoisie to the emergence and evolution of consumer capitalism. Lears perceptively notes that this emergence entailed the shift from perpetual work to periodic leisure, compulsive saving to compulsive spending, civic responsibility to apolitical passivity, Protestant self-denial to therapeutic self-fulfillment. The move from solid character to sparkling personality, steadfast morality to upbeat morale, self-control to self-release signaled the rise of new cultural values and sensibilities—secular values and sensibilities efficacious for undergirding consumer capitalism. And though these values and sensibilities often opposed the increasing impersonalization and rationalization of American society, they also reinforced these processes by promoting new experts and professionals to manage the new anxieties.

In addition to therapists, psychologists, and "liberal" preachers, the major ascendant group consisted of national advertisers, equipped with a budding national market and advancing technological capacities. The exemplary case here is automobile advertising, which soon dropped rational appeals to technical details and instead promoted styles, status, and utopian longings. Needless to say, Henry Ford's ingenious idea—

From *Christianity and Crisis* (Mar. 5, 1984); review of Richard W. Fox and T. Jackson Lears, eds., *The Culture of Consumption: Critical Essays in American History, 1880-1980* (New York: Pantheon, 1983).

the affordable automobile—became the embodiment of this change and the cornerstone of consumer capitalism.

The role of religious elites was crucial in this episode of American history. Faced with the declining authority of churches, many highbrow Protestant ministers began to preach the Christ of G. Stanley Hall's *Jesus Christ, in Light of Psychology* (1917) and Bruce Barton's *The Man Nobody Knows* (1925); that is, Jesus Christ as adolescent superman or the founder of modern business. Even Harry Emerson Fosdick was, at times, seduced by the vitalistic therapeutic ethos (see his *Adventurous Religion,* 1925).

Christopher Wilson's incisive essay examines the rise of the new managerial elites in publishing who created the sensationalist metropolitan tabloid, the frenzied "best seller," commercial images and slogans, and the beginnings of mass entertainment. He focuses on the "cheap magazines," specifically *McClure's, The World's Work,* the *Saturday Evening Post,* and the *Ladies Home Journal.* These magazines not only transformed the reading experience of their audiences; they also made available for the first time a consumer rhetoric that penetrated family life, politics, and contemporary affairs. With the shift from subscription income to advertising revenue as the source of financial support, the "cheap magazines" displaced literary substance with timely, topical items of practical import: intellectual cultivation with domestic efficiency and titillating gossip of glamorous "heroes." In short, the "rhetoric of consumption"—with its themes of spectatorship and passivity—was promoted by managers of manipulated responses to their own consumer products.

Jean-Christophe Agnew's essay enacts a highly complex reading of Henry James's novels, especially *The Golden Bowl,* as mirrors refracting the American bourgeoisie's creation and contestation of the culture of consumption. James's animus against the values and sensibilities of market society is well known. Yet, Agnew claims, in James's fiction we witness "a model of possessive or acquisitive cognition"; James becomes "an entrepreneur of observation." In *The Golden Bowl,* active verbs turn into passive participles and participles into nouns; actions and movements slowly dissolve into thoughts, perceptions, and things. Agnew argues that this insatiable acquisitive model of cognition in James—with its sense of weightlessness and cotton candy–like character—is the very model of activity which sustains consumerism in capitalist society. In this sense, James's "consuming vision" displays the process of cultural reproduction in emerging consumer-oriented American society.

Robert Lynd, the famous author of *Middletown* (1929) and *Middletown in Transition* (1937), is the focus of Richard Wightman Fox's fascinating essay. Lynd becomes a paradigmatic figure whose life exemplifies

189

a basic trajectory of WASP elites and whose work popularized the idea of America as a consumer culture. Raised in the Midwest, Lynd was the son of a self-made banker who was a devout Presbyterian layman. A graduate of Princeton and Union Theological Seminary, Lynd began his career as a muckraker unveiling the dehumanizing conditions of a Wyoming oil camp. Ironically, though his early attacks were pointed at John D. Rockefeller, Jr., whose company owned the camp, the support of Raymond Fosdick (Harry's brother and Rockefeller's lawyer) resulted in Rockefeller's financial backing of Lynd's "small city study," his classic *Middletown*. Guided by John Dewey's progressive educational theory, Lynd and his wife, Helen, highlighted the process by which the residents of Muncie, Indiana, were abandoning their Protestant democratic heritage and becoming captive to "a culture in which everything hinges on money." This book thrust Lynd into the academic limelight. With no higher degree, he was offered tenured professorships at the University of Michigan and Columbia University. He accepted the latter, obtained his doctorate by submitting *Middletown* (omitting the sections written by Helen) and found himself working on the second volume.

Middletown in Transition is quite different in perspective. Dewey's influence gave way to that of Walter Lippmann and Graham Wallas: Lynd renounced his earlier belief in the rational capacity of common people and instead accepted their irrationality. This crucial shift was mediated by his investigation of advertising propaganda during the depression. In "The People as Consumers" he concluded that the power of advertising was irresistible: consumers were powerless against the machinations of consumerism. The only salvation lay in enlisting professional managers to mold public institutions for the common good. Lynd's own political activism was as a professional manager; he became chairman of the Committee on Standards of the National Recovery Administration's Consumers' Advisory Board.

After this second book, Lynd became depressed. Although he taught at Columbia until 1960, he published only one more book, *Knowledge For What?* (1939), which heralded the Soviet Union's social planning because it embodied elements of his own theory of professional management. In a letter to his old Union Seminary professor, the pro-Soviet leftist Harry F. Ward, Lynd wrote of his loneliness and despair. The culture of consumption had tamed, incorporated, and dismayed one of its major critics.

Marketing People and Things

Robert Westbrook's timely treatment of the commodification of modern American politics—the packaging and sale of candidates to voters/consumers—depicts the reduction of elections to market campaigns. Nineteenth-century elections were highly competitive, with high turnout (averaging 80 percent between 1876 and 1896 in presidential elections) and deeply partisan voters. With the erosion of the patronage system and the transfer of the entertainment and informational functions of political parties to mass culture and journalism, the process of party decomposition escalated. With the rising importance of professional campaign managers and consultants equipped with "attitude" psychology and survey research, the advent of television (1952 elections and after), and the marriage of candidates with ad agencies, the reduction of politics to a mode of consumption was complete. As Westbrook concludes, "voting has become for most Americans little more than one of a myriad of consumption choices in a high-intensity market in commodities."

In the final essay Michael Smith explores the making of "commodity scientism"—the elevation of technological display in the American quest for nuclear and lunar supremacy. Prior to World War II, the emphasis on display value over technical function could be seen in the Corliss steam engine at the 1876 Centennial Exposition in Philadelphia and the symbols of technocracy (Trylon, Perisphere, and DemocraCity) at the 1939 New York World's Fair. With the development of the atomic bomb (in full secrecy), commodity scientism emerged full-blown. The very justification for the use of the atomic bombs in Hiroshima and Nagasaki put forward by the Target Committee to President Truman was: (1) obtaining the *greatest psychological effect* against Japan; (2) making the initial use *sufficiently spectacular* for the importance of the weapon to be internationally recognized when publicity on it was released.

Similarly, the decision to opt for a *manned* space program when nearly every significant space objective, from weather monitoring to communications, could be achieved at less cost and with more effectiveness with automated satellites, rests upon its dramatic impact through television. The process of elevating astronauts over aims combined the WASP pioneering image with technical mastery. As Project Mercury gave way to Gemini and Gemini to Apollo, the focus shifted from astronauts to the gadgetry of the spacecraft, with the appropriate obfuscating "techno-jargon." The image of national purpose, the drive for national pride, and the ingenuity of consumer culture blended together in order to "sell the moon." And it worked.

The essays in *The Culture of Consumption* are far from perfect. First, they suffer from a kind of "Johnny-one-note" character; that is, they often make the same point over and over. Second, the authors' wit sometimes degenerates into mere intellectual cuteness, thereby exemplifying the very histrionic values they are denigrating. Third, they simply lack vision: their analyses do not inform either an alternative way of life or the modes of resistance presently at work against the culture of consumption. In this regard, their theoretical frameworks are far inferior to those of Aronowitz, Genovese, Gutman, and Berkovitch. Notwithstanding its limitations, however, the book is significant because it forces us to confront the old bugbear of American exceptionalism: Is effective resistance and fundamental transformation possible in this country?

If the essays in *The Culture of Consumption* tell persuasive stories, then we are imprisoned in the iron cage of capitalist commodification and bureaucratic rationalization—in which resistance is grist for the mill of further imprisonment. It sometimes seems that way: the very cultural and communal sources of resistance—working-class neighborhoods, trade-union enclaves, Afro-American cultural forms, feminist lifestyles—are undergoing subversion and co-optation. Ironically, the traditional bastions of stability—churches and universities—become more and more the central terrains of politicization. But apart from keeping alive the memory and presence of resistance, these institutions do not constitute possibilities for fundamental change.

Is it a distinctive feature of capitalist America that it digs not its own grave from which rises a more egalitarian society (as Marxist mythology once held), but that it digs the grave of civilization itself rather than permit an alternative to itself? I pray not and act accordingly. But it is difficult not to think this is so. It may be that only religious visions and moral convictions sustain such wishful aspiration and engaged action.

PART THREE

Religion and Contemporary Theology

Christian Theological Mediocrity

The distinctive feature of Christian thought in our postmodern times is its mediocrity. We live in the age of theological epigones. The Christian fold presently contains neither a great thinker nor a towering prophet. There indeed are many talented theologians and courageous religious leaders—but none compare with Ernst Troeltsch and Karl Barth or Elizabeth Cady Stanton and Martin Luther King, Jr. Is the present moment the nadir of Euro-American Christian theology? If so, why?

This situation results principally from two brute facts: the failure of nerve of Euro-American Christian thought and the superficial success of liberation theology. The failure of nerve consists of the inability of European and, especially, American religious thinkers to respond creatively to the turbulent 1960s and the eclipse of U.S. world hegemony in the seventies. The modern Christian traditions of liberalism (Whitehead and Wieman), neoorthodoxy (Barth, Brunner) and realism (Reinhold Niebuhr) were unable to generate powerful and persuasive responses to the issues of racial degradation, patriarchal domination, and imperialist aggression.

The superficial success of liberation theology amounts to a filling of this intellectual vacuum. With the exceptions of Jurgen Moltmann, Mary Daly, James Cone, and a few others, little theological effort has been made to delve into the depth of the European and American experience. For American religious thought, this is not new. Rarely have Americans seriously probed into their own circumstances in order to meet new theological challenges—with the glaring counterexamples of Edwards, Channing, Emerson, Dickinson, Bushnell, Rauschenbusch, and the Niebuhrs exemplifying this rarity.

Instead, Americans have tended to rely on European sources, especially German ones. Yet after Hitler, concentration camps, and national partition, German theology has had little energy to confront the problems of race, gender, and war. Encapsulated French Catholic thought and mutilated British theologies have provided few guides. In short, the European well has run dry, leaving most American theologians holding an empty pail—hence easily seduced by the mirages of a golden past or a revolutionary future.

Contemporary American religious scholars can be divided roughly

From *Christianity and Crisis* (Nov. 26, 1984).

into two camps: those who nostalgically harken back to the grand old days of Whitehead, Barth, or the Niebuhrs, and those who naively point to the originary paradigms of Cone, Daly, and Gutiérrez. The former camp rightly upholds the great achievements of past intellectual giants yet reinforces the present paralysis by a debilitating deference that diverts attention from the uniqueness of the postmodern challenges. The latter camp correctly directs energies toward the present crisis but possesses neither the intellectual patience nor the theological scope to respond adequately. These two camps have left American theological education oscillating between a seemingly exhausted liberalism, a perceived discrediting of neoorthodoxy and realism, and a limited though relevant liberationism. Needless to say, old-style conservative American fundamentalism and evangelicalism (with newly found money!) thrive in such circumstances.

There is little doubt that the decline of highbrow humanist education in Germany—which once transplanted emulations across the American pedagogical landscape—has affected the quality of philosophical, historical, and linguistic knowledge in theological education. In addition, the pressures of a leveling mass culture and a shrinking of teaching positions render it more difficult to convince assimilated fourth-generation immigrants, mainstream WASPS, and first-generation seminary-attending minorities and women that the past educational models are pertinent and productive. Therefore intellectual dilution along with healthy political awareness has occurred in our divinity schools—as in all of our institutions of higher learning. It is important to note that the political awareness is not fully responsible for this intellectual dilution; rather, the dilution is caused primarily by the pervasive crisis in theological education and the bureaucratic encroachment of once humanistic centers of learning. In fact, the political awareness has contributed to an honest encounter with the crisis and has enabled resistance to the managerial ethos slowly creeping into these centers.

Our present Christian theological mediocrity will be overcome neither by nostalgic remembrances of past glory nor by naive hopes for future achievements. Both merely satisfy cathartic needs of the present. Only renewed intellectual preoccupation with the challenges of our time, equipped with a firm grounding in the past and a comprehensive vision of the future, can promote a move beyond mediocrity. There is as much talent around today as there has ever been. The question is whether the postmodern realities of education, culture, and politics will permit this talent to flourish. Without this cultivated talent, the Christian presence in this country will not only remain mediocre; this presence also will become, more than it already is, a menace to the Christian faith.

On Juan Luis Segundo's
Faith and Ideologies

Liberation theologies are the principal forms of Christian prophetic thought and action in our contemporary age. They present the ways of life and struggle of Christians around the world who have convinced remnants of the church to open its eyes to human misery and oppose socioeconomic systems and political structures that perpetuate such misery. Like all serious modes of inquiry, liberation theologies are predicated on crisis—on human situations of tremendous danger and incipient possibility. Such concrete crises invariably generate forms of critical consciousness. Liberation theologies are the predominant forms of critical consciousness within the Christian church that respond to the dangers of class, racial, and sexual privilege, and project the possibility of class, racial, and sexual equality.

Black, feminist, Native American, Hispanic, and especially Latin American versions of liberation theology have made major contributions to Christian thought and the life of the church. The theological theme of God's identification with the poor and oppressed now resounds throughout our seminaries, takes shape in some of our ecclesiastical agencies, and regulates the practices in a select few of our churches. The methodological mandate for systemic social analysis of structures of domination in light of the good news of Jesus Christ is forcing many theologians, preachers, and laity to take seriously the works of Karl Marx and Max Weber, Simone de Beauvoir and W. E. B. Du Bois, Anthony Giddens, and Christopher Lasch. In short, liberation theologies have pushed religious thinkers beyond their usual parochial concerns and challenged churches to become more enlightened participants in the great political and economic issues of our time.

But beneath this intense intellectual ferment and heated political discourse lurks a hidden truth: *the high moment of liberation theology has passed*. The original texts of James Cone, Mary Daly, and Gustavo Gutiérrez spawned widely diffused and dispersed theological currents. As with all ground-breaking upsurges, liberation theologies emerged with impressive power and insight and presently have evolved in diverse and multiple forms.

From *Commonweal* (Jan. 27, 1984); review of Juan Luis Segundo, *Faith and Ideologies* (Maryknoll, N.Y.: Orbis, 1983).

197

This evolution of liberation theologies is particularly noteworthy in that these theologies ushered forth from an academic discipline which suffers from an immense identity crisis. Hence, the early enthusiasm for liberation theologies can be attributed not only to the relevance of their perspectives for the oppressed but also to the hope that these theologies would breathe new life into a fading and faltering mode of intellectual reflection. To put it crudely, liberation theologies were expected to both change the world and keep theology alive.

Yet as the zenith of liberation theological reflection fades, we witness the proliferation of philosophical investigations, cultural critiques, social analyses, and historical reconstructions from Christian liberationist perspectives. The theological concerns of liberation theology are now shifting to their philosophical, cultural, social-analytical, or historical concerns. This move requires not only rigorous interdisciplinary tools, but also more intense interaction with secular colleagues—thereby facilitating more religious participation within the larger public conversation in society and culture at large.

This positive dialogue and candid alliance with both the Academy and political movements helps break down the walls of demarcation between divinity schools and universities, preachers and political activists. But it also could result in a new kind of theological evasion, a refusal to take seriously the difficult task of specifying Christian identity in a pluralistic world. And as the tentacles of secular professionalism and vulgar politicization further pervade our seminaries and divinity schools, even the theological task itself could become passé.

In regard to this precarious though pregnant situation, liberation theologies more than likely will move in one of four directions. They will: (1) relapse back into traditional kinds of systematic theology equipped with new themes, motifs, and insights—as in Jon Sobrino's *Christology at the Crossroads;* (2) retreat into versions of philosophical anthropology (i.e., a philosophy of human existence) which appeal to Kant, Hegel, Feuerbach, or the early Marx, and thereby subvert systematic theology—as in Juan Luis Segundo's *The Liberation of Theology;* (3) spill over into social theory, cultural criticism, and historical reconstruction which may take either Christian or post-Christian forms—as in Elisabeth Schüssler Fiorenza's *In Memory of Her* or Mary Daly's *Gynecology,* respectively; or (4) resort to practical writings in journalistic styles which attempt to reach the general literate laity and clergy—as in James Cone's *My Soul Looks Back.*

The first alternative is essential but limited; it preserves precious links with elements of the tradition and church but at the inescapable expense of intellectual marginality in our secular intellectual milieu. The second option, philosophic anthropology, is a trap to be avoided by both theologians and philosophers alike; it succumbs to a seductive quest for universal categorical schemas that yield either formal results too empty for usefulness or transcendental frameworks that conceal their historicity. The third line of development is the most fruitful and challenging; it sidelines many narrowly trained theologians and gives prominence to Christian and secular social theorists, cultural critics, and historians. The last direction performs a crucial propagandistic role, but provides little, if any, intellectual depth.

Juan Luis Segundo's *Faith and Ideologies* exemplifies the second option. This book builds on his earlier work and puts forward a full-blown philosophical anthropology—a detailed specification of "the universal dimensions of human beings." Segundo is the most ambitious and audacious of the Latin American liberation religious thinkers. He disregards the traditional intellectual division of labor in the university and eagerly pursues a daring idea, no matter how half-baked that idea may be. In this book, Segundo's ambition and audacity lead to organizational fragmentation and philosophical confusion.

Segundo's aim in this text is threefold: first, to infuse new content in the categorical notions of faith and ideology; second, to explore how these two ideas relate to one another, using Christianity and Marxism as interlocutors; third, to examine the concrete situation of present-day Latin America in light of his philosophical perspective. Like Immanuel Kant and Matthew Arnold, Segundo wants to preserve the transcendent character of moral conduct yet create a comprehensive secular discourse which subsumes religion. In short, his primary intention is to displace theology and put forward a new philosophical anthropology.

But in Chapter I entitled "Toward A New Statement of the Problem," it becomes quite clear that Segundo's philosophical anthropology is not new at all. Rather, it is a warmed-over version of neo-Kantianism—much less refined than those found in Wilhelm Dilthey or Jurgen Habermas. Segundo's two "basic anthropological dimensions" are faith and ideology. He understands "faith" to be the human acquisition of meaning and value principally by means of socialization. "Ideology" is taken to be the human techniques of efficacy and predictability necessary to actualize one's value-laden ends or goals.

Following Gregory Bateson's *Steps to an Ecology of Mind*, Segundo defines faith as a "partially self-validating" set of "epistemological and ontological premises" which human beings impose on "the flux of happenings" for purposes of order and coherence. Since these "premises" circumscribe the limits of human knowledge, they are immune from rational validation, hence "self-validating." Yet Segundo also defines faith as a "certain type of knowledge." Here confusion sets in. Can faith be a set of "premises" which delimit what we can and do know and also be a certain type of knowledge? Is the latter a transcendental form of knowledge, a special kind of knowledge that enables us to know the premises that constitute preconditions for knowledge? Is this not viciously circular? Or does Segundo mean that the premises are socially derived and hence we know them through social and historical analysis? If so, then can he consistently claim that faith is "an anthropological dimension as universal as the human species itself"? Surely not. He must either fall back on neo-Kantianism and provide an account of faith as an anthropological dimension or adopt a Mannheimian sociology of knowledge and give up talk about such dimensions. At one point in his text, Segundo endorses Mannheim's "real sociology of knowledge" yet still characterizes the indispensable unconditional absolute as a value, a "transcendent datum." Like Kant of the *Critique of Practical Reason,* philosophical anthropology has solely a self-validating, that is, a moral basis. But, following Mannheim, if morality is socially constituted, philosophical anthropology is undercut.

To add more confusion, Segundo understands faith as "the fund of saved energy on which all human planning is based." In addition to this technocratic image of faith, Segundo's attempt to link this conception of faith to his overarching theory of evolution—with its desirable homeostatic mechanisms and the "best energy calculus"—is utterly unconvincing. Owing to his imprecise and amorphous definitions of faith, it is difficult to follow his comparative criticisms of Pannenberg's notion of trust and Tracy's conception of religion.

In his discussion of faith, Segundo relies upon a pre-Wittgensteinian view of language. That is, in contrast to Wittgenstein's view that language constitutes our social world, Segundo holds that language expresses private worlds. In order to make clear how people "express in words their values-structure, their meaning-world," Segundo engages in some close readings of poems—especially Gustavo Adolfo Bécquer's famous *Rima.* After a rather idiosyncratic though interesting interpretation, Segundo highlights human "access, through the medium of language, to the vast, structured realm of meaning and values." This neo-Kantian vocabulary, found in Ernst Cassirer and Susanne K. Langer, is highly suspect. Yet, ironically, Segundo persists with this expressivist view of language even after invoking the work of the later Wittgenstein which precludes any such view. At this point one is forced to conclude that Segundo's intellectual project yields philosophical confusion.

Similar to Habermas, Segundo fears that meaning-structures (faith) are "structured in terms of efficacy (ideology) alone." That is, issues involving value are reduced to technical matters. And this fear is justified. But is not his own technocratic conception of faith a reduction of meaning to mere use, planning, and efficacy? If so, he promotes the very program he fears. Segundo rightly exposes the dimension of faith in modern and postmodern science—a point noted by David Hume and refined by Michael Polanyi—yet his means-ends mode of philosophical and political analysis reeks of technocratic rationality. Even John Dewey, no friend of modern Luddites like Martin Heidegger, grappled more seriously with the reductionist implications and managerial consequences of crude means-ends analyses.

The second and third parts of Segundo's book are much better than the first. The section on Christianity and Marxism is, though far from original, competent. His claims regarding Marx's rejection of philosophy for science and opposition to ontological materialism are persuasive. Yet his defense of Erich Fromm's claim that Marx put forward a philosophical anthropology—which is true for the early Marx but rejected by the later Marx—is perplexing. Segundo rightly suggests that the continuity between the early and later Marx consists of his "ideal conception of the human being." But does such an ideal constitute a philosophical anthropology? Does the mere possession of values mean that one adheres to a philosophical anthropology? Surely not. So why defend Fromm's exorbitant claim?

The last section of Segundo's book is a sketch of "a Latin American anthropology"—a reading of Latin American realities from 1950 to 1975 in light of his philosophical perspective. After brief generalizations of the periods of consciousness raising, violent action, and repression, Segundo tries to go beyond mere economic and political analysis and accents "the ecological state of human beings" in relation to nature, the state, and class exploitation. He ends his book calling for the creation of "an effective cultural tradition"—a task to be achieved only if the supreme evolutionary quality, flexibility, is internalized and transmitted to the younger generation of freedom fighters.

In stark contrast to *The Liberation of Theology*, Segundo's *Faith and Ideologies* is more a phenomenon than an event, a symptom of the second alternative in the evolution of liberation theologies rather than a mover and shaker on the contemporary scene. His book illustrates the severe limitations of opting for a full-blown philosophical anthropology. And even if one decides to do so, it is better to revise already refined versions rather than create one's own out of thin air or derived from anthropologists and psychologists.

In my opinion, the major intellectual task of liberation theologians is to continue to reexamine and reshape the traditional doctrines of the church, engage in more serious efforts of social theory, cultural criticism, and historical reconstruction, and write palpable and intelligible essays and texts for the nonacademic literate laity and clergy. Needless to say, these three activities require different persons working on different terrains. The church theologians are not likely to put forward sophisticated social analyses, just as the more broadly engaged social theorist cannot possibly do justice to the complexities of church theology—though both can write for a wider audience.

Furthermore, if liberation theologies have taught us anything, it is that Christian thinkers must be organically linked with prophetic churches and progressive movements. An uncommitted and detached liberation theologian is a contradiction in terms. Without some form of ecclesiastical and political praxis, critical consciousness becomes as sounding brass and theological reflection a tinkling cymbal.

On Franz Hinkelammert's
The Ideological Weapons of Death

Liberation theology at its best is a worldly theology—a theology that not only opens our eyes to the social misery of the world but also teaches us better to understand and transform it. Academic theology in the first world, true to its priestly role, remains preoccupied with doctrinal precision and epistemological pretension. It either refuses to get its hands dirty with the ugly and messy affairs of contemporary politics or pontificates at a comfortable distance about the shortcomings of theoretical formulations and practical proposals of liberation theologians. Yet for those Christians deeply enmeshed in and united with poor peoples' struggles, theology is first and foremost concerned with urgent issues of life and death, especially the circumstances that dictate who lives and who dies.

Franz Hinkelammert's *The Ideological Weapons of Death* marks a new point of departure for liberation theology. First, it is the first product of a unique institutional setting—the renowned Departmento Ecumenico de Investigaciones (DEI) in San Jose, Costa Rica—that is intentionally interdisciplinary and explicitly political. Shunning the narrow confines of the intellectual division of labor in academic institutions, DEI rejects the compartmentalized disciplines of our bureaucratized seminaries and divinity schools. Instead DEI promotes and encourages theological reflection that traverses the fields of political economy, biblical studies, social theory, church history, and social ethics. In this way, DEI reveals the intellectual impoverishment of academic theologies that enact ostrichlike exercises in highly specialized sand—with little view to the pressing problems confronting ordinary people in our present period of crisis.

Second, Hinkelammert's book is significant in that it tries to ground liberation theology itself in a more detailed social-analytical viewpoint and a more developed biblical perspective. For too long liberation theologians have simply invoked Marxist theory without a serious examination of Marx's own most fecund analysis of capitalist society—namely, his analysis of fetishism. As Georg Lukács noted in his influential book, *History and Class Consciousness* (1923), the Marxist analysis of fetishism in *Capital* brings to light the hidden and concealed effects of commodity relations in the everyday lives of people in capitalist societies. These

From the Foreword to the Orbis edition, 1986.

effects result from the power-laden character and class-ridden structure of capitalist societies which make relations between people appear as relations between things. This deceptive appearance presents capitalist realities as natural and eternal. A Marxist analysis of this veil of appearance discloses these realities to be transient historical products and results of provisional social struggles.

Hinkelammert's book takes as its point of analytical departure the three central stages of Marx's analysis of fetishism—the commodity fetishism, money fetishism, and capital fetishism. The magical power people ascribe to commodities produced, money acquired, and capital expanded has idolatrous status in capitalist societies—a status not only rarely questioned but, more important, hardly analyzed and understood by Christians. Too often Christians merely condemn seductive materialism or pervasive hedonism with little or no grasp of the complex relations of the conditions under which commodities are produced, the ways in which money is acquired, and the means by which capital is expanded. Positing these complex relations as objects of theological reflection is unheard of in contemporary first world theology. Yet, if theologians are to come to terms with life-and-death issues of our time, there is no escape from reflecting upon and gaining an understanding of these complex relations.

Such a monumental step requires a grounding in the history of economic thought and contemporary social theory. In this regard, working knowledge of the classical economic theories of Adam Smith and David Ricardo, the neoclassical economic formulations of Alfred Marshall and Stanley Jevons, the intricate debates between followers of Karl Marx, Max Weber, and Émile Durkheim in social theory, and the present-day viewpoints of Milton Friedman, Paul Samuelson, and Ernest Mandel become requisite for serious theological engagement with the burning life-and-death issues of our day. Needless to say, the immediate intellectual risk is a debilitating dilettantism that obfuscates rather than illuminates. Yet to refuse the risk is to settle for an arid academicism that values professional status and career ambitions at the expense of trying to lay bare the richness of the Christian gospel for our time. Therefore Hinkelammert's text may seem strange to first world Christians—with his analyses of the links between Milton Friedman's thought to the economic policies of the Chilean dictator Pinochet or his critique of the Trilateral Commission's recommendations for the third world. In fact, many first world academic theologians may balk at such exercises that seem to fall outside more tame theological investigations. Yet, it should be apparent after reading Hinkelammert's text that he simply is attempting to come to terms with the array of ideological weapons of death deployed against the wretched of the earth—and the books and blueprints of academic and political elites are not spared.

His critiques also apply to contemporary biblical scholarship in the first world. This culturally homogeneous guild of highly trained yet narrowly socialized academicians have, in many ways, yet to enter the postmodern age of epistemological disarray, cultural upheaval, and ideological contestation. This guild remains the last bastion of first world male hegemony over the methods and results of a branch of theological investigations. Most biblical scholars remain uncritically and unjustifiably wedded to sophisticated models of research—models that emerged from problematics of a bygone period. Hinkelammert boldly contests the complacency of this guild by putting forward a highly controversial and provocative reading of Pauline conceptions of life and death in light of his own analysis of fetishism. Whatever one's views are on the complexity of Pauline theology, this perspective cannot but broaden the conversation in New Testament studies and thereby deepen our readings of Paul's letters.

Last, Hinkelammert examines the implications of his views on modern Catholic thought. Recent pastoral letters from the Catholic and Methodist churches in the USA have alerted us to the crucial role of denominational pronouncements on social and political issues. These pronouncements cannot be fully understood without some knowledge of the history of the churches' social teachings. This is especially so in regard to the issue of private property—an often uncritically examined cornerstone of much of these teachings. As Hinkelammert notes, the aim is not simply to substitute socialist notions of property for earlier conceptions of private property, but rather to interrogate the very act of hypostasizing property as such. Historical questions concerning how private property became an unquestioned presupposition of Christian social ethics, the relation of churches to social systems based on slave and wage labor, and theoretical issues about the relation of conceptions of personhood to private property and the links between slaves and women to rights of property possession loom large here.

Hinkelammert's book provides neither full-fledged solutions nor panaceas to the broad range of issues it raises. Rather, it is a groundbreaking work-in-progress that alerts us to contemporary forms of captivity to which most first world theologies are bound. Like the first wave of liberation theologies from Latin America, Asia, Africa, and first world women and minorities (especially Afro-Americans), his book opens new discursive space in our theological work. The seriousness with which Hinkelammert takes Marxist analyses of fetishism, biblical studies, modern Catholic social ethics, and the current shortcomings of liberation theologies indeed may initiate a second wave—I hope a tidal wave—that fundamentally transforms how we do theology and act out our precious Christian faith.

On Sharon D. Welch's Communities of Resistance and Solidarity

As we move toward the end of the twentieth century, the crisis in liberal theology deepens. Modern theological claims regarding the knowledge and reality of God remain problematic at best and downright unconvincing at worst. Debate over appropriate theological methods is bogged down in the seemingly irreconcilable differences in approach between liberal theology and the various versions of liberation theology. Meanwhile, theological education leaves most Christian teachers and preachers ill-equipped to engage complex issues of social and political theory and economics in an informed and intelligent manner. In the process pressing political challenges remain unmet.

Liberal theology, with its noble aim of taking seriously the many dimensions of modern experience, is in crisis primarily because it has failed to do so. While celebrating the grand achievements of the modern era, it has not come to grips with the *underside* of that experience. As Marx, Nietzsche, Freud, De Beauvoir, and Du Bois have taught us, modernity is not marked solely by the triumph of science and technology, the expansion of liberal capitalist democracy, and the proliferation of cultural pluralism. It includes also the extension of new forms of planetary destruction and bureaucratic surveillance, blatant kinds of state repression and imperialist exploitation, and various types of racism, patriarchy, and homophobia.

It is not as if liberal theology ignores these manifestations. But rather than make them central to its theological inquiry, it relegates them to the category of "practical theology" and then goes on with the "serious" business of justifying its truth-claims about God. It is no accident, therefore, that the initial reaction of most liberal theologians to liberation theology was to confine it to the "practical fields" within the seminary curriculum. Yet the moral and political challenges of liberation theologians will not go away—not so much because their arguments are convincing but because the "underside" of modernity, which the liberationists

From *Christianity and Crisis* (Oct. 14, 1985); review of Sharon D. Welch, *Communities of Resistance and Solidarity: A Feminist Theology of Liberation* (Maryknoll, N.Y.: Orbis, 1985).

207

address, more and more affects and influences our lives, our societies, our theologies, and our churches.

Sharon Welch's new book courageously and intelligently speaks to this present situation—this dangling between the insights and blindnesses of the past and the dreams and possible holocausts of a future era. It is, moreover, unique in that it attempts to speak candidly to both the "old" liberals and the "new" liberationists.

This "double-identity" is openly acknowledged in Welch's self-description as a "feminist, white, middle-class, American Christian theologian—oppressed by patriarchy yet participant in oppressive structures of race, class, and national identity." Following the seminal yet controversial work of the late Michel Foucault (whose explicit gay orientation and death allegedly from AIDS in June 1984 are surprisingly never mentioned), Welch claims that Western knowledge is undergoing a shift. We are moving away from a model of knowledge that highlights science and historical teleology and toward a model that emphasizes the politics of scientific inquiry and the clash of cultural traditions in history. This shift results in a wholesale nihilism, skepticism, and relativism, and a concomitant stress on practices, on the consequences and effects of human action. The crucial intellectual battles of the day, therefore, are no longer over Truth but rather over the production of truths—and this truth-production is a fully historical and political affair. That is, we do not passively accept the Truth from a static past, but rather we contribute to the creation of new truths by reinterpreting old truths of dynamic traditions in light of new circumstances and challenges. The new model highlights historical consciousness, societal transformation, and political engagement.

Welch argues that the rise of liberation theologies exemplifies this shift in models. Liberation theologies constitute what Foucault terms an "insurrection of subjugated knowledges." That is, oppressed people in opposition to the dominant theories of the theological establishment are pointing out the limitations and shortcomings of the traditions upon which mainstream theologians rely. By delving into the past and present experiences of women, Africans, Hispanics, gays, lesbians, and Indians, liberation theologians unearth suppressed traditions and cast new light on old ones.

It is in this context that Welch sets forth her own feminist liberation theology. Her perspective differs from other feminist theologies in that she accepts Foucault's historical relativism; that is, she holds that "truth" is more a product of political power and practice than rational argument. On this view, rational argument is a rhetorical strategy in the quest for power. In fact, Welch goes so far as to reject both Scripture and the person and work of Jesus as grounds for her theology. Rather, she justifies her viewpoint by appeal to the practices and experiences of communities of faith struggling against sexism and other forms of oppression. Instead of invoking prophetic ideals in the Scriptures or marginal prophetic groups in the Christian tradition, Welch employs explicit political and practical standards from and for the present. Hence, her ecclesiology follows "not denominational but political divisions."

Welch tries to speak to the central concerns of the "old" liberals by conceiving of liberating practice as "both a hermeneutic key and a means of verification." In other words, concrete actions against oppression provide the proper context for interpreting the Christian tradition and the ultimate test for authentic Christian faith. Yet she harbors great skepticism about the possibilities of historical fulfillment of such liberating practice. She supports the "new" liberationists, but she remains preoccupied with "the paucity of resistance" among poor persons and the unlikelihood that they will win. This uneasy conjoining of historical consciousness, skepticism, and a political "leap of commitment" yields a tragic radical stance on the margins of activist Christian communities.

Struggling with Skepticism

Welch's book is courageous in that it articulates for religious readers the deep sense of pessimism among academic intellectuals with progressive convictions, historicist sensibilities, and skeptical epistemologies. Her gallant struggle with this predicament is quite poignant.

In the end, however, Welch's stance leaves us wanting. It does not hang together enough to persuade or sustain us. This is so because Welch does not take seriously enough her key notion, "practice."

As Ernst Troeltsch and John Dewey—two pertinent figures absent in her text—suggested years ago, a wholesale historicism leads to at least four possible responses: a paralyzing skepticism, a "might makes right" cynicism, an unacknowledged intuitionism, or a critical self-situating contextualism. Welch rightly rejects an immobilizing skepticism. At times, she leans toward cynicism, but she refuses unequivocally to affirm it. Rather than opt for the fourth alternative, however, she adopts a form of intuitionism—what she calls "a pretheoretical commitment to the oppressed." Welch's stance amounts to a belief that certain truths—in this case the claims of the oppressed—are self-evident and thereby require acceptance prior to theoretical scrutiny. Her intuitionism is almost an *a priori* allegiance to a political form of confessionalism, to the belief that fundamental convictions are less than authentic if they are the result of or motivated by rational argument. But since Welch's intuitionist/confessional political commitment is neither self-evident nor singular, she must give good reasons for it. Ideological fideism will not suffice. Furthermore, reasons couched in historical narratives and social analyses will sustain vital communities and possibly persuade those outside only as long as they can be justifed to oneself and those within one's context; that is, only as long as there is a critical self-situating within the language of a struggling community. Practice possesses a reflective *and* activist component. To overlook the critical and theoretical aspects of practice is to miss its dialectical character. It is to reduce practice to customary habit or egoistic impulse.

Yet Welch is highly suspicious of such communal language because she believes it easily leads to universal discourse, absolutist values, and ahistorical grounding of beliefs. She holds that such discourse, values, and grounding are the language "of the privileged" and are "intrinsically correlated with oppression." I find this claim philosophically unconvincing, but, more important, it is demonstrably unwarranted. If one examines the *practices* of the resistance movements of the oppressed (Christian or non-Christian), one finds that the critiques of the present and their visions of the future are usually put forward in universal discourses, absolute values, and ahistorical grounding of beliefs.

In fact, the use of universal discourse by the privileged to mask oppression is a modern affair enacted by the European bourgeoisies who could not resort to the kinds of particularistic justifications for oppression used by past kings, lords, patriarchs, and slaveholders. It is skepticism that has constituted a major stance of the disaffected privileged: some kind of privilege is required to deal with *and remain in* the deep horror of the absurd. Most ordinary people struggling within and against oppression tend not to adopt skeptical outlooks. We middle-class intellectuals, therefore, may entertain skeptical views about the status of universal and absolutist claims, but we must bring *enabling* forms of criticism to the communities of faith and struggle we inhabit. And to link *all* forms of universalism and absolutism to domination is to overlook how some such forms have and can morally regulate and politically mobilize people to resist domination. In other words, critique is the major task of intellectuals, but it is never an end in itself. Rather, it is inseparable from, though not reducible to, practical strategies for greater human freedom.

For Welch, primary evidence of truth rests on "successful historical actualization." On those grounds, she concludes that "Christianity has failed." It is at this point that I find her theology too thin, her faith too fragile, and her sense of struggle too abstract. A theology of worldly skepticism and liberation commitments without genuine openness to ameliorative historical possibilities and/or transhistorical hopes amounts to excessive skepticism with a pessimistic twist I refuse to accept. A faith based solely on contemporary struggle for liberation is too presentist and unmindful of unpredictable future developments. And a sense of struggle that focuses more on the improbability of ultimate triumph than on the necessity and possibility of gaining the next penultimate victory reflects a distance from practical engagement that can never disarm skepticism. For is not the alternative for victims sheer insanity and a hopeless living death?

And yet, Welch's tragic radical viewpoint might be true. If so, we are all the worse for it since we can do little about it. If not, we are much the better for her sobering book: now we can go about our prophetic liberationist Christian work with a deeper sense of urgency and hope.

On Harvey Cox's
Religion in the Secular City

In his revealing poem "The Grande Chartreuse" (1855), the exemplary bourgeois humanist Matthew Arnold portrayed the crisis of modernity as "Wandering between two worlds, one dead/The other powerless to be born." The proponents of the most powerful critique of bourgeois humanism—Karl Marx and Friedrich Nietzsche—would have agreed, with some qualifications, with Arnold's statement. All three figures pointed out what they perceived as the decay and decadence in modernity and projected alternatives for renewal and regeneration.

Arnold's bourgeois humanism—which conjoined the neoclassicism of the Enlightenment with the historical progressivism of German Romanticism—highlighted the sanctity of individual achievement, the hope for incremental change, and the fear of social instability; that is, values and sensibilities held by the enlightened elements of the literate middle class. His grand effort to reduce Christianity to moral sentiments and inspiring poetry echoes the project of liberal theology. Arnold's perennial fear was the cosmic absurdity and nihilistic hedonism that often surfaced in his intellectual hero, Heinrich Heine, just as the Achilles' heel of liberal theology was its refusal to take seriously tragedy, dread, and despair. Yet bourgeois humanism and its religious sidekick, liberal theology, are neither dead nor dormant. Rather, they have been updated, as in Lionel Trilling's criticism or Schubert Ogden's theology, or reformulated, as with Thomas Nagel in philosophy or David Tracy in theology.

Marxism, like liberation theology, is a distinctive response to modernity which both extends and subverts bourgeois humanism (and liberal theology). Like Arnold, Marx refuses to succumb to catastrophic nihilism and complacent cynicism. Instead, he promotes even more utopian hopes—hopes for full-scale societal transformation. Such social projects of liberation are attractive to those on the margins of modernity, especially those who are victimized by modern structures of domination. Revolutionary Marxism extends bourgeois humanism in that it retains the aura of human achievements in history; it subverts bourgeois humanism because conscienticized groups rather than cultivated individuals become the major agents for social change. In this sense, Her-

From *Christianity and Crisis* (Feb. 20, 1984); review of Harvey Cox, *Religion in the Secular City: Toward a Postmodern Theology* (New York: Simon and Schuster, 1984).

bert Marcuse's Marxism is to F. R. Leavis's moralism what Gustavo Gutiérrez's liberation theology is to Walter Rauschenbusch's social gospel—similar in motivation, yet radically different in orientation.

Nietzsche's critique of modernity is the beginning of something new, though not necessarily better. His deconstruction of history, including quests for liberation in history, undermines the projects of Arnold and Marx, Rauschenbusch and Gutiérrez. With this move, we have the early stirrings of postmodern sentiments. To put it crudely, Nietzsche's move flattens out latent depths into manifest surfaces, underlying harmonies into contingent quandaries, emerging unities into dispersed differences, and pregnant paradoxes into random incongruities. Postmodern artistic strategies of play, performance, and silence (such as the works of Beckett, Nabokov, and Cage) enact these sentiments. Yet Nietzsche never fully accepted the consequences of his critique. He kept one foot in modernity. Like his rebellious student, Martin Heidegger, Nietzsche heralded some form of enhancement for a select few. Only Jacques Derrida's poststructuralism follows through on Nietzsche's postmodern perspective.

With the emergence and evolution of late capitalist culture—the culture of consumption, shot through with corporate domination, managerial norms, and polymorphous selves in search of therapeutic release—Nietzsche's profound postmodern sentiments are vulgarly packaged and fed to a relatively passive consumer populace. In this sense, Nietzsche's catastrophic nihilism and Derrida's barren skepticism surreptitiously regulate and legitimate the pervasive narcissism and hedonism of postmodern culture.

There is no doubt that we are living in a transitional period. The old authority of science is now undergoing demythologization and demystification. The prevailing institutions of oppression, such as state repression, class exploitation, patriarchy, and racism, are under severe attack. And the premodern bastions of socialization, churches and families, are changing rapidly. The quest for an appropriate Christian response to this complex and confusing situation sits at the top of the theological agenda.

Harvey Cox's *Religion in the Secular City* is a significant and serious example of such a response. First, his perspective is a global one which acknowledges the demographic dwarfing of the North Atlantic societies and the relative eclipse of modern Euro-American theological frameworks. Needless to say, this dwarfing does not preclude economic dependence and this eclipse should not prescribe intellectual insularity. Cox takes seriously third world critiques of first world theologies which conceal their particularity, in form and content, behind self-professed universality and hide specific problems beneath general problematics. Cox is a reliable guide through the labyrinthine postmodern situation because he and Christian communities. And he neither denigrates nor romanticizes these life-worlds. He rightly views acceptable responses to postmodernity as those that creatively build upon, rather than naively reject, the modern sensibilities of critical consciousness and intellectual clarity.

A Saving Hope

Yet it is important to note that Cox's response to postmodernity is put forward by a leading *modern* theologian. His own modern and Christian prejudices—such as the quest for hope, liberation, and deliverance—lead him to highlight primarily those possibilities that lend themselves to such a quest, for example, basic Christian communities in the Americas, Europe, Africa, and Asia. From the perspective of Nietzsche and Derrida, it is this quest itself that is, in part, responsible for our woes and hence worthy of rejection. At this point, the distinction between "postmodern" as an adjective describing a historical period and "postmodern" as a term for a set of cultural sentiments looms large. Fortunately, Cox's response to our postmodern situation is a modern Christian response, not a postmodern one. Hence, he realizes we must confront, characterize, and understand our postmodern situation in light of the best of our modern and Christian traditions.

What I find missing in Cox's challenging text is precisely that with which Arnold spent his life struggling: the tenacity of the nation-state and the entrenched and educated middle classes who help sustain it. Like Marx and Nietzsche, Cox has few insights regarding these two crucial modern phenomena which carry over into postmodernity. Yet a theological perspective that does not speak adequately of the state or to the middle classes can be neither relevant to our time nor pertinent to realizable liberation projects. This absence also reinforces the image of prophetic intellectuals as free-floating individuals rather than progressive petit bourgeois persons who are intentionally marginal to their own middle-class group. Cox indeed is quite aware of this matter, but the theoretical challenge of postmodern theorists of the state and intellectuals like Michel Foucault, and the practical obstacles which impede more effective resistance, require his and our attention.

Postmodernity confronts us as a frightening and dangerous world. Yet, even before possible nuclear annihilation, the world was frightening and dangerous. The Christian response is neither conservative escapism which refuses to come to terms with new realities, nor Jacobin enthusiasm which tosses out tradition and apes contemporary perspectives. Rather, as Cox suggests, we must preserve the Christian notions of struggle and hope, refine analytical tools that discern structural and personal forms of dehumanization, and be not despairing of present troubles, even postmodern ones.

On Leszek Kolakowski's Religion

Leszek Kolakowski is a unique and fascinating figure on the American intellectual scene. Born in Poland, he was expelled from Warsaw University in 1968 owing to his self-styled humanist Marxism and oppositional political commitments—represented in his influential book, *Towards a Marxist Humanism*. His writings cover a broad range of subjects, from Spinoza, Husserl, Anglo-American positivism, and seventeenth-century sectarian movements to his recent controversial three-volume history of Marxist thought. He also has written three books of tales and some plays.

Since the early seventies, Kolakowski has energetically and persistently defended religious experience within the secular world of English-speaking highbrow intellectual culture. In valuable contributions to *Encounter, London Times Literary Supplement, Salmagundi* and numerous other periodicals, he has tried to convince his peers that religious insights are indispensable for understanding the major events of this century.

In his book *Religion: If There Is No God . . . On God, the Devil, Sin and Other Worries of the So-called Philosophy of Religion* (Oxford, 1982), Kolakowski makes his strongest case for religious experience. Although the book appears in Frank Kermode's *Masterguides* series and is intended to be an introductory treatment of the discipline of philosophy of religion, Kolakowski puts a deeply personal stamp on it. In fact, the book is not so much a standard introduction to philosophy of religion; rather, it is a collection of philosophical fragments on being religious. The text indeed provides illuminating encounters with classical perspectives in the Western and Eastern traditions of religious thought. But it also contains brilliant existential insights and words of wisdom about life. There are few sustained positive philosophical arguments primarily because Kolakowski spends much time attempting to show why philosophical arguments are inappropriate for understanding religious experience. In short, this text is in the tradition of Montaigne, Pascal, and Kierkegaard not Descartes, Kant, and Hegel.

For Kolakowski, the primary task of philosophy of religion is neither rationally to ground particular religious beliefs nor comprehensively to

From *Old Westbury Review* (fall 1986); review of Leszek Kolakowski, *Religion* (Oxford: Oxford University Press, 1982).

systematize existing religious doctrines. Rather, the role of the philosopher of religion is to preserve the integrity and irreducibility of forms of "socially established worship of eternal reality," that is, religion. This task of preservation entails sidestepping the dilemmas created by both religious liberals and fundamentalists and showing how the major religions speak to the most basic feature of human existence, namely, the need to cope with powerlessness, helplessness, weakness, and frailty.

Kolakowski does not believe that philosophical inquiry can persuade or dissuade one from adopting particular religious worldviews. But rational discourse can help in pointing out what is at stake in adopting one worldview over another.

> I rather tend to accept the law of the infinite cornucopia which applies not only to philosophy but to all general theories in the human and social sciences: it states that there is never a shortage of arguments to support any doctrine you want to believe in for whatever reasons. These arguments, however, are not entirely barren. They have helped in elucidating the *status quaestionis* and in explaining why these questions matter, and this is what I am concerned with here. (P. 16)

What is ultimately at stake is one's sanity; that is, the ability to make sense of a deeply tragic and flawed existence without succumbing to meaninglessness and hopelessness. Kolakowski's defense of religious experience holds that human beings must learn how to be failures and how to cry for help while acknowledging that this very capacity to learn and wisdom to cry out is a form of empowerment from a Reality greater than human beings that keeps people struggling and living. The major foes are self-deception, for example, forms of happiness which are really types of bad faith, and self-deification, for example, the refusal to acknowledge the need for divine help or aid.

From the vantage point of this Augustinian framework, Kolakowski examines the question of evil in the world, the various gods of the philosophers, mystical traditions in Christianity, Judaism, Islam, and Eastern religions, the relation between fear of death and religious faith, and the uniqueness of the language of the Sacred within the context of worship. Kolakowski is most provocative and profound on the issues of theodicy and mysticism. Both sections are powerful *tours de force* in and of themselves.

Kolakowski links the religious conception of learning how to be a failure yet avoiding insanity to God's inability to commit suicide. This crucial divine inability (even Nietzsche has God killed by humans!) confines evil to a separation from God—that is, Sin—that is moral, not ontological. The world is viewed as essentially good yet existentially evil.

On this Christian view, a deep sense of the tragic is required, yet the world is not inherently tragic.

For religious traditions, be they Christian, Islamic, Buddhist or whatever, the problem of evil cannot be "solved" or even understood theoretically. Rather, it can only be met with a practical response: trust God or go insane. This basic trust or confidence is based neither on an objective reading of history nor the workings of nature. Rather, it is an unconditional trust, a nonfalsifiable assent that insures continued sanity, that is, meaning and hope. In other words, some form of such trust is requisite for psychic health, yet there are no philosophical grounds for such trust.

> To summarize this part of the discussion: an acceptance of the world as a divinely ordered cosmos wherein everything is given a meaning is neither self-contradictory nor inconsistent with empirical knowledge, and yet it can never be a consequence of such knowledge, however vastly expanded. Both moral evil and human suffering, including everybody's inevitable failure in life, can be accepted and mentally absorbed, but it would be preposterous to pretend that, starting with the terrifying chaos of life, we can, as a result of logically admissible procedures, end up with a cosmos full of sense and of purpose. The act of faith and trust in God has to precede the ability to see His hand in the course of events and in the sadness of human history. In brief: *credo ut intelligam.* (Pp. 53-54)

Kolakowski highlights the anthropocentric character of Judaic and Christian thought on evil and suffering. Eastern traditions affirm the unity and sanctity of all life whereas Jews and Christians uphold the dignity of human life while promoting the human right to master and exploit nonhuman organisms, especially animals. Furthermore, the Christian perspective implies that there is some unredeemable evil, that some forms of suffering and hardship stand outside the domain of redemption and punishment. In this regard, the absurdity of the world or insanity in life seeps in even from a religious (in this case, Christian) perspective.

In the section on mysticism, Kolakowski reaches an interesting conclusion: "that it is not inconsistent or monstrous to be a sceptic and a mystic at the same time" (p. 145). In epistemological matters, both skeptic and mystic claim that knowledge is essentially a practical not cognitive affair; that is, silence is the appropriate response to whether we can really know that we know, yet since out of necessity we must speak and act knowledge becomes a tool to cope with reality, not a mirror which depicts reality.

Kolakowski's experiential attitude and skeptical approach to religious experience would seem to imply that he is either a closet pragmatist stripped of the privileging of the scientific method in all cognitive matters or a full-blown conventionalist informed by a sociology of knowledge. Yet one would be wrong to accept such implications. Kolakowski indeed possesses a deep sense of historical contingency and a critical disposition toward all philosophical traditions. But he also is fearful of relativism, nihilism, and cynicism. At moments in his text he moves toward a philosophical transcendentalism in order to defend the possibility of God's existence. At the heart of the book, he claims,

> I will try to argue for the following, quasi-Cartesian assertion: Dostoyevski's famous dictum, "If there is no God, everything is permissible," is valid not only as a moral rule but also as an epistemological principle. This means that the legitimate use of the concept "truth" or the belief that "truth" may even be justifiably predicted of our knowledge is possible only on the assumption of an absolute Mind. (P. 82)

> Thus I follow the Cartesian formula insofar as it asserts that human claims to truth are empty without reference to the divine being. No reference to God's veracity is thereby implied; but I admit that the predicate "true" has no meaning unless referred to the all-encompassing truth, which is equivalent to an absolute mind. The transcendental approach is thus far vindicated.
>
> The argument has nothing to do however with the proofs of God's reality: it can neither reinforce nor enfeeble any of the arguments in existence. Its aim is not to show that God does exist, but to expose the dilemma which we seem to face when we cope with the question of truth and of the very possibility of an epistemology: either God or a cognitive nihilism, there is nothing in between. (Pp. 90-91)

Yet he finally must reject any such philosophical transcendentalism since we have no access to an Archimedean point which would permit us to adjudicate rationally between the conflicting perspectives.

> My point is negative: since we have no key to the treasury of transcendental rationality, all restrictions imposed on the implicit everyday criteria of meaning are royal commands issued *ex nihilo* by philosophers and carry no other legitimacy; they are enforceable only to the extent of the philosophers' sheer power. (P. 164)

I suggest that Kolakowski's struggle between the Scylla of transcendentalism and the Charybdis of nihilism yields a unique philosophical position—a religious form of cultural ontology which shuns a glib objectivism and stresses the contingency of human cultural practices yet which holds out for convergence and unity in the long run. This convergence and unity is not simply a regulative ideal but rather features of a humanly incomprehensible God. Like Charles Pierce's conservative version of pragmatism (and similar to Hilary Putnam's recent work), Kolakowski wants to preserve a bedrock notion of Reality and Truth by means of an eschatology. Unlike Pierce and Putnam, his eschatology is not a matter of the scientific community ultimately grasping Truth, that is, convergence as rational agreement, but rather of religious persons ultimately "being in Truth," that is, convergence as existential deliverance. I find the makings of such a viewpoint in the following statements.

Jesus's saying that the truth will make us free does not mean that the mastery of technical skills will lead to a desirable result; for Him, and for all great religious teachers, people realize the nature of their bondage in the same act of illumination that includes the means of shaking it off and the understanding of the divinely ordained destiny of the world. . . .

No philosophical speculation can perform this task. In spite of the claims of philosophical transcendentalism it is only by reference to the all-knowing and eternal mind that the convergence of goals and knowledge is attainable. . . .

It would be utterly wrong to infer from the foregoing discussion that the conflict between the Reason of the Enlightenment and religious certitudes or, on a larger scale, between the Profane and the Sacred, may be in my view explained in terms of logical mistakes, conceptual confusion or misconceived ideas about borderlines between knowledge and faith. Such an approach would appear to me grotesquely inadequate. The conflict is cultural, not logical, and it is arguably rooted in the persistent, irreconcilable claims imposed on us by various forces within human nature. . . . Do we have to do with an accidental collision or rather with a fundamental conflict which might have remained latent here and there yet was bound to emerge as a result of the sheer growth in human abilities to master the world?

The factual elements which are required to answer such a question would encompass the complete history of all religions, whereas its unavoidable speculative components must necessarily be derived from the ontology of culture. (Pp. 219, 220, 224)

This embryonic religious version of cultural ontology builds on the best of the skeptical, pragmatic, and historicist traditions, without succumbing to theoretical self-contradiction or internal inconsistency. It is neither tied to a particular religious set of doctrines nor even confined to Western forms of religiosity—yet it preserves the integrity and irreducibility of religious experience.

I find this perspective highly attractive. Yet I remain unconvinced that this view can do anything more than project possible kinds of convergence and unity—hence function essentially as regulative ideals. Favoring Dewey's version of pragmatism over that of Pierce, I hold that there can be no ontological assurance of convergence and unity without our reading into cultural practices the very projected convergence and unity presupposed by our own perspectives, that is, vicious circularity. So all we can have, as cultural agents and historical beings, is regulative ideals of convergence and unity dependent on our own perspectives. This view still avoids vulgar relativism and nihilism, but it stops short of any sort of ontology. It keeps us in history and culture without history and culture—as Kolakowski rightly desires—disposing and casting our dignity and worth "in the wanton and boundless sea of chance." In this way, Kolakowski helps us deepen the historicist turn in philosophy of religion while holding on to the profound insights of the multiple religious traditions of humankind.

On Nicholas Lash's
A Matter of Hope

Anglo-American Christian thought rarely has taken the Marxist tradition seriously. The exemplary texts of English-speaking Christian socialists— George Washington Woodbey's *The Bible and Socialism* (1904), Walter Rauschenbusch's *Christianity and the Social Crisis* (1907), Vida Scudder's *Socialism and Character* (1912), Reinhold Niebuhr's *Moral Man and Immoral Society* (1932), John C. Bennett's *Social Salvation* (1935), John Macmurray's *Creative Society* (1936), Harry Ward's *Democracy and Social Change* (1940), F. O. Matthiessen's *From the Heart of Europe* (1948), Alasdair MacIntyre's *Marxism: An Interpretation* (1953), Charles West's *Communism and the Theologians* (1958), and Terence Eagleton's *The New Left Church* (1966)—fail to engage in a sustained examination of Marx and Engels. These valuable works often employ Marxist insights, but (with the slight exception of MacIntyre) they do not confront the primary Marxist sources with care and caution. Instead, Anglo-American Christian socialists have tended to regard Marxism more as an antiquated intellectual system akin to those of Hobbes and Malthus than as a vibrant cultural legacy comparable to that of Freud or Nietzsche.

Furthermore, these texts are silent regarding the sophisticated versions of Marxism put forward in Antonio Labriola's *Socialism and Philosophy* (1907), Georg Lukács's *History and Class Consciousness* (1923), or Karl Korsch's *Marxism and Philosophy* (1925). Labriola's penetrating critique of mechanical materialism and vulgar economism would have corrected many of the Christians' misleading associations of narrow determinism with Marxism. Lukács's provocative claim that cultural life in capitalist society is pervaded by dehumanization would have provided fertile ground for refined Christian-Marxist dialogue. Instead, such ground did not emerge until the 1960s with the translations of Marx's manuscripts of 1844—his writings on alienation. Lukács's book was not translated until 1971! Korsch's powerful critique of the metaphysical monism of orthodox Marxism and the managerial elitism of Leninist politics would have preempted many standard Christian rejections of Marxism.

From *Christianity and Crisis* (Apr. 18, 1983); review of Nicholas Lash, *A Matter of Hope: A Theologian's Reflections on the Thought of Karl Marx* (Notre Dame, Ind.: University of Notre Dame Press, 1982).

This failure and silence are symptomatic not only of intellectual insularity among prophetic Christian intellectuals; they also exemplify the thick walls of demarcation between progressive Christian activists and socialist movements in Britain and the United States. In short, there have been (and are) no Anglo-American Christian socialists comparable to Germany's Paul Tillich, Helmut Gollwitzer, and Dorothee Sölle, India's M. M. Thomas, Brazil's Hugo Assmann, or Peru's Gustavo Gutiérrez. This is so primarily because the indigenous forms of radicalism in Britain and the U.S. veer far from Marxist theory and practice.

In Britain, working-class deference to ruling authorities and middle-class allegiance to aristocratic sensibilities have left little space for Marxist influence. For example, visible opposition to capitalist Britain has been led mainly by Fabian socialists such as Sidney and Beatrice Webb or British Labor party leaders like Anthony Crosland who owed more to the radical libertarianism of John Stuart Mill and the subversive traditionalism of William Morris than to the revolutionary vision of Karl Marx. In the U.S., the ethnic and racial heterogeneity of the working class, deep loyalty to the two-party system, and unprecedented economic growth have confined populist, black, feminist, and labor movements to programs of correcting the abuses within capitalist society rather than to projects of fundamentally transforming this society.

The consequences of this refusal to take Marxism seriously have been twofold. First, they have imposed constraints on public discourse regarding the future of these societies, including the social visions of their churches. By confining the available options to either liberal reform or conservative austerity (both of which ignore the basic problems of structural unemployment, prison overcrowding, ecological imbalance, sexual freedom, racist violence, and third world impoverishment), political despair and disillusionment set in. Such lethargy may take the form of apathy, crime, or corruption; but its content is a seething dissatisfaction that could burst through the brittle social fabrics of Britain and the U.S. The major prophetic challenge of our time is to provide religious vision, moral guidance, and organizational structure for these eruptive forces— more prisons, more police, and more military recruitment will not suffice.

Second, refusal to take Marxism seriously has contributed to the deterioration of Anglo-American intellectual life. The demoralization within the Academy is quite apparent: intense careerism and professionalism mimicking technocratic bureaucracies conceal the paucity of intellectual visions. The deep crisis of political liberalism—still with us long after Barth and Niebuhr undermined theological liberalism—has rendered liberal education suspect. Yet the Anglo-American aversion to Marxism stifles open conversation and dialogue, thereby precluding possible growth and development. Marxism indeed has begun to acquire a foot-hold, but its defensiveness tends to render it pedantic and pedestrian. Only recently have seminaries and divinity schools caught up with this emerging Marxist renascence on the margins of academia, and typically seminarians grasp at the more moralistic varieties (e.g., Jurgen Haber-mas) or ape the more exotic versions (Latin American liberation the-ology). There have been few serious efforts to develop an indigenous Marxist analysis within a Christian framework.

This situation presents prophetic Christian intellectuals with a double challenge. First, a serious encounter with Marxist thought is required. Second, this encounter must uncover and delineate the strengths and weaknesses of Marxism in the light of British and American contexts. Nicholas Lash's *A Matter of Hope* is a gallant attempt to meet the first challenge. This book is an important beginning toward engaging Marx's thought. Its significance lies precisely in the care and caution he brings to bear on Marx's own texts. I often disagree with his particular inter-pretations or his specific characterizations, but it is quite clear that he has confronted Marx with Christian candor and critical intelligence.

What is distinctive about this book is that it takes the reader by the hand and walks delicately through Marx's major texts with the guide of an uncompromising yet sympathetic Christian perspective. Lash as-sumes that he cannot only learn something from Marxism but, more im-portant, that he can strengthen his Christian faith (and his under-standing of his Christian faith) by scrutinizing Marx's texts. For example, Marx's historical materialism led him to ponder the radical in-carnational implications of Christianity, the seriousness with which Christians ought to take history—and these reflections send him to Wil-liam Temple's formulations of "Christian materialism." Lash's persuasive remarks regarding Marx's relative silence on the ultimate form of aliena-tion—death itself—impels Marxists to reexamine the limited character and content of their notion of liberation. Finally, his contrasting inter-pretations of orthodox Marxist optimism, which sacrifices the present, bourgeois despair, which surrenders the future, and Christian hope, which draws from the past, remains engaged in the present, and is linked to an ever-invading future, are illuminating. This kind of face-to-face en-counter with the primary sources should prove refreshing both to Chris-tians who uncritically appropriate Marxism and to those who prema-turely eschew it.

The major limitation of Lash's fine book is that it relies upon a rather selective British Marxist discourse. Lash acknowledges that even a direct reading of Marx requires some mediation by contemporary Marxist thinkers. Yet noteworthy Continental Marxist thinkers make only brief appearances in his book. Instead, Lash leans heavily upon the distinguished British Marxist E. P. Thompson, whose historical works are magisterial but whose theoretical inquiries are weak. The most important intervention in Marxist theory, that of Italy's Antonio Gramsci, is overlooked, hardly mentioned. Thompson is a "humanist" Marxist with strong empiricist leanings. But, as his provocative, yet tendentious, attack on the French Marxist Louis Althusser made clear (see *The Poverty of Theory*), Thompson's grasp of the subtlety and complexity of contemporary theoretical issues in Marxism is limited. Lash's distance from Gramsci's monumental work on the central role of culture, religion, and the state *(Prison Notebooks)* is surprising in light of the fact that some of the most pioneering recent neo-Gramscian work, especially that of Ernesto Laclau, Chantal Mouffe, and Bob Jessop, has been done in Britain.

This neo-Gramscian work is not only the most fruitful terrain for secular leftist intellectuals interested in the relation of race and gender analyses to Marxism; it also is the starting point for prophetic Christians who hold that religious life is a privileged site wherein the forces of liberation, liberalism, and reaction clash, where salvation, survival, and death struggle for primacy. Notwithstanding his omission of Gramsci, Lash's book quietly contributes to the clarifying of this struggle and prophetically points toward its Christian goal of abundant life.

On Paul Holmer's
The Grammar of Faith

The present theological scene in North America is perplexing. In the past, theological controversies were central features and crucial episodes in our culture. Presently, such controversies and debates continue, but they take place in ghettolike atmospheres, insulated from the circumstances and problems of the believing laity and isolated from unbelieving men and women of letters. This situation tends to render vital theological discussions innocuous and irrelevant to general intelligent audiences. And, often, the response of theologians is only to intensify such discussions among themselves. As with other disciplines in the humanities, especially philosophy and literary criticism, professionalization and specialization seem to have significantly sapped theology's quest for wisdom, its involvement and engagement in the general intellectual and political life of our nation.

There are four major paradigms in North American theology today. And, to my dismay, all four seem to confirm my observations. The first paradigm, dominant years ago and still persisting, derives from H. Richard Niebuhr's powerful dissertation on Troeltsch's philosophy of religion. I shall call it the *historicized Kantian paradigm*. It confronts the most important philosophical issue in contemporary theology—the encounter of history with necessary and universal faith-claims, and the ensuing debate between historicists and transcendentalists. The major proponents in our generation have been Gordon Kaufmann and his younger, unorthodox students such as George Rupp and Wayne Proudfoot. This paradigm thrives on dialogue with academic philosophers who are disenchanted with the ahistorical character of Anglo-American analytic philosophy. Its method ranges from appropriating the later Wittgenstein and J. L. Austin to rendering the insights of Stephen Toulmin, Richard Rorty, and Stanley Cavell relevant to contemporary theology.

The chief shortcoming of this paradigm is inseparable from the nature of the philosophical issue it addresses. The history/faith or historicist/transcendentalist controversy is a perennial one and quite possibly an insoluble one. It is not merely a philosophical problem but, more im-

From *Union Seminary Quarterly Review* (spring-summer 1980); review of Paul Holmer, *The Grammar of Faith* (New York: Harper & Row, 1978).

portant, a clash of cultural descriptions of what it is to be human. By focusing primarily on the philosophical aspects of this problem rather than on the internal dynamics of these clashing cultural descriptions, this paradigm tends to spin its wheels while traveling little distance, and subsequently to hold the broader theological, cultural, and political issues of the day at arm's length.

The second major paradigm—the *process paradigm*—rests upon the works of Alfred North Whitehead and Charles Hartshorne. It is the most vital paradigm on the academic theological scene today. Its proponents are the most enthusiastic theologians in the Academy. It has enlisted in its ranks the most talented cluster of academic theologians, including such figures as Schubert Ogden, John Cobb, Langdon Gilkey, and gifted younger thinkers such as David Griffin, and (with qualifications) Robert Neville and David Tracy. Despite periodic adverse publicity and frequent sneering remarks by mainstream theologians, process theologians are extremely serious thinkers engaged in a philosophical and theological revision of the Christian tradition. Unlike proponents of the first paradigm, process theologians have been unable to create and sustain any meaningful and longstanding dialogue with academic philosophers. The antimetaphysical disposition, and specifically an indifference to Whiteheadian metaphysics, of academic philosophers has prevented such a dialogue. This situation has contributed to the undoing of process theologians insofar as it has ensured their isolation. Armed with an alien philosophical vocabulary and a novel and unique theological worldview, and crippled by an embarrassing silence on ethics and politics, the process paradigm remains the possession of Christian academicians who are marginal to the nontheological Academy, Christian laity, and the general intelligent audience in the country.

The profound and often obscure philosophical writings of Husserl and Heidegger undergird the third major paradigm—the *hermeneutical paradigm*. Giant theological figures of the past generation, such as Paul Tillich and Rudolf Bultmann, and more recent thinkers, such as Hans-Georg Gadamer and Gerhard Ebeling, have enriched this paradigm. Aside from its prevailing presence in New Testament studies, this paradigm has been kept alive by the provocative and prolific work of Paul Ricoeur. The influence of Ricoeur on North American theologians has been immense, yet, it has always been unclear to me what this influence has actually amounted to, or what it has concretely yielded or produced. It surely informs the sophisticated theological formulations and illuminating literary insights of Nathan Scott; it also plays a crucial role in the promising eclectic theology of David Tracy, but this paradigm seems more and more to be the possession of Ricoeur. It is uncertain whether there will emerge any group of creative theological disciples to sustain it.

The last paradigm I will consider is the *liberation paradigm*. The proponents of this paradigm tend to be vehement, often vociferous, social critics who invoke Christian themes of justice and liberation to complacent, conforming Christians. The initiator of this paradigm was James Cone, who focused on the most visible and vicious form of oppression in North America—namely, racism. This paradigm differs fundamentally from the others in two ways. First, despite its similarity to the social gospel, it became a serious theological alternative in our own time (in the late sixties and early seventies). Second, it was initiated by a member of one of the most oppressed and exploited groups in North America, namely James Cone, a black American.

With the help of Latin American liberation theologians, this paradigm has now become the heartthrob of left-liberal Christians, with feminist, Native American, Hispanic, and gay variations on the liberation theme. This paradigm confronts theologically the most important ethical and political issues in postindustrial North America—those of class, racial and sexual exploitation and oppression, and the maldistribution of wealth.

The major limitation of this paradigm is that although it is more successful than the others in this regard, it remains primarily an academic affair, with little penetration into local congregations. Second, it has not been able persuasively to distinguish its voice, message, and aims from left-liberal, non-Christian voices. Hence it risks being relevant to the most crucial ethical and political issues of the day while losing its distinctively Christian character and content. This paradigm raises the crucial question as to whether being engaged as Christians in the central controversies and issues of our day renders one's Christian identity superfluous.

Enter Paul Holmer. Holmer's new book, *The Grammar of Faith,* is best understood against a scenario of the present theological scene. I have just sketched a crude scheme in order to situate his work historically. Let it first be said that it is a wise book, an unpretentious book, free of theological jargon. It is informed by an academic concern for subtlety, and yet it is not directed toward academic theologians. It is written primarily for Christian laity. It possesses a personal tone without degenerating into fashionable self-indulgence. It shows the Christian lay reader why and how academic theologians have failed to keep the faith alive.

And why have academic theologians failed to keep the faith alive? Precisely because they have been so obsessed with keeping the faith alive, and hence have looked in places—philosophy, metaphysics, science, politics—which end by deadening this faith. Holmer is a traditional evangelist. But what makes him so interesting are the radical metaphilosophical and metatheological moves he employs to justify his traditional evangelism.

Holmer is an important theologian because his viewpoint represents a nascent and emerging fifth paradigm, a *Wittgensteinian-Kierkegaardian paradigm,* which links radical efforts to overcome academic philosophy and theology with attempts to lay bare the structure, content, and vitality of the life and language of the faithful. He is one of the few theologians in the Academy, along with Geoffrey Wainwright, James Cone, and a few others, who take seriously the common activities and practices of Christian laypeople. He also is one of the few philosophers in Christian seminaries to offer a highly plausible philosophical position which puts these activities and practices at the center of theological reflection.

Holmer's metatheological thesis is that theology ought to be a *part of* the language of the faithful, not *about* this language. Theology has a participatory dimension which precludes objective, disinterested attempts to "ground" the language of the faithful in some ontology, metaphysics, or upon some set of "undeniable facts." "Theology must always move towards a present-tense first-person mood" (p. 24). Theology should be done in an "of" mood rather than an "about" mood. Theology sets forth the structure of Christian faith or the rules and grammar of the life and language of the faithful with "the form of personal appropriation built in" (p. 25).

Holmer's conception of theology breaks down the modern academic distinctions between theology and preaching, and between theory and practice. Theology becomes, as Kierkegaard conceived it, concerned first and foremost—in form and content—with the quality of one's life and the quality of the message thereby communicated. Holmer states,

> The thesis of these pages is that when Christianity is made into something primarily theological and doctrinal, then the nature of faith becomes malformed, as if it were chiefly an act of belief in the doctrine. Subsequently, every person would then be required to understand the theology, and the gist of being a Christian would be a matter of comprehension, just as one might say that being a geologist is a matter of ever deepening and broadening the intellectual grasp. (P. 185)

Theology becomes a form of preaching in that it reveals what the faith is about by disclosing the emptiness of fashionable theological forms of bad faith. Theology tries "to intensify and purify religious passion" (p. 67), and "to root believers firmly in the Christian life" (p. 50). Like preaching, theology has an evangelical aim: to discover, encourage, promote, cultivate, and refine Christian virtues, values, sensibilities, and capacities. Holmer asks seriously, "For what else is good preaching but vernacular theology?" (p. 14) and notes that "the positive projection of real preaching becomes theology in action" (p. 27). He is neither reducing theology to mere didactic preaching nor elevating preaching to propagandistic theology. Rather, he is highlighting their common aim—to convert and sustain souls for Christ—and accenting the subtle ways in which both participate in the language of the faithful.

Holmer also is concerned with breaking down the distinction between theory and practice in the life and work of theologians. For him, theology, like the Christian life for all believers, is not a profession but a vocation, not specialized teaching but life activity. It is a risky affair, not because its subject matter is often hard to get a hold on but because it calls one's own life continually into question. Theologizing, like preaching, singing, and praying, is a Christian practice which contributes to one's self-development and self-formation in the faith. It is the broadening of the lens, derived from the Scripture and tradition, through which one views oneself in order to become a fuller and more faithful self in Christ.

Holmer's conception of theology presupposes controversial philosophical views on truth, objectivity, rationality, and validity of which he is well aware. His discussion contains the traditional philosophical debates about realism vs. idealism, correspondence vs. coherence theories of truth, univocal vs. equivocal (or "polymorphic") rationality, universal vs. contextual validity. It is at this point that we see clearly Holmer's radical Wittgensteinian viewpoint. He undercuts the realist/idealist debate by revealing how both are sides of the same coin; both are tied to the quest for foundations. Only by checking this quest, this urge for grounding beliefs in some ontology, metaphysics, or set of scientific "facts" do we come to see that the Christian beliefs we hold are never based on privileged foundations but rather are incomplete descriptions of ourselves, the world and God we adopt, accept, and adjust to:

> The overwhelming point to remember, which lays to rest the ghost of those peculiar philosophical longings that grip us ever and anon, is that there is no indisputable, no indubitable starting point—no fact—for any and all inquirers. (P. 106)

Holmer deals with the traditional debates about truth, objectivity, rationality, and validity by contextualizing these notions. Like a good Wittgensteinian, he refuses to grant them a factual or transcendental foundation which is free of an interest-laden description or theory. In the most revealing philosophical paragraph in the book, he answers the Platonists, Cartesians, or Kantians who would insist upon context-free conceptions of knowledge, truth, objectivity, rationality, and validity:

> What I have said about the word *knowledge*—namely, that it is context-determined and hence is used for a variety of conceptual pur-

poses—must also be said about *objective, true,* and even *real.* Thus, when someone says: "What I want to know is whether theology is 'objective' and not just a party line," the question does not permit the plain and unequivocal answer that is often being sought. The better part of wisdom is not to answer the question directly; for either *yes* or *no* tends to buttress the vulgar academic prejudice that lurks in the question. A prejudice is, among other things, an idea about which one refuses to think. And it is an academic and hence a confoundedly difficult prejudice to eradicate—namely, that *objective, real, true, logical, rational,* and other words of this extensive criteriological sort are manifest in meaning, unvariegated in use, simple to understand, and plainly rudimentary and underived in import. Though we use them in every context, and though we all are endowed with sufficient capacity to use some of them in telling ways, they are still not transcendentals and context-free. The fact is that they are used in several contexts, and they become context-dependent. So we have to be clear about the specifics in each case. *Rational, objective, true, real,* etc. are always "in respect to so and so"; and then the expressions make sense and engage a subject matter and a thinker. (Pp. 189-90)

This viewpoint raises unsurprising accusations of relativism, skepticism, even "closet" nihilism. Is not contextualism a form of relativism? If truth is contextual, how do we know what really *is?* If rationality is polymorphic, how do we know what we really ought to believe? If validity depends on a context, how do we know what we really ought to accept? Holmer's Wittgensteinian aim is to rid us of this "really-disease" and force us to face the topsy-turvy world as mortals rather than as gods, and to look at the world from the viewpoint of fallen, limited, finite, and sinful human beings rather than *sub specie aeternitatis.*

Yet despite my agreement with Holmer's philosophical Wittgensteinian position to support his theological Kierkegaardian views, I believe he is neither Wittgensteinian nor Kierkegaardian enough. He is not Wittgensteinian enough because he tends to freeze the rules and grammar of the life and language of the faithful. For Wittgenstein, the dynamic rules and grammar of language replace static Platonic forms, Aristotelian essences, Cartesian egos, and Kantian categories. Holmer often seems to talk about the rules and grammar of the language of the faithful as if they are stationary, as if they were not part of the flux of human history. For instance, he writes,

> . . . I want to stress that fact that not all concepts wane and wax, live and die, so that we cannot say blandly about them, as a class, that they are all historical. That theory is wrong. That generalization is

too sweeping and stifles our sensing many differences. Most of the concepts that inform our esthetic, moral, and religious concerns have a striking nonhistorical character about them. . . . By the term *nonhistorical,* I do not suggest anything ethereal or otherworldly. Rather, I am only drawing attention to the fact that the concept does not need any particular historical surrounding in order for it to acquire vitality. All or any historical settings are sufficient. (P. 150)

For Holmer, concepts like "I" and "God" are nonhistorical, which can only mean that they are ultimately context-free. If this is so, he seems to retreat from his radical Wittgensteinian view. Since the rules and grammar of the language of the faithful are seen as human activities and social practices, he remains within the Wittgensteinian camp. But he is no longer a radical Wittgensteinian because of his tendency to downplay the dynamism of these activities and practices.

Holmer is not Kierkegaardian enough because he puts too little emphasis on the radical character of the existential risk and uncertainty attached to the perennial process of becoming a Christian. He is aware of this character, but it does not seem to be an integral element in his view of Christian living. We find little talk about the leap of faith or the tortuous move from abstract possibility to concrete actuality which is required by Christian faith. It is plausible that his tendency to freeze the rules and grammar of the life and language of the faithful leads him to downplay the risk and uncertainty in life and language. In this way, his conservative readings of Wittgenstein and Kierkegaard complement one another.

Holmer's refusal to be Wittgensteinian or Kierkegaardian enough is inextricably linked to his attitude toward tradition in Christian thinking and living. He has a Burkean view of tradition. For him, the Christian tradition is organic, "rich, many-sided," and requires little change. If there are to be any changes, they should be slight, "sheer increments." He appears to experience little anxiety in referring constantly to "the faithful," "the Christian scripture," and "the liturgy." In short, "the tradition" is more easily identifiable for him than for many of us.

I am not suggesting that Holmer ought to be a Jacobin about tradition and discard it. In a sense, all good Wittgensteinians are Burkeans on tradition. Yet, what most Burkeans often overlook is that some aspects of the tradition may promote and encourage radical changes of the tradition in order to preserve the tradition. The Burkean insight, the inescapable need for tradition, doesn't necessarily lead to Burkean ideology, the view that any changes of the tradition must be slow and gradual.

This brings me to a general point about Holmer's illuminating and fascinating book. It bears the stamp of ideological innocence. He acknowledges the polemical aim of the book—to counter the ideological character and academic isolation of contemporary theology—and then he quips, "True, there is no ideology here" (p. xi). And it is true that there is no moral didacticism or political propaganda in the book. But despite all his Wittgensteinian sophistication, he still assumes the possibility of a face-to-face encounter with the Christian Scriptures and tradition which is unencumbered by our fallenness, our sinfulness, and our ideological biases and prejudices. It is one thing to criticize convoluted theological attempts to show what the biblical texts express or stand for, but it is another thing to suggest that we can understand the texts unmediated by some interpretation. And, indeed, every interpretation and counterinterpretation contains the indelible imprint of our fallenness. In a revealing passage, Holmer writes,

> Of course, when we speak with emotion, we are not doing science or writing treatises. But we do often understand ourselves and others in such crisis situations. It is the plain task of theology, whatever its point of departure, be it a glorious and extravagantly endowed genius of the past or a school of thought that sweeps all opposition before it, to move towards such simplicity. (P. 16)

One may partly endorse this task of theology, but it seems false to say that when we speak with emotion we often understand others, because it is in precisely such situations that disagreement, and often disagreement based on misunderstanding, prevails. Holmer's statement rings true only in those situations in which there has been close personal contact, or when a group is culturally homogeneous or held together by bonds of trust—in short, in those situations in which an organic, cohesive tradition exists. Within such a tradition, general consensus on interpretations of the Scripture, liturgy, and so forth, makes it look as if a face-to-face encounter with the Christian tradition is occurring. Only then does the show of emotion prompt empathy and understanding. But it is precisely these kinds of situations and this ideal of tradition which are being called into question by the realities facing our churches, our seminaries, our communities, our society, our world.

Holmer has performed an invaluable service by presenting and promoting a new and exciting viewpoint—the Wittgensteinian-Kierkegaardian paradigm—on the North American theological scene. It is the most noteworthy viewpoint I know that begins and ends with the laity without surrendering intellectual rigor. Yet, such a viewpoint must be more radically Wittgensteinian, more radically Kierkegaardian, and more open to change and innovation of the tradition—especially its ethical and political practices—if it is to disclose more fully "the grammar of Christian faith" in our troubled times.

On Pascal's Significance

The immeasurable impact of Pascal is rarely appreciated or understood by contemporary thinkers. On the one hand, Pascal is lauded by literary critics for his writing style yet his philosophical contributions are overlooked. On the other hand, Pascal is trivialized by analytic philosophers who view his wager argument as but a poor instance of decision theory. Nicholas Rescher's book is distinctive in that it takes Pascal seriously as a philosopher in light of past and present theological modes of argumentation. As a distinguished historian of pragmatic philosophy, Rescher understands Pascal to be the great innovator of the major philosophical trends of our day: the theological use of practical reason, the diversity of modes of rationality, and the focus on praxis in contemporary hermeneutics.

Rescher's fundamental thesis is that Pascal promotes a basic shift in theological argumentation—a shift from theoretical proof and demonstration of facts concerning God to practical justification of trust and hope (i.e., faith) in God. For Pascal, theological arguments are less like validating scientific data and more like legitimating a practice. As Rescher notes, this shift was guided by the "shrewd psychological insight that despair brings no benefits and hope exacts few penalties" (p. 115). Rescher persuasively shows how Pascal's wager argument presupposes a skepticism regarding the capacity of evidential modes of rationality to arrive at convincing theological conclusions. Yet this skepticism does not lead to an irrationalism or a crude pitting of reason against blind faith. Rather, Pascal's mitigated skepticism—harkening back to the praxis-oriented thinkers of the Middle Academy and prefiguring the thought of Kant and James—invokes prudential modes of rationality to motivate decisions regarding theological options for actual human beings. In short, there may be rational grounds to believe in God, yet these grounds are practical ones that may engender faith in a particular God of a specific religious tradition. And over against Jules Lachelier and William James, for Pascal, these grounds have to do with what one will gain in the world to come, that is, eternal life, as opposed to this world, for example, empowerment, sense of dignity.

Rescher's sophisticated treatment of Pascal is significant in that he historicizes Pascal's thought without rendering Pascal a vulgar historicist.

This essay has not been previously published. Review of Nicholas Rescher, *Pascal's Wager* (Notre Dame, Ind.: University of Notre Dame Press, 1985).

234

That is, he acknowledges that Pascal's apologia for Christianity was not directed at Everyperson to accept a God-in-general, but rather a rational case for nominal Christians of "slack religiosity" seduced by this-worldly interests and concerns to return to the Christian fold. Pascal's project of practical reasoning in theology has a specific audience in mind, namely, the Christian acculturated yet straying freethinking *libertine* of his social circle.

The major problem of Pascal's project—and Rescher's treatment of it—is that it assumes that an evidential mode of reasoning leaves the case of God's existence "up in the air." I do not believe that a persuasive rational case can be made against the existence of God, but given the perennial problem of evil in theology I hold that evidential modes of rationality yield conclusions *against the probability* of God's existence. The seminal thought of Kant and the radical formulations of Kierkegaard, James, and Barth acknowledge that God-talk hits up against the evidential modes of rationality in our culture. In this sense, a rational though practical case for God's existence is more a defense of a particular religious tradition than an attempt to conceive of another mode of rationality. Rescher's rejection of the exorbitant claims of James reveals his own preference for Kant as the legitimate heir of Pascal's basic shift. And I believe he is right. Yet this simply shows the degree to which both Pascal and Kant refuse to realize just how nonrational (not irrational) God-talk is in a culture permeated by evidential modes of rationality. To call such nonrational talk a mode of practical reasoning should not conceal just how such talk is against the modern grain.

On Hans W. Frei's
The Eclipse of Biblical Narrative

Hans Frei's book deserves much more attention than it has yet received in historical, philosophical, and literary circles. His text is the best historical study we have in English of developments from post-Renaissance hermeneutics to the modern hermeneutics of Schleiermacher and Hegel. Frei's fascinating interpretation is intertwined with a complex argument regarding the problematic status of modern theological discourse. This argument rests upon conceiving "the Bible as writing," which thereby requires appropriate literary-critical tools. Frei's philosophical perspective is inspired by Karl Barth and indebted to Gilbert Ryle, Peter Strawson, and Stuart Hampshire. His literary-critical approach is guided by the monumental achievement of Erich Auerbach. And Frei's historical interpretation is wholly original—an imaginative reshaping of the terrain of early modern interpretation theory.

Frei's fresh interpretation demonstrates the specific ways in which forms of supernaturalism, historicism, classicism, moralism, and positivism have imposed debilitating constraints on the emergence of modern hermeneutics. These constraints resulted in a discursive closure which prohibited the development of a perspective which viewed biblical texts as literary texts depicting unique characters and personages. Instead, early modern hermeneutical discourse conceived such texts as manifestations of divine presence, sources for historical reconstruction, articulations of the inner existential anxieties of its authors, bases for moral imperatives, or candidates for verifiable claims. In a painstaking and often persuasive manner, Frei examines the "precritical" (a self-serving adjective coined by modern hermeneutical thinkers) interpretive procedures of Luther and Calvin, the pietistic viewpoint represented by Johann Jacob Rambach, the rationalistic approach of Spinoza, and the proto-*heilsgeschichtliche* outlook of Johannes Cocceius.

At the turn of the eighteenth century, the major split arose between narrative and subject matter, literal explicative sense and actual historical reference. In short, the texts no longer render the reality of the history they depict. Following the pioneering work of Mark Pattison and Sir

From *Notre Dame English Journal* (spring 1982); review of Hans W. Frei, *The Eclipse of Biblical Narrative: A Study in Eighteenth and Nineteenth Century Hermeneutics* (New Haven: Yale University Press, 1974).

Leslie Stephen, Frei locates the crystallization of this split in England. With the decline of the metaphysical poets, the rise of Bunyan's allegorical stories, and the emergence of the authority of scientific discourse, the Deist controversy—the search for external evidence for divine revelation—acquires a position of eminence in theological discourse. For Frei, this controversy constitutes the beginning of modern theology.

In Germany—traditionally regarded as the cradle of modern theology—the issues of the factuality of revelation and the credibility of the Bible loom large, but the Lutheran tradition linked them to the broader issue of the meaning of biblical texts. This latter issue focused on the semantic conditions under which the biblical texts support human salvation. The exegetical and theological notion of "positivity"—the endorsement of a direct divine intervention in the finite realm manifest in the unique "miracle" of character and being of Jesus Christ—emerged as the major candidate to satisfy the semantic conditions.

The exemplary Deist debate between the literalist William Whiston and the skeptic Anthony Collins in England and the line of development from the sophisticated supernaturalist Sigmund Jakob Baumgarten to the neologist Johann Salomo Semler signify the radical fissure between biblical words and biblical subject matter, between biblical realism and "real" facts, between biblical historylike stories and "actual" historical events. And the weight of modernity, especially modern science, accented and elevated the side of subject matter, facts, and events. Thereafter, the major traditions in modern theological hermeneutics remained caught in this fissure, oscillating between allegory and historical occurrences (Kant), apologetics and historical facts (Schleiermacher), and myth and historical events (Hegel, Strauss). In each tradition, the biblical texts as writings are reduced to mere sources for moral allegories, springboards for theological apologetics, or launching pads for existential myths—all against the backdrop of unverifiable historical occurrences, events, and facts.

Frei's ingenious tale about the emergence of this situation in eighteenth- and nineteenth-century hermeneutics demonstrates the way in which viewing the biblical texts as writings was unable to gain a foothold in early modern theological discourse. Furthermore, he argues that modern theology and hermeneutics is the worse owing to this situation. Frei's central culprits are German historicism and British positivism. The former precluded realistic narrative analysis of the Bible because of its rigid conception of the Bible as an object of scholarly commentary; the latter prompted the rise of realistic narrative form in the novel but did not permit a corresponding tradition of criticism viewing the Bible as such.

Frei's conception of biblical texts as literary texts depicting unique

237

characters and personages achieves saliency in theological discourse upon the appearance of Karl Barth's powerful section on the humanity of Jesus Christ entitled "The Royal Man" in his *Church Dogmatics*. For Barth and Frei, biblical narratives render an agent whose identity—whose intentions and actions—serves as the center of theological reflection. Following Ryle, Strawson, and Hampshire, Frei refines Barth's treatment of identity-descriptions by understanding intentions as implicit actions and actions as enacted intentions. This understanding—delineated in his book *The Identity of Jesus Christ*—allows Frei to view biblical narratives as constitutive writings wherein the unique character and being of Jesus Christ is depicted.

Frei's argument appeals to Auerbach's *Mimesis* primarily because of Frei's insistence on the realistic character of biblical narratives and the central role of "figura" traditionally invoked by Christian thinkers to hold the Bible together. Yet this appeal to Auerbach is the least convincing component of Frei's argument. First, Frei's project rests upon an internal realism within the biblical texts (with the appropriate exclusions such as Psalms, Ecclesiastes, Proverbs, the Gospel of John, and others)—a realism readily apparent on the surface which depicts human actions and intentions in historylike fashion. In contrast, Auerbach's conception of realism is regulated by his Hegelian viewpoint. Auerbach's realist texts reflect the unfolding of underlying processes and forces within a changing social context in the literary form of mixed styles. Therefore Auerbach can view Zola's *Germinal* as the exemplary realist novel and read Virginia Woolf's *To the Lighthouse* as realist literature (since it reflects inner processes of consciousness). In short, Frei's anti-Hegelian Barthian position flies in the face of the Hegelianism of Auerbach.

In a more philosophical vein, Frei rightly exposes the limitations of historicism and positivism on early modern hermeneutics, but his appeal to Auerbachian realistic narratives only reenacts the problematic of historicism by reinvoking the Hegelian reality/appearance distinction. Auerbach's *Mimesis* not only depends on this distinction; it also begins with it in the initial opposition between Homer and the Bible, foreground and background, externality and interiority, presence and hiddenness in the famous "Odysseus' Scar" chapter. In other words Frei seems inclined to reduce the biblical texts to mere historylike narratives which render identity-descriptions accessible by ignoring Auerbach's Hegelian conception of reality. In so doing, Frei too easily sidesteps an inescapable hermeneutical problem: the problem of radical indeterminacy in textual interpretation.

Even if we accept Frei's position and view the Bible as principally narrative-texts-rendering-agents, we still are left with little theoretical machinery to face the problem of indeterminacy. This is so because the very act of "rendering agents" is an interpretive act. It seems Frei either wishes the biblical texts were more Homeric (i.e., with little hidden meaning) or dreads the perennial interpretive process of separating reality from appearance, meaning from significance, sense from reference.

Frei's nostalgia for figural interpretation—though he is too sophisticated to call for a return to precritical hermeneutics—reveals his dismay regarding radical indeterminacy. Figural interpretations provide precisely what hermeneutics of radical indeterminacy preclude: totalizing frameworks, unified texts, homogeneous readings, chronological continuities, and recuperative strategies. In contrast to these aims, contemporary interpretation theory promotes antitotalizing approaches, dissemination of textual meanings, heterogeneous readings, antiteleological discontinuities, and deconstructive efforts. Ironically, such consequences seem to result from recent attempts to view all texts as writing. Frei indeed would shun the textual idealism and interpretive freeplay of avant-garde literary critics who promote a slogan similar to his own. Yet, crucial questions remain. Is this textual idealism and interpretive freeplay the logical consequence of Frei's own efforts to view "the Bible as writing"? If not, what kind of hermeneutics lurks beyond "the eclipse of Biblical narrative" in our time?

Despite Frei's powerful critiques of the major developments in eighteenth- and nineteenth-century hermeneutics, he remains much closer to the aims of these developments than to those of contemporary interpretation theory. Frei's intellectual achievement lies primarily in his profound insights regarding the "path not taken" by these developments. His insights generate an intricate and incisive argument which constitutes the major Christian intervention in contemporary criticism in which the very nature of theological discourse is at stake. Frei's intervention is hardly a modest achievement in this post-Christian and postmodern age.

On George Stroup's
The Promise of Narrative Theology

The twentieth century has been the setting for the development of two important and interdependent movements: the emergence of narratology in literary criticism and the subsequent rise of narrative theology in religious studies. In the course of my review of George Stroup's book *The Promise of Narrative Theology* I shall argue that the diverse literary-critical and theological work focused on the amorphous category "narrative" is noteworthy not because it constitutes the beginning of a new breakthrough nor because it sheds new light on old problems. Rather, this work deserves our attention primarily because it clearly exemplifies and amplifies the content and character of the present crisis in contemporary philosophical, literary-critical, and theological thought and practice. In other words, narratology and narrative theology, though aspiring to overcome the present crisis, is (in its dominant professional form) itself a paradigmatic symptom of this crisis.

For our purposes, an insightful genealogy of narratology should begin neither with the Russian formalism of Vladimir Propp and Viktor Shiklovsky, the Prefaces of Henry James, nor the linguistic acrobatics of French structuralists. We must start with the unpopular defenses of literary realism advanced by Georg Lukács and Erich Auerbach against the rising tide of high modernist literature. This tide was promoted and encouraged by the New Criticism of I. A. Richards, Allen Tate, John Crowe Ransom, and, above all, T. S. Eliot. The realism of Lukács and Auerbach can be characterized by the following claim made by Lukács in his famous 1936 essay "Narrate or Describe?":

> Only through deeds do people become interesting to one another. Only through deeds do they become worthy of poetic portrayal. The basic features of the human character can be revealed only through deeds and actions in human practice. (*Marxism and Human Liberation*, p. 119).

Similarly, both supported Auerbach's depiction of literary realism in his powerful chapter on Stendahl, Balzac, and Flaubert in his magisterial work, *Mimesis*:

From *Union Seminary Quarterly Review* (spring 1982); review of George Stroup, *The Promise of Narrative Theology* (Atlanta: John Knox Press, 1981).

The serious treatment of everyday reality, the rise of more extensive and socially inferior human groups to the position of subject-matter for problematic-existential representation, on the one hand; on the other, the embedding of random persons and events in the general course of contemporary history, the fluid historical background.... (P. 491)

Lukács and Auerbach are appropriate starting points for our inquiry because they defend precisely what the category of "narrative" connotes in Anglo-American narratology and narrative theology: the primacy of intentional human agency (be it radical choice for Kierkegaardians, nuanced confession for Barthians, or praxis for Marxists and liberation theologians), the centrality of community, and the quest for historical and personal intelligibility. Yet, like Lukács and Auerbach in decades past, contemporary Anglo-American narratologists and narrative theologians are put on the defensive in our culture owing to persistent assaults on those three central theses by modernist and postmodern literature, theory, and ethics.

Strategies of play, silence, and performance, as developed within contemporary literature, call into question intentional human agency, the possibility of nourishing human relationships, and the value of historical and personal continuity. In philosophy and literary criticism, epistemological holism, linguistic contextualism, and textual idealism—all formidable attacks on the referential power of language—transform quests for intelligibility into either local linguistic affairs or elusive rhetorical operations. In fact, for Jacques Derrida, the late Paul de Man, and other deconstructionists, narratives are the opium of the people. They are rhetorical operations of conventional codes which not only sustain illusory sequences of linguistic constructs (such as selves or agents) and rhetorical effects (such as actions and events) but also conceal the linguistic play of differences that make possible these illusory sequences, agents, and events.

In regard to ethics, the breakdown of political liberalism has made suspect its two major pillars: utilitarianism and Kantianism. As Alasdair MacIntyre has persuasively argued in his provocative book *After Virtue*, the secular pleasure-centered teleology of utilitarianism and the universal categorical status of Kantian-supported norms have been unmasked by Marx, Nietzsche, and Freud. The fiction of utility which regulates our bureaucracies and the fiction of rights which guides our political behavior have been disclosed as disguised wills to power.

In light of this crude and sketchy picture of the modernist and postmodern malaise, the emergence of narratology and narrative theology is to be understood as a barricade against the onslaught of critical attacks on human agency, history, meaning, intelligibility, community, virtue, character, and, most important, narrative. In this sense, narratology and narrative theology are first and foremost nostalgic attempts to revive lost traditions (Aristotelian, Christian, *Gemeinschaften*) and recover waning values. Such attempts are similar to the sophisticated nostalgic anti-modernist responses in the later W. H. Auden (of *About the House* and *City Without Walls*), Hannah Arendt's longing for classical public inter-course in *The Human Condition,* Heidegger's obsession for pre-Socratic conceptions of Being, and the later Lionel Trilling's veneration of the small-scale intimacy of Jane Austen's world.

If my sketch is plausible, then it should appear as no accident that nar-ratology and narrative theology arise in staunchly antimodernist camps: that of humanists marginalized by a scientific, technocentric culture, of religious humanists even more marginalized by a post-Christian Academy as well as alienated from middlebrow religious constituencies, and of intellectuals of the downtrodden on the edges of modernity. To put it crudely, the emergence of narratology and narrative theology is symptomatic of contemporary humanist, religious, and/or political re-sistance to the processes that have resulted in the fragmented communi-ties, lives, and discourses—the ruins of the West—that we inhabit: the Weberian processes of rationalization (e.g., bureaucratization, imper-sonalization) and the Marxian processes of commodification (e.g., de-humanization, thingification).

Yet each form of resistance bears the mark of the context from which its specific version of narratology and narrative theology arises. Humanist narratology (over which hovers the ghost of Auerbach) is pre-eminently Kantian in its major structuralist and Anglo-American forms; this Kantian foundation is evidenced by its search for the fundamental nature of necessary and sufficient conditions for narrative. Religious nar-ratology (or narrative theology) is primarily Barthian with Wittgenstein-ian and metaphysical realist poles; it attempts to defend the rendering of the revealed Word of God, that is, Jesus Christ, in the biblical narratives of the Christian tradition. Narratives of the downtrodden (over which hovers the ghost of Lukács) are basically Marxist, although they may have feminist and racial additions in modern contexts and some religious manifestations in third world contexts. The Marxian influence is easily recognizable in their concern to organize and mobilize newly industrial-ized peoples against prevailing structures of domination.

George Stroup's *The Promise of Narrative Theology* is an exemplary text of the second sort, of narrative theology with a Barthian slant. What is distinctive about this text is not its smooth hypnotic prose which is pal-pable to a general readership, nor its Barthian reformulations in a narra-tive mode. Rather, its distinctiveness lies in its professed provincialism, in both its content and scope. It not only speaks to church people; it also speaks exclusively about the church and its practices. Its central problematic is the crisis in Christian identity.

> The crucial theological issue of our day is . . . whether the Church can rediscover the sense in which it stands in and lives out of a tradition, reinterpret that tradition so that it is intelligible in the contemporary world, and offer a clear description of Christian faith which makes it relevant to the urgent questions and issues of modern society. (P. 24)

As a Christian and one who takes the life of the church seriously, I view this project as notable and desirable. It has been the task of Christian theology since the advent of modernity. Surely Schleiermacher, Ritschl, Harnack, Barth, Brunner, and Tillich would assent to such a task. Yet Stroup's prejudices, prejudgments, and presuppositions become apparent in his characterization of the four central symptoms of this crisis in Christian identity: the silence of Scripture in the life of the church, the church's loss of its theological tradition, the absence of theological reflection at all levels of the church's life, and the inability of many Christians to make sense out of their personal identity by means of Christian faith. Even if these symptoms are widespread in most middle-class and ruling-class American churches, this conception of the present theological crisis leads one to suspect that it may be self-serving. This suspicion grows from the fact that this conception constitutes a central portion of the Barthian problematic, with glib liberal moralism and captivity to modernity as its major culprits, and is confirmed when a few pages later we read,

> The attack on neo-orthodox interpretations of revelation reflect at the level of the Church's intellectual life the crisis in identity which Christians were experiencing at the more primordial level of lived experience. (P. 40)

My point here is not to diminish the monumental theological achievement of Barth nor to downplay Stroup's ingenious recasting of Barthian insights and doctrine in narrative terms. Rather, I want to accent the degree to which the attempt to understand our present postmodern crisis as roughly the same as Barth's problematic is itself indicative of a much deeper and more profound crisis of Christian identity in religious narratologies of the second sort. In agreement with Stroup I should also add that Ebeling's naturalization of revelation in human words or Pannenberg's warmed-over Hegelian notions of universal history do not suffice in such matters.

Although the external manifestations of many characteristics of postmodern industrial societies may appear to resemble similar phenomena in times past, these characteristics, for example, the biblical illiteracy, historical amnesia, ecclesiastical obsession with finance and public image, and the congestion of narratives in the marketplace of identity-formation, have different roots, roles, and functions than their predecessors. As Guy Debord has argued in his influential *Society of the Spectacle* and Jean Baudrillard in his *Toward a Critique of the Political Economy of the Sign,* we live in amnesiac societies saturated with flashing images, quick information, and consumer sensibilities. Similarly, Stanley Hauerwas writes in his notable essay "Story and Theology,"

> In our everyday life we are often impatient with the storyteller. . . . Stories were for slower times when we did not need to get things done. (*Truthfulness and Tragedy,* p. 77)

And Walter Benjamin adds in his masterful piece "The Storyteller,"

> Every morning brings us the news of the globe and yet we are poor in noteworthy stories. This is because no event any longer comes to us without already being shot through with explanation. In other words, by now almost nothing that happens benefits storytelling. Almost everything benefits information. (*Illuminations,* p. 89)

In other words, the very processes which inform consumer societies render problematic the authority of the story—communal, familial, religious, or personal forms of memory—and leave us with nothing more than a series of random experiences organized according to no "hierarchy of significance." Such fractured living constitutes the content and character of what Alan Wilde has called the suspensive irony of postmodern literature, the radical vision of multiplicity, randomness, and contingency in a world with no hope of coherence, continuity, and community. "With a true sense of the randomness of life's moments, man is at peace with himself—and that peace is happiness" (Jerzy Kosinski, *Contemporary Literature,* 1978, p. 142).

The theological response to this situation is not simply to reinvoke Barthian conceptions of Scripture and faith in narrative modes. Rather, it may be to envision a mode of theological discourse which no longer assumes a position of privilege, which preserves its distinctiveness while immersing itself into the personal and collective struggles of the day. A ritualistic gesture of asserting the authoritative status of biblical narratives without an elaborate defense of such narratives over against the major competing narratives in the culture will only further frustrate the formation of Christian identities. In this regard, Christian students of contemporary literature are far ahead of Christian theologians.

On the philosophical front, two problems continue to plague any sophisticated Barthian formulation of narrative theology: an allegiance to metaphysical realism and a maintenance of a version of the Myth of the Given, the appeal to interpretation-free events and experiences. Wittgensteinian and functional perspectives (like those of Charles Wood and Hans Frei) in narrative theology sidestep metaphysical realist claims about the referential character of biblical narratives yet tend to obscure the divine self-disclosive character of these narratives.

In contrast to such perspectives, Stroup is open to nonreferential claims about the creation and patriarchal stories (p. 233), yet he holds strongly to the referential claims of the crucial New Testament narratives. In cautioning narrative theologians about reducing truth into meaning, he writes,

> There may be other narratives, even religious narratives, in which the question of truth and meaning can be collapsed, but such is not the case with Christian narrative, for at its center it makes claims about what has taken place in history and those truth claims are historical assertions. (P. 236)

Given his admittance that metaphysical speculation about the reality and nature of God "is a necessary theological task" (p. 245), it is quite plausible to hold that Stroup subscribes to some version of metaphysical realism. Lastly, Stroup's crucial distinctions between chronicle and history (p. 114) and history and narrative (p. 236) are confusing. On the one hand, he is cautious against any form of the Myth of the Given. On the other hand, if chronicles are interpretation-laden, then history is an interpretation of a primitive interpretation and narrative is an interpretation of an interpretation of a primitive interpretation. It then becomes unclear how this latter claim is to be reconciled with his referential or metaphysical realist claims about certain gospel narratives.

In conclusion, narratology and narrative theology will continue to flourish primarily because their very existence is rooted in fundamental symptoms of and noteworthy responses to the contemporary crisis. There are good reasons to believe that the nostalgia upon which they feed will grow. And the talent they have attracted ensures development. Yet they will prosper and progress when—like their political counterparts on the edges and margins of modernity—they confront more fully the realities of postmodern culture, consumer society, and post-Barthian Christian thought and practice.

Winter in the West

Gibson Winter's "Hope For The Earth: A Hermeneutic of Nuclearism in Ecumenical Perspective" is the most provocative and powerful meditation I have read on the urgent issues of possible nuclear annihilation and actual nuclear weaponry buildup. Based on his ontological framework set forth in *Liberation Creation: Foundations of Religious Social Ethics,* Winter argues that nuclearism is not simply a logical consequence of Western technological development; it also is an effect of the modern Western way of "Dasein-in-der-Welt" (Being-in-the-World). This fundamental insight permits Winter to go beyond the usual confinement of nuclearism to the concerns of peace activists and move toward making crucial links to U.S. and Soviet forms of imperialism and colonialism. Furthermore, like Nietzsche, Winter discerns a basic will to power at the heart of the modern Western project which posits an autonomous, calculating Subject that defies and degrades historicity, temporality, spatiality, and sociality for the purposes of mastery and manipulation.

The work of Robert J. Lifton, Richard Falk, George Kennan, and Jonathan Schell have informed and alerted the public to various dimensions of nuclearism. Winter's reflections move to the archaeological dimension of this matter; that is, he provides a philosophical excavation of the ontological terrain wherein the hegemony of modern European *techne* has reigned since Descartes and Hobbes. Winter's inquiry cuts deeper than a mere history of ideas, depiction of possible nightmares, and prescriptions of *Realpolitik* primarily because it attempts to lay bare the hermeneutical horizons and existential symbols which promote and encourage dispositions of destruction and annihilation. His perspective not only provides a profound characterization of the philosophical depths of nuclearism; it also suggests a new way of Being-in-the World which takes seriously openness to the disclosure of Divine Mystery, thereby facilitating a *periagoge* (Turning) toward a historically informed humility, a spatially anchored sociality, and an ecumenically oriented communality.

I applaud Winter's motivations. For too long the political and moral aspects of nuclearism have been accented at the expense of its religious aspects. Surely, issues concerning the common good and normative character of nuclear weaponry warrant close attention. Yet, our concep-

From *Religion and Intellectual Life* (spring 1984).

tions of goodness, power, and ultimacy in relation to nuclearism also demand our rational scrutiny. In this regard, Winter has performed a valuable service.

I also deeply resonate with Winter's intentions. His attempt to elevate the dialogue to a more sophisticated level of investigation is salutary. And I believe he has succeeded well in rearranging the domain in which discourses on nuclearism take place.

Yet, I disagree in significant ways with Winter's perspective. First, my conception of the Western project is more radically pluralist and heterogeneous than his. I find the roots of Western nuclearism in far more than the mechanistic tradition of Descartes and Hobbes. In fact, I find some of these roots in the organicist tradition of which Winter is a product. Second, I am not persuaded that the valorization of a root metaphor of *poesis* or *phronesis* avoids the Western will to power. Third, the particular way in which *periagoge* comes about in Winter's perspective remains quite vague, with hints of mere moral persuasion and idealist reflection.

Winter is right to ground the modern Western will to power in the disembodied and deracinated *cogito* of Descartes and in the psychological hedonism of Hobbes. The autonomous world-seeking and power-hungry Subjects of the exemplary early modern thinkers indeed constitute a kind of prototype of the destructive monstrous forces now haunting us—as Mary Wollstonecraft Shelley's *Frankenstein* illustrates. But I suggest that there are many other possible grounds for the modern Western will to power. These grounds include the organicist and historicist traditions.

The organicist tradition—from Herder to Hitler, Hegel to Heidegger—usually incorporates a mystical dimension, which promotes an openness to the mystery of *Geist, Volk*, Being, Presence, or the Whole that sits well with authoritarian subordination and passive submission. My point here is not that Winter's beloved Heidegger was a Nazi for a few months, but rather that the organicist tradition bears as much intellectual responsibility for our present predicament as the mechanistic tradition of Descartes and Hobbes. In his book, Winter calls for a new synthesis of the creative powers of the mechanistic tradition and the participatory communitarianism of the organicist tradition. Yet, I remain unconvinced that the kind of radical democratic participatory values Winter and I favor are rooted in the organicist tradition. As Jacques Derrida, Gilles Deleuze, and Michel Foucault have pointed out, organicist notions of unity, harmony, and totality have led not only to the Unhappy Consciousness of the modern West, but also to premature closures and debilitating constraints which are but forms of the Western will to power. Such dangerous notions often elude and elide difference and heterogeneity (the very ingredients for radical participatory democracy) which results in dominating and destructive dispositions.

Similarly, the historicist tradition—from Nietzsche to Gadamer, Marx to Gramsci—which tries to take seriously historicity, sociality, and community bears some culpability for nuclearism. The discovery of history in the modern West—principally a nineteenth-century affair—meant the control of and mastery over historical forces. As Engels noted, freedom is the recognition of necessity and necessity is history as *Ananke,* as preexistent material to shape and mold for human purposes. Again the modern Western will to power looms large.

In short, I am not disagreeing with Winter's powerful critique of the mechanistic tradition. I am merely extending it to other precious traditions in the modern West, including his own. My point here is simply that the major traditions in the modern West fall prey to his critique—none are free of spot or wrinkle. Furthermore, these traditions (though some more than others) contain elements useful for launching such critiques. For example, the mechanistic tradition—though worthy of devastating criticism and ultimate rejection—produced Hume's associationism which bequeathed to us a valuable mitigated skepticism that promoted a Fallibilism requisite for an acceptable historicism. The organicist tradition—though limited and romantic—yielded the rich system of Hegel and the profound insights of Heidegger which made possible penetrating critiques of technological rationality. Lastly, the historicist tradition—which I prefer though still criticize—gave us Marx's illuminating social analyses and Gramsci's revisions which still partly guide our conception of and activities against modern forms of oppression. Yet, despite these grand contributions, these traditions contribute in significant ways to the modern European will to power and our present nuclear predicament.

I support Winter's claim that the complex linking of Cartesian and Hobbesian epistemologies to modern *techne* more readily results in dominating dispositions. But I am not convinced—by either Winter, MacIntyre, Gadamer, or Bernstein—that its replacement by some notion of *poesis* or *phronesis* will in itself necessarily or probably void the Western will to power or dilute the nuclearism in our world. In fact, Nietzsche may be right: the very attempt to recover and recuperate our Greek heritage—both pre-Socratic and post-Socratic notions—is debilitating and reveals our parochialism. I do not follow Nietzsche in such a direction, but his radical viewpoints warrant serious attention. To put my cards on the table, I hold that a particular religious and political form of *phronesis*—a practical wisdom linked to specific prophetic religious and progressive political movements—might redirect the Western will to power and constrain the nuclearism in our world. But this position remains a hope and a risk. Even openness to the disclosure of Divine Mystery does not guarantee it. For there is, in my Christian view, the slight chance that Christianity might be false.

In other words, Winter must spell out in more detailed terms the concrete political content of his alternative to Cartesian and Hobbesian *technes*. I find his characterization of the effects of these *technes* persuasive. But precisely what the relation of "dwelling" is to political praxis and "sharing" is to movement building remains unclear. Furthermore, I think such praxis and movement building can be done without assuming that "the rhythms and energies of the play of life lend a common base to human aspirations and struggles." Such romantic naturalism is not warranted by the commonsensical or scientific evidence we have and surely no transcendental justification can stand the scrutiny of Winter's historicist sentiments. So what does sustain such an optimistic assumption? Like Whitehead's consequent nature of God, it is an understandable but unacceptable naturalist leap of faith. The impossible possibility of Divine Grace might sustain and enable such a leap, but not "the relational processes of species life."

Lastly, Winter's account of how the *periagoge* is to take place is underdeveloped. At one point, he suggests this to be the role of the "servant church." Yet "in the Between" even this cloud of witnesses "has no special protection from the painful rupture of power and goodness." At another point, he suggests that the choice of life over death "*can* come when people begin to reflect on where the path of deterrence is leading."

My point here is not that Winter should put forward elaborate strategies and tactics to resist and overthrow nuclearism, but rather that he must specify more clearly the conditions under which new ways of being-in-the-World—with their concomitant new hermeneutical horizons and existential symbols—come about. To put it bluntly, the pedagogical dimension of his perspective remains vague—and there can be no *periagoge* without a distinct *paideia*.

In conclusion, Winter's essay elevates the contemporary discourse on nuclearism in an admirable and impressive manner. His critique is powerful—yet its scope needs broadening. His alternative is pregnant—though it lacks historical concreteness. And his pedagogy is perspicacious—but it remains rudimentary. We all should be grateful to Professor Winter for his meditation—his grand vision, acute analysis, and propitious praxis—because he surely helps us to think more clearly and work more effectively for the preservation and humanization of the earth.

On Elisabeth Schüssler Fiorenza's In Memory of Her

Elisabeth Schüssler Fiorenza's *In Memory of Her* is a ground-breaking work. For the first time, we have a powerful defense of new theological emancipatory models of hermeneutics, critical method, and historical reconstruction and an application of these models in one book. This intentional traversing of academic disciplines—theology, ethics, church history, and biblical studies—for the pursuit of knowledge and empowerment of women represents a coming of age for liberation theology. In this chapter I shall focus solely on Schüssler Fiorenza's hermeneutical and methodological formulations, without losing sight of her broader concerns.

Any major challenge to prevailing paradigms in scholarship must build upon the profound and persuasive insights generated by mainstream scholars yet call into question their uncritically accepted presuppositions, prejudgments, and prejudices which deter new breakthroughs. Schüssler Fiorenza adopts this strategy with great effectiveness. She begins by accepting the starting point of biblical historical criticism: the acknowledgment of biblical texts as neither verbally inspired revelation nor doctrinal stipulations but rather as historical responses within the context of religious communities over time and space. Following the feminist claim that such contexts are patriarchal and androcentric, Schüssler Fiorenza demystifies mainstream biblical scholarship by revealing its captivity to androcentrism—its relative silence on and marginalization of women's lives in the past and present—and by disclosing the oppositional Christian women's culture concealed by traditional church his-story.

Schüssler Fiorenza moves from this "hermeneutics of suspicion" to hermeneutical combat by putting forward an alternative model of interpretive criteria and methodological orientation for unearthing, understanding, and undergirding women's individual and collective agency in the past and present. This move is neither a glib attack on the cult of objectivity in the Academy nor a vulgar call for women's freedom. Rather, it is a sophisticated fusing of hermeneutics, social theory, Christian

From *Religion Studies Review* (Jan. 1985); review of Elisabeth Schüssler Fiorenza, *In Memory of Her: A Feminist Theological Reconstruction of Christian Origins* (New York: Crossroad, 1983).

ethics, and church history which specifies standards for evaluation and appropriation of past texts and histories, highlights gender system (women's oppression and resistance) as a fundamental category of historical and social analysis, and promotes Christian women's heritage.

Schüssler Fiorenza's feminist critical hermeneutics quickly dismisses the doctrinal and historical exegetical models of biblical interpretation by rejecting the former's ahistorical claim of revelational immediacy in the Bible and the latter's positivistic commitment to "value-free" inquiry. Of course, Schüssler Fiorenza realizes that both models have been severely criticized and thoroughly discarded by most twentieth-century biblical scholars—yet residues such as the quest for timeless truth and an allegiance to detached, value-neutral investigation persists. The model of dialogical-hermeneutical interpretation is predominant in biblical scholarship. The philosophical influence of Heidegger, Gadamer, and Ricoeur ensures biblical interpretive sensitivity to the "otherness" of the text, the inescapable prejudices of the interpreter, and the pervasive web of language, tradition, and community. For Schüssler Fiorenza, this model is important yet limited. It is important because it takes *historicity* seriously by acknowledging the temporal situating of the interpreter and the illuminating potential of the interpreter's biases. Yet it is limited in that it does not take *history* seriously; that is, the model refuses to dig into the depths of the cultural, political, and societal contexts of texts and interpreters. Heidegger, Gadamer, and Ricoeur have taught biblical scholars to accent the existential interestedness of interpreters while listening to the "strangeness" of past texts; but this important insight does not encourage biblical scholars to examine also the social, political, and economic interests of interpreters contained in texts. The model of liberation theology highlights these interests and brings to the surface the ideological commitments of interpreters and texts within the context of class struggle, cultural/racial conflict, and feminist resistance.

Schüssler Fiorenza suggests that feminist Christian scholars—since Elizabeth Cady Stanton's monumental *The Women's Bible* (1895)—have appropriated liberation themes without critically examining the problems of the hermeneutical models they adopt. She focuses on two such models: the neoorthodox model and the sociology-of-knowledge model. Feminists such as Letty Russell, Phyllis Trible, and Rosemary Ruether have put forward influential claims regarding the patriarchal language of the Bible while holding that there is a nonpatriarchal content therein. This apologetic move presupposes fundamental distinctions between revelatory essence and historical accident, timeless truth and culturally conditioned language, constant Tradition and changing traditions. The aim of such neoorthodoxy is to confront candidly the specter of historical conditionedness without succumbing to historical relativism and to specify the biblical grounds for Christian identity (by preserving Christocentric revelation) in the face of objections by natural theologians.

Schüssler Fiorenza's critique of feminist neoorthodoxy is threefold. First, she argues that neoorthodox models ultimately put the burden of historical agency on God, not women. The worldly skepticism of neoorthodoxy can accommodate liberation themes, but it cannot rest transformative powers in the praxis of oppressed peoples. Therefore the reinterpretation of the gospel from a liberationist perspective can yield, at most, a moral ideal and an abstract prophetic tradition with little grounding in the flesh-and-blood past and present of struggling peoples. Second, this model—against the intentions of its feminist representatives—idealizes the biblical and prophetic traditions by refusing to come to terms with the oppressive androcentric elements of these traditions. This idealization produces rather romanticist claims about the "liberating" effects of recuperating past prophetic traditions. The intent is admirable; yet the effect is rather empty. To put it crudely, the model yields theological critique, moral outrage, and ahistorical tradition posturing, but not engaged empowerment of the downtrodden. Third, neoorthodoxy posits an "Archimedean point" which attempts to meet secular (or religious post-Christian) feminist objections regarding the patriarchal and even misogynist character of Christianity: this "Archimedean point"—divine revelation in Jesus Christ—preserves the liberating kernel within the patriarchal husk.

The sociology-of-knowledge model, best exemplified in Mary Daly's work, accents the overwhelming sexism shot through biblical texts and church traditions. This model holds that reconstruction and revision of such texts and traditions is anachronistic. Instead of disclosing a liberating essence in such texts and traditions, the model calls for new construction and new vision: the creation of feminist life-centers that will generate alternative ways of naming reality and modes of women's empowerment. It assumes that the medium is the message, that patriarchal language can yield only patriarchal content. Therefore new mediums and languages must be constructed by feminists. Schüssler Fiorenza is enchanted by the audacity of this model, especially with its willingness to push Christian feminists to the edge with its sober assessment of patriarchy in Christian texts and traditions. Yet she refuses to construe complex Christian practices as mere patriarchal enactments. Since the model focuses primarily on sexist language and sado-ritual repetitions of Goddess repression and murder, it provides shock effects to the novice (feminists-to-be). Yet it does not deal in any serious manner with concrete socioeconomic structures of oppression and feminist opposition to these structures. The model opts for marginality, "Otherworld sisterhood," and "sacred space" which reinforces the peripheral status imposed upon women in patriarchal society and gives the "center," the "old territory," namely, human history, to oppressive men and subjugated women. This model surely heightens feminist awareness of patriarchy in history, but it elides specific historical forms of patriarchy, abstracts from the social and historical relations that shape these forms, and, most important, denies the protracted struggles of women at the "center," in the "old territory," within human history.

Schüssler Fiorenza's new model of feminist critical hermeneutics of liberation moves the focus from questions concerning the authority of biblical revelation to discussions regarding feminist historical reconstruction of the background conditions under which biblical texts were constituted—from androcentric texts to patriarchal-historical contexts in which women contest and resist as well as defer and lose. Such reconstruction proceeds not only by delving into the liberating impulse within the biblical texts, but, more important, by going beyond the texts to examine women's struggle against patriarchal canonization. Since these texts are not objective, factual reports of the past but rather pastorally engaged responses to particular circumstances, it is not surprising that they represent the views of (and for?) the "historical winners." By critically scrutinizing the canonization process itself, Schüssler Fiorenza goes beyond the neoorthodox model as well as that of liberation theology. No longer can one simply turn to the canonical Christian texts for insights and even imperatives for present social and political struggles. Rather, the formation of the biblical texts becomes a terrain of ideological and historical contestation. To start with the biblical texts, the final canon, and infer liberation themes, deliverance motifs, salvific principles which then serve as sources to criticize the texts themselves still dehistoricizes and depoliticizes the canonization process.

For Schüssler Fiorenza, the revelatory criteria for theological evaluation and appropriation of the Christian past and present is transbiblical; that is, linked to biblical texts yet substantively beyond them. At times, Schüssler Fiorenza nearly excludes the biblical texts and offers only Christian women's struggle for liberation from patriarchal oppression. At other times, she admits that this struggle in the past produced nonpatriarchal elements in the biblical texts. This ambiguity is seen in her metaphor for biblical revelation as a historical prototype not a mythic archetype—as an all-too-human process open to critique and change rather than an ideal, timeless form. The ambiguity arises in that if one locates revelation first and foremost in the Christian (or non-Christian) feminist struggle for freedom, and if the biblical texts are fundamentally androcentric, it is unclear why the adjective "biblical" is used in "biblical revelation."

This dilemma haunts Schüssler Fiorenza's hermeneutical and method-ological discussion. Her critiques of the prevailing interpretive models are often persuasive. And her attempt to analyze seriously the historical context with gender system as a fundamental category as well as highlight the ideological conflicts within the canonization process is wel-come. Yet her model seems to lead her into feminist history about Chris-tian women rather than *Christian* feminist historical reconstruction. Does she pull the Christian rug from under her project and relegate her work to historical inquiry on Christian feminist women by failing to generate Christian normative criteria to regulate her interpretation and appropriation of the past? I think not. She pushes us to the edge of the Christian tradition precisely to help us understand it as a deeply histori-cal yet revelatory phenomenon.

Schüssler Fiorenza's conception of truth and justification—her im-plicit ontology and epistemology—within her new hermeneutical model provides us with clues to her Christian identity. In contemporary her-meneutics there are three basic philosophical strategies regarding the separate yet related problems of truth and justification. The first strategy follows Hegel by discerning Truth within the depths of the historical process. This discernment consists of keeping track of the active, reflec-tive, autonomizing *Weltgeist* who ultimately overcomes the historical process in order to achieve absolute self-consciousness and self-transparency. Refined versions of this perspective—put forward in re-ligious form by Wolfgang Pannenberg and in Marxist form by Georg Lukács—holds that every hermeneutics requires some degree of tran-scendental, that is, totalistic viewpoint. Therefore every hermeneutics, if honest about itself, presupposes a philosophy of history and hence is but a disguised form of Hegelianism.

The second strategy incorporates Kierkegaardian insights regarding the radical transiency of historical claims and the ultimate mystery (or utter "absurdity") of God's self-disclosure in Jesus Christ. This strategy, developed by Barth and others, sits at the center of the neoorthodox model. It employs sophisticated modes of historicist argumentation and, contrary to Schüssler Fiorenza's claim (culled from Peter Berger) that it invokes an "Archimedean point," refuses to look at the world *sub specie aeternitatis*. Yet this strategy claims that the existential power and world-view generated by an encounter with Jesus Christ in the preached Word of the Christian community warrants the truth-status of Christian rev-elation.

The last strategy rests upon Gadamer's historicist perspective, which understands Truth as revealment *and* concealment, as part and parcel of the perennial process of cultivating and refining inescapable traditions in relation to particular situations and circumstances. On this view there can be no transcendental standpoint, but there indeed are transcending possibilities which build upon prevailing finite standpoints. The criterion for Truth here resides neither in Hegelian transcendentalism nor in Kierkegaardian fideism, but rather in the regulative ideal of the *Vorgriff der Vollkommenheit* ("anticipation of perfection")—the openness to newness and novelty on the way to a perennially deferred unity. Like Dewey's pragmatism, this strategy shuns a Derridean unregulated free play of truth-effacing which lacks an applicatory, praxis-dimension and any form of closure. Instead this strategy promotes regulated historical praxis with only provisional closure without a constitutive telos.

This third strategy runs deep throughout Schüssler Fiorenza's philosophical discussion. Her fundamental concern with human agency, the dialectical interplay of revealment and concealment, the situating of texts within *Wirkungsgeschichte* (continuously operative and influential history) shot through with social conflict and the conception of biblical texts and subsequent interpretations as human practices are all compatible with Gadamer's historicism. Yet, Schüssler Fiorenza refuses to go all the way down the historicist road. And if she did so the Christian locus of truth and justification would be sacrificed. Contrary to the perceptions of many, the consequences of full-blown historicism are neither nihilistic relativism nor promiscuous pluralism; but for the Christian such historicism does result in a radical deprivileging of Jesus Christ as rendered in the biblical texts. One can surely follow the historicism of Gadamer and Dewey and sidestep vulgar relativistic traps. But for Christians to follow such paths means giving up the unique status of Jesus Christ. This is so because if one's historicism "goes all the way down" (like Hegel's) but resists neo-Platonic-like epistrophes (unlike Hegel's and like Gadamer's), then Jesus Christ becomes not only a historical person but also permeated by contradiction and imperfection. For the Christian, historical status of Jesus is crucial, but mere peer status of Jesus Christ is ultimately to reject the Hegelian and Gadamerian strategies—and remain on Kierkegaardian terrain. This does not mean subscribing to a neoorthodox model, simply that a neoorthodox element sustains one's Christian identity.

The privileged status of Jesus Christ looms large in Schüssler Fiorenza's text. Given her shift from androcentric texts to patriarchal contexts, one would expect a thorough interrogation of the patriarchal sensibilities and practices of Jesus, in and beyond the biblical texts. Instead, we are offered a view of Jesus as a "woman-identified man" with a *basileia* vision of a discipleship of equals, as if a reincarnate Jesus would join the contemporary feminist struggle against patriarchy. Such a presentist reading of the Synoptic Gospels reeks of Christian confessionalism and ahistorical moralism—the very charges Schüssler Fiorenza makes against feminist neoorthodox Christian scholars.

My point here is neither to promote a secular deprivileging of Jesus Christ nor to return to prefeminist readings of biblical texts and the Christian tradition. Rather, my point is to acknowledge the degree to which the Kierkegaardian-Barthian touchstone of modern Christian identity remains intact in Schüssler Fiorenza's work. I applaud this element in her text, but I remain unconvinced that it follows from her new hermeneutical model. The irreducible life, death, and resurrection of Jesus Christ—whose power and perspective is always found in human communities in dialogical form—is the mark of modern Christian identity. Schüssler Fiorenza's presentist portrait of Jesus Christ affirms this mark. Given her deep feminist commitments, this portrait becomes her way of preserving the privileged status of Jesus Christ. Without this status, the struggle for women's liberation has no Christian normative source. The struggle may warrant support, but there would be no Christian grounds to arrive at this conclusion. I believe that Christian texts and traditions—without a presentist reading of Jesus Christ yet while preserving the irreducibility of Jesus Christ—justify feminist liberation movements. But this justification is a historically informed moral one.

Is it contradictory and disempowering that Jesus Christ (male in human form) normatively grounds women's fight for freedom? I think not. Just as it is not contradictory that Jesus Christ (Jewish in ethnic origins) normatively grounds Arabs' struggle for human dignity in Israel—even as it grounds any struggle for human dignity. Only in an age obsessed with articulations of particularities (e.g., gender, race, nation) often relegated to the margins by false universalities (e.g., technocratic rationality, value-free and value-neutral inquiry) could such questions arise with potency. And only with a sophisticated emancipatory hermeneutics can a new conception of differential universality emerge which provides the framework for new perspectives and practices. Schüssler Fiorenza's powerful Christian interpretation and reconstruction of the biblical texts and early church move us closer to such a conception.

Martin Luther as Prophet

A few days ago we celebrated the 500th anniversary of the birth of that Augustinian monk from Saxony who shook the foundations of Western Christendom: Martin Luther. This celebration of his birth is inseparable from the theology he taught and the life he lived. Blinded by our anachronistic assumptions, we often reduce the rich complexity of this world-historical figure to the dimensions of caricature. Owing to his notorious justification of the suppression of the peasants' revolt in 1525, for instance, Luther is frequently viewed as primarily a defender of the political status quo. But it was Luther, not Calvin, who introduced the concept of active resistance into the political theory of the magisterial Reformation, as set forth in his *Warning to His Dear German People* in April 1531 which invokes the private-law doctrine that it may sometimes be legitimate to resist an unjust emperor violently.

It is crucial not to lose sight of Martin Luther the prophet whose understanding of the Christian faith led him to stand up against the most dominant and hegemonic institution in his society. This profound understanding highlighted the gift character of divine grace, the utter unworthiness of sinners like ourselves who can miraculously receive this grace, and the inexhaustible power of this grace to sustain our lives and communities in struggle. Luther's theological attempt to link his conception of grace to oppositional Christian praxis led him to call for the existing priesthood to commit a kind of class suicide, for the Catholic church to decapitate and democratize itself, for the Holy Scriptures to be translated into vernacular language, and for the laity to take responsibility for their religious lives, rituals, and theology.

Luther's prophetic stance prompted him to stand up, armed solely with the armor of the Word of God, against the powerful repressive and ideological apparatus of the Catholic Church; to nail his famous Ninety-five Theses to the door of the castle church in Wittenberg against Roman imperialism and Pope Leo X's theological consumerism; and, four years later, to stand trial before the powers and principalities of his day—before Emperor Charles V and the Imperial Diet at Worms—and declare:

> Since then your serene majesty and your lordships seek a simple answer, I will give it in this manner, neither horned nor toothed:

From *Christianity and Crisis* (Nov. 28, 1983).

Unless I am convinced by the testimony of the Scriptures or by clear reason (for I do not trust either in the pope or in councils alone, since it is well known that they have often erred and contradicted themselves), I am bound by the Scriptures I have quoted and my conscience is captive to the word of God. I cannot and I will not retract anything, since it is neither safe nor right to go against conscience.

I cannot do otherwise, here I stand, may God help me. Amen.

Luther's audacious declaration initiated a religious movement and intellectual current of which we are a part 463 years later. His penetrating theological critique of the existing order and his persistent resistance against the prevailing religious hierarchy exposed a decadent Christianity and corrupt church. Like Jesus Christ in the temple that had become a den of thieves, Luther realized that the church and even the gospel are terrains of contestation. Luther's own alternative to religious decadence and ecclesiastical corruption was not free from flaws and defects. For God never chooses perfect prophets. And every prophet who claims perfection or access to a flaw-free vision is a false messiah. We must never demand of our prophets more than we ask of ourselves. Yet God does choose peculiar prophets. Never before or after has a biblical professor in a university performed such prophetic gestures of gargantuan proportions, nor has a traditional intellectual engaged in organic activity with such astounding results. It is no accident that Antonio Gramsci, an Italian Marxist thinker in a Catholic country, should call his own revolutionary project a "modern popular Reformation" which tries to complete the process begun by Martin Luther.

The genius of Martin Luther was that he transformed Christian identity from a glib and innocuous ecclesiastical affiliation into an intense Christocentric phenomenology of standing—a standing which requires all of one's heart, soul, and mind. Luther's prophetic Christian legacy comes to us in the form of four fundamental questions:

- Do we have a Christianity which requires us to stand up against personal and institutional sin?
- What do we stand for? Do we take seriously the biblical injunction to do justice, love mercy, and walk humbly with God?
- With whom do we stand? Is our Christian witness in solidarity with those who suffer existential anguish, cultural degradation, political repression, and class exploitation?
- Upon what do we stand? Is our Christian practice grounded on a solid rock or does it rest on sinking sand? (I am referring here not to epistemological foundationalism but rather existential anchorage.)

For Luther, Christian witness against personal and institutional sin, for human freedom and with the prophetic wing of the church, is grounded in Jesus Christ. We are nourished by his blood and the struggling community that drinks thereof. We are motivated by his example and the comrades who act thereon. We are captive to his promise and the kingdom which enacts it. In short, we speak the truth in love and fight for freedom with humility.

This is, in part, the legacy Martin Luther bequeathed to us. And no one has embodied this legacy in such a clear and poignant manner as has Martin Luther's fellow Christian and contemporary namesake, Martin Luther King, Jr. This great son of the black church did for Protestant USA what the Saxon monk did for Catholic Europe: both reclaimed and recovered in their own ways the salvific and liberating power of Jesus Christ. As we move toward the end of the twentieth century amid the ruins of capitalist and communist civilizations—aware of their colossal crimes against humanity and their feeble efforts of internal transformation—the prophetic stand of Martin Luther and his towering progeny Martin Luther King, Jr., should remind us that, even among the driest of bones, the kingdom of God may proleptically lurk within.

A Philosophical View of Easter

I

The joyful attitude of a Christian toward the resurrection claim that "Jesus arose from the dead" seems to preclude the philosophical dispositions of disinterest, detachment, and distance. Yet, as a Christian and philosopher, I believe that the resurrection claim can be both dispassionately defended and enthusiastically exalted. In this brief chapter I will suggest philosophical strategies for such a defense and existential reasons for such an exaltation. In my treatment of the resurrection claim, I shall move from its philosophical testability to my own personal testimony.

There are three basic aspects of the resurrection claim, namely, its truth-value, its epistemic status, and its significance. First, we must ask what it means to say that the resurrection claim is true or false. Second, how do we know whether the resurrection claim is true or false? Third, what significance should the resurrection claim have for us as Christians?

II

Before we begin to examine what it means to say that the resurrection claim is true or false, we must have some idea of what it means to say that any claim is true or false. A commonsensical view would be that a claim is true or false if it can be correlated with a particular set of experiences or observations such that all and only members of that set are evidence for or against the claim. For example, the resurrection claim would be true if we could persuasively demonstrate that reliable observers saw Jesus physically dead, put in Joseph's tomb, and either arise from the dead or alive after his death.

There are two major problems with this commonsensical view. First, it rests upon the reliability of those friends and disciples of Jesus who are purported to have made observations which may serve as evidence for the veracity of the resurrection claim. David Hume's powerful essay on miracles convincingly renders this reliability problematic. Second, this

From *Dialog: A Journal of Theology* (winter 1980).

view assumes that the resurrection claim is the kind of claim whose truth-value can be determined by a particular set of observations. This assumption is questionable because it presupposes the dogma of sentential reductionism, namely, the view that sentences have their evidence for or against their truth or falsity isolated from and independent of other sentences.

I will suggest that the truth-values of crucial claims or important sentences in the two major kinds of descriptions, versions, or theories of the self, world, and God—religion and science—can be determined neither in isolation from other sentences nor by a particular set of observations. My suggestion rests upon the insight put forward by the Catholic philosopher of science, Pierre Duhem, and popularized in our time by W. V. Quine and Thomas Kuhn: that the truth-value of our claims about the self, world, and God are determined by marshaling evidence for or against the descriptions, versions, or theories of which these claims are a part. This insight leads us to examine the truth-value of particular descriptions, versions, or theories of the self, world, and God, not isolated claims or sentences within these particular descriptions, versions, or theories.

If we hold to the dogma of sentential reductionism and observational criterion in determining the truth-value of claims or sentences in scientific descriptions, versions, or theories of the self, world, and God, we reach the same dead end that Hume reached in his narrow dogmatic rejection of the resurrection claim in Christian descriptions, versions, or theories. The dogma of sentential reductionism for scientific descriptions amounts to the claim that any scientific statement could be reduced to an equivalent statement consisting solely of observation terms or observables. But the most important sentences in any scientific description, version, or theory contain nonobservation terms, such as disposition terms, metrical terms, and theoretical terms. For example, terms such as *recessive trait, conductor of heat, magnetic,* or *elastic* are not observable characteristics of objects, but rather dispositions of objects to behave in certain ways under specific circumstances. Terms such as *length, mass, temperature,* or *electric charge* are numerically measurable quantities which also cannot be reduced to observable attributes of objects. And terms such as *force, pressure, electron,* or *black holes* are neither observable characteristics of objects nor observable objects, but rather theoretical constructs whose positing within a theory is warranted by the explanatory and predictive power the theory yields.

I suggest that just as it is inappropriate to apply the dogma of sentential reductionism and the observational criterion to the most important claims or sentences in scientific descriptions, so it is inappropriate to apply this dogma and criterion to the resurrection claim in Christian descriptions. We must acknowledge that truth-values pertain to bodies of knowledge, descriptions, versions, or theories of the self, world, and God, not to atomic sentences, autonomous statements, or isolated claims. If we do not acknowledge this Duhemian insight, then we must admit that it is impossible to determine the truth-value of scientific laws (which contain nonobservation terms) in scientific theories and the resurrection claim in Christian descriptions.

So, in reply to our first question about what it means to say that the resurrection claim is true or false, we conclude that to raise the question of the truth-value of this claim is to raise the question of the truth-value of Christian descriptions, versions, or theories of the self, world, and God of which the resurrection claim is central.

III

Now that we have some idea of what it means to say that the resurrection claim is true or false, how do we know whether the resurrection claim is true or false? Since the truth-value of the resurrection claim is inseparable from the truth-value of particular Christian descriptions, versions, or theories of which this claim is central, the crucial question becomes, how do we know particular Christian descriptions are true or false?

It is important to point out here the different senses of "know" or kinds of knowledge in the various scientific and religious language-games we play. For example, when one puts forward knowledge claims from the viewpoint of a scientific description, version, or theory about the self, world, and God, one is attempting to support or defend a particular description, version, or theory which tries to provide reliable predictions and trustworthy explanations of future experience in light of past experience. When one puts forward knowledge claims from the vantage point of a religious description, version, or theory about the self, world, and God, one is attempting to support or defend a particular description, version, or theory which tries to promote the valuing of certain insights, illuminations, capacities, and abilities in order honestly to confront and effectively to cope with the inevitable vicissitudes and unavoidable limit-situations in life.

In drawing this distinction between scientific "knowing" and religious "knowing," I do not want to suggest that science and religion require different methodologies or different standards by which to adjudicate conflicting descriptions. Rather, I am suggesting that both consist of social practices and human activities with different aims to achieve and different problems to address. I make this distinction between scientific practices and religious practices in order to avoid category mistakes, such as asking science to achieve the aims or address the problems of religion or vice versa.

In coming to terms with the question, how do we know particular Christian descriptions, versions, or theories of the self, world, and God are true or false and hence whether the resurrection claim within these descriptions, versions, or theories is true or false, we are forced to acknowledge that there are no *ultimate* courts of appeal presently available to us. Every penultimate court of appeal is linked to a particular description, version, or theory of the self, world, and God. To confine ultimate courts of appeal to the spheres of either science or religion is reductionistic. To believe that Truth is a property solely of scientific theories which yield reliable predictions and trustworthy explanations is to fall prey to a narrow positivism. To believe that Truth is an attribute solely of religious descriptions which promote certain insights and capacities for living is to fall prey to an expedient existentialism. And to believe that there is a description-free, version-free, theory-free standard which enables us to choose the true descriptions, versions, or theories in science and religion is to fall prey to an Archimedean objectivism.

Since we should neither reduce Truth to the spheres of either science or religion nor assume we can view the world *sub species aeternitatis,* we must acknowledge our finitude, fallenness, and sinfulness as human beings. This acknowledgment entails that when we say we "know" that a particular scientific or religious description, version, or theory of the self, world, and God is true, we are actually identifying ourselves with a particular group of people, community of believers, or tradition of social practices. There indeed may be good reasons why we identify ourselves with particular groups, communities, or traditions. But there are, ultimately, no reasons with the force of logical necessity or universal obligation which could rationally compel others to join us. In this sense, there is no true description, version, or theory of the self, world, and God which all must and should acknowledge as inescapably true, but rather particular descriptions, versions, or theories put forward by various people, groups, communities, and traditions in order (usually) to make such views attractive to us.

At this point, it is appropriate for me to cast off my dispassionate philosophical disposition and openly acknowledge my own membership in the Christian community. This "casting off" is essentially a rejection of the conception of philosophy which does not permit one openly to acknowledge the particular tradition and community from which one speaks. By accepting a particular (i.e., Kierkegaardian) Christian description and therefore accenting our fallenness, I am led to adopt a radical historicist view which renders all "truthtalk" a contextual affair, always related to human aims and human problems, human groups and human communities.

As a self-avowed Christian, it seems redundant to say that a particular Christian description of the self, world, and God is true. But, more important, it is misleading to say this. Christians believe in various Christian descriptions which do not claim their descriptions are true but rather that these descriptions are acceptable and possibly sufficient for their aims. Christian descriptions hold that our fallenness will never permit our Christian descriptions to grasp the Truth. This is so because, for Christians, Jesus Christ is the Truth and Jesus Christ always rests outside our particular Christian descriptions.

The philosophical implication of this view is that, for Christians, Truth is not a characteristic of a description, not even of a Christian description. Rather, Jesus Christ is the Truth or Reality which can only be existentially appropriated by fallen human beings caught in their finite descriptions. And the fact that this view itself is but part of a finite Christian description only further accents our fallenness and supports the view.

I am suggesting that the primary test for the "truth-value" of particular Christian descriptions and their resurrection claim is their capacity to facilitate the existential appropriation of Jesus Christ. This means that any "true" Christian description makes the Reality of Jesus Christ available, that it promotes and encourages the putting of oneself on the line, going to the edge of life's abyss and finding out whether the Reality of Jesus Christ, though understood through one's finite Christian description, can sustain and support, define and develop oneself in one's perennial struggle of becoming a fuller and more faithful self in Christ.

So, in reply to our second question about the epistemic status of the resurrection claim or how do we know that particular Christian descriptions and their resurrection claim are true or false, we conclude that truth-claims about descriptions in science and religion are contextual and that for Christians "Truth-talk" precludes disinterest, detachment, and distance because Jesus Christ is the Truth, the Truth which cannot be theoretically reified into a property of an abstract description, but only existentially appropriated by concrete human beings in need.

IV

What significance should the resurrection claim within particular Christian descriptions of the self, world, and God have for us as Christians?

This question can be adequately addressed only after we have some notion of what the biblical understanding of the resurrection claim is. How did the first Christians view the resurrection claim? What significance did it have for them?

These questions take us into the muddy waters of New Testament scholarship. But this need not discourage us, for such controversy indicates that first-rate Christian minds are still grappling with the meaning of the resurrection claim. Following the powerful and penetrating 1955 Ingersoll Lecture by Oscar Cullmann, I believe it is first important to point out that the resurrection claim should not be confused with the Greek claim about the immortality of the soul. The Christian resurrection claim assumes that the sting of death was once deadly, that its power was once definitive, whereas the Greek immortality claim presupposes that the soul is intrinsically eternal, hence death is a release, a liberation for the soul out of the prison of the body. On the Christian view, the sting and power of death is conquered and overcome by the death and resurrection of Jesus Christ. On the Greek view, this victory over death is superfluous and unnecessary since the soul has always belonged to the eternal world, the world of Being and Essence.

The radical character of the Christian resurrection claim is found in its salvation-history perspective. The Christian claim that "Jesus arose from the dead" or that Jesus is "the first-born from the dead" is a proclamation of a divine miracle of creation in that God has called back to life a new creature from the old, a new creation from the old, a new history from the old. In this sense, the resurrection claim essentially refers to the inauguration of a new future, a future which promises redemption and deliverance.

The resurrection claim should mean to us that Jesus' victory over death ushered in a new age, an age in which the almighty power of God is already fulfilled but not yet consummated, an age in which death is conquered but not yet abolished. This new age is an interim period in which this divine power in the form of the Holy Spirit is at work among us. In this interim period, this Holy Spirit can be understood as the Reality of Jesus Christ to be existentially appropriated by fallen human beings for life sustenance, self-formation, self-maturation, and societal transformation.

The significance of the resurrection claim within "true" Christian descriptions of the self, world, and God is that, despite how tragic and hopeless present situations and circumstances appear to be, there is a God who sits high and looks low, a God who came into this filthy, fallen world in the form of a common peasant in order to commence a new epoch, an epoch in which Easter focuses our attention on the decisive victory of Jesus Christ and hence the possibility of our victory over our creaturehood, the old creation, and this old world, with its history of oppression and exploitation. So to be a Christian is to have a joyful attitude toward the resurrection claim, to stake one's life on it, and to rest one's hope upon its promise—the promise of a new heaven and a new earth.

Dispensing with Metaphysics in Religious Thought

A historicist turn has occurred in contemporary philosophy which has not yet awakened some theologians from their dogmatic slumber. Ironically, this turn—enacted by Thomas Kuhn, Richard Rorty, and others—is less radical and thorough than that initiated in theology by Ernst Troeltsch at the turn of the century. But who among our most influential religious thinkers invokes Troeltsch these days?

In this brief chapter I shall argue that historicism is indispensable for contemporary religious thought. I understand historicism as the view that structured social practices constitute the sources for standards which adjudicate between conflicting theories and interpretations. I then will suggest that this acceptance of historicism (an acceptance of our finitude and fallibilism) entails a rejection of old-style metaphysics.

Historicism in itself is a philosophically uninteresting perspective. It functions primarily in a critical and negative manner. It becomes philosophically controversial only when one tries to make it into a philosophical viewpoint. I hold that historicism should be understood as merely claiming that background prejudices, presuppositions, and prejudgments are requisite for any metaphysical or ontological reflections on the way the world is. This means that those metaphysical or ontological projects which hide and conceal their background conditions are deceptive and deficient. There is no doubt that metaphysical and ontological reflections should continue. In fact, these reflections are inescapable for finite human animals suspended in webs of significance we ourselves spin (to invoke Max Weber's famous phrase popularized by Clifford Geertz). Yet since these metaphysical or ontological reflections are never free of a particular set of presuppositions, prejudices, and prejudgments, metaphysics and ontology in the grand mode or in the old sense are anachronistic, antiquated, and, most important, unwarranted. Instead, metaphysics and ontologies are always relative to specific traditions, theories, and particular sets of social practices. In short, the Age of Metaphysics is over, yet inescapable metaphysical reflections will and must go on.

My conception of historicism requires that we try to approach the

From *Religion and Intellectual Life* (spring 1986).

metaphysical schemes of contemporary philosophers as anthropologists approach the cosmological schemes of Hopi Indians. The aim here is not to remove ourselves from our own background assumptions and presuppositions, but rather to demystify the highbrow philosophical debates, to demythologize the aura of profundity and solemnity of the debates themselves.

Seen in this way, crucial philosophical debates are less about the way the world is or the legitimate grounds of knowledge and more about how self-critical interlocutors (as bearers of particular traditions) in specific modes of inquiry project and preserve regulative self-images and guiding vocabularies that promote various aims and purposes. For example, the basic aim of philosophical realists in our time is to defend what some authoritative institutional practices, such as those of the scientific community or of some religious community, say that the world really is. Secular realists hold that what the secular priesthood, that is, the scientific community, says about the world is the way the world really is. For secular realists, the self-correcting character of scientific practices ensures that their grasp of Reality is the most reliable we have.

Religious realists hold that what an ecclesiastical priesthood says about the world is the way the world is. For them, the nonrational character of religious discourse signifies just how right they must be regarding an entity or power that transcends human reason. For both types of realists (secular or religious), it is Reality which ultimately serves as the arbiter of which theories or interpretations are accepted and warranted.

For historicists, secular realism is an intellectual strategy adopted by those who promote the authority of the secular priesthood. The aim of this strategy is to convince themselves and others that their acceptance of this authority is rational *independent of the aims and purposes of the secular priesthood*. I reject secular realism because its notion of rationality is deceptive and deficient. The predominant concepts of rationality accepted in the scientific community are inseparable from the aims and purposes of this community, that is, to predict and control phenomena. Yet even if one accepts, as good historicists do, that the scientific community fulfills this aim better than any other competitors, for example, communities of magicians or numerologists, one need not be seduced by an ideology of secular realism. The issue of whether scientific explanations provide the best predictions of phenomena because they are true or whether they are true because they yield the best predictions becomes a perennially circular one—precisely because the notion of truth in the scientific community is value-laden, that is, integral to its aims of prediction and control. To put it crudely, the idea of a true theory that predicts poorly is unintelligible and unacceptable in the scientific community.

Similarly, religious realism is an intellectual strategy adopted by those who accept the authority of particular ecclesiastical (or personal) interpretations. The purpose here is to convince one's self and others that these interpretations are true *regardless of their role and function in one's life*. I reject religious realism because it rests upon a faulty notion of religious "truth." The truth-claims of religious communities are inseparable from the aims and purposes of those communities, that is, to provide meaning and value in human lives. Yet if one holds, as some Christian historicists do, that certain Christian communities do this better than other communities, one need not accept religious realism in order to be religious. The issue of whether certain religious communities provide the best meaning and value in human lives because they are true or whether they are true because they yield the best meaning and value in human lives becomes inescapably circular—precisely because the notion of truth in religious communities is value-laden, that is, integral to its aims of providing meaning and value. The notion of a true religion that does not sustain people through the crises and traumas of life is unintelligible and unacceptable for religious communities. In fact, as Pascal and Kierkegaard noted, the ideology of religious realism may sap some of the authenticity of religious faith by robbing it of existential risk and anxiety. In this way, old-style metaphysics may even harm one's religious faith.

Historicists have often been accused of being closet idealists or vulgar relativists. Since they reject using Reality as the ultimate standard to adjudicate between conflicting viewpoints, they are portrayed as either disbelieving in sense-independent objects or claiming that there are no rational standards to distinguish better and worse interpretations. My sort of historicism indeed rejects Reality as the ultimate standard since reality-claims are theory-laden, that is, our truth-claims are mediated by our theories. But sense-independent objects indeed do exist according to our best theories. So to reject Reality as the standard by which we accept theories of reality is not the same as rejecting the existence of Reality per se. Rather, it is to reject value-neutral and theory-free notions of Reality as standards for philosophical arbitration.

Nor is my historicism reducible to vulgar relativism. There are rational standards to adjudicate between better and worse theories or interpretations, yet these standards are relative to our common aims and purposes. Intersubjective agreement is requisite for feasible and effective standards. This does not mean that Reality is simply what people can agree on. Rather, it means that common aims and purposes are required if there are to be rational standards which help determine acceptable and unacceptable theories and interpretations.

In conclusion, I suggest that acceptable forms of metaphysical reflections are those of synoptic narratives and overarching vocabularies that provide enhancing self-images and enabling coping techniques for living. The greatness (and weakness) of the grand metaphysicians of old is not the logical consistency and theoretical coherence of their systems but rather the qualities of mind and forms of life that are imaged and enacted in their discourses. My sort of historicism does not see the threat to legitimate metaphysical reflection coming from philosophers but rather from the deep crisis in synecdochic narrative practices in our postmodern culture.

Since the high modernism of Proust, Joyce, and Kafka, our narrative strategies have shunned self-confident notions of social belonging and innocent ideas of "capturing the whole" of things. And as Jean-François Lyotard has argued in *The Postmodern Condition,* we are witnessing an increasing incredulity toward master- or meta-narratives, be they Christian, Marxist, or liberal. We live in a time of cultural disarray and social decay, an age filled with ruins and fragments. Hence, our intellectual landscapes are littered with allegorical tales of deterioration rather than dramatic narratives of reconciliation. The only truly totalizing story that can credibly encompass all of us is a nuclear holocaust narrative.

In stark contrast to Huston Smith, my historicism compels me to conclude that dispensing with old-style metaphysics is a crucial step toward more legitimate (and much less ambitious) modes of metaphysical reflection. Yet even these more legitimate narrative modes may have highly limited potency and pertinence in a world in which any sense of the whole has been lost. Without such a sense, there can be only truncated (especially nostalgic) forms of metaphysical reflections. And without vital narratives, narrativity itself becomes more and more an object of metaphysical reflection. In fact, the great metaphysical project of our time—Paul Ricoeur's metaphysics of narrativity in *Time and Narrative*— may be symptomatic of the end of old-style and legitimate forms of metaphysics. If this be so, both Huston Smith's metaphysical realism and my narrativistic historicism are "vestigial clingings to long lost ways, the planting of feet on a world that is gone."

On Christian Intellectuals

In his influential *Prison Notebooks,* the Italian Marxist Antonio Gramsci makes an important distinction between "organic" and "traditional" intellectuals. To put it crudely, the former are those who, because they are organically linked to prophetic movements or priestly institutions, take the life of the mind seriously enough to relate ideas to the everyday life of ordinary folk. Traditional intellectuals, in contrast, are those who revel in the world of ideas while nesting in comfortable places far removed from the realities of the common life. Organic intellectuals are activistic and engaged; traditional intellectuals are academic and detached.

Like most such constructs, Gramsci's distinction is too broad and vague to do full justice to the complexity of intellectual activity. Yet it is useful. Prior to the emergence of modernity, intellectuals primarily were organically linked with either the church or rich patrons. Contrary to popular opinion, medieval intellectuals were organic intellectuals, often involved in public turmoil. Today most intellectuals are employed by educational institutions. They are traditional intellectuals preoccupied with academic affairs.

A distinctive feature of religious traditions in the modern world—represented in seminaries, ecclesiastical agencies, and especially churches—is that, at least ideally, serious intellectual activity is understood as inseparable from moral and political practice. In contrast to predominant modern conceptions of knowledge, which subordinate ideas to technical control and manipulation, religious notions of knowledge accent ethical accountability and political fruition. This is especially so for the Christian tradition in which the principal form of intellectual activity consists of making clear and plain the content and character of Christian living.

Christian intellectuals should differ from others by refusing either to exalt or to denigrate the life of the mind. They should raise questions about the modern "objective" search for truth and the enthusiasm for social engineering. The ideal Christian intellectual is neither a detached seminary professor teaching potential elites of the church nor an engaged layperson in solidarity with the downtrodden, but rather the dedicated and devoted Christian member of a group or community informed by the best available systemic social analysis of self and society and guided by the most insightful interpretation of the Scriptures and tradi-

From *Christianity and Crisis* (Mar. 19, 1984).

271

tion. This ideal Christian intellectual is an organic intellectual, simultaneously immersed in the tortuous realities of the day and enticed by the felicities of the mind.

What Is the Task?

Contemporary circumstances make it difficult for such Christian intellectuals to emerge. First, the professional ethos of the secular academy continues to seduce many seminaries and divinity schools. Principled and fruitful interaction with the academy is indispensable; yet the academy cannot serve as either model or paradigm for Christian cultivation. Second, increased denominational concerns breed parochial modes of intellectual activity that are narrowly defensive and obsessed with internal operations. This reversion to premodern sentiments—aided by modern capital—is nostalgic and escapist. Third, the world of highbrow journalism offers stimulation but it does not lend itself to the kind of intellectual depth requisite for profound Christian vision, analysis, and practice.

The tasks of Christian intellectuals are to uphold the centrality of prophetic preaching of the Word, preserve the richness of the Christian past, and put forward informed Christian ways of life and struggle. These tasks include traditional and organic types of intellectual work—but their aim should be the production of sermons and texts which become potent within the lives of everyday people. This does not mean that sermons and texts should simply cater to parishioners but rather that they should be directed to the pertinent issues that fundamentally affect the lives of church people.

The critical function of Christian intellectuals remains a crucial item on the theological agenda. And none of the schools of thought and action on the scene contain acceptable perspectives on this issue. This is so primarily because theologians and preachers are reluctant to engage in what Gramsci calls a "self-inventory"—a critical examination of their own middle-class status, academic setting, or social privilege. Yet a more self-critical viewpoint is imperative if the Body of Christ is to function in a more Christian manner.

The Crisis in Theological Education

Preparation for the Christian ministry has always been a difficult affair. We can look back to any historical period and see enormous shortcomings and blindnesses in the education and cultivation of mature Christian ministers. Yet in our present moment, the inescapable difficulties have mushroomed into structural deficiencies. Our seminaries and divinity schools are not simply in intellectual disarray and existential disorientation; our very conceptions of what they should be doing are in shambles. For example, students come ill-equipped for and unaware of what they will encounter in our theological schools; faculty often are uninterested in and unrewarded for meeting the *practical* demands of educating refined and relevant Christian ministers; and administrators usually have little vision of or capacity for guiding our theological schools in a prophetic (as opposed to a cost-benefit) manner.

These symptoms can be understood as manifestations of a more fundamental problem: *the problem of what it means to be a Christian minister in our time*. The sources of this problem are threefold. First, the institutional matrices in which preparation for the Christian ministry takes place have been in the grip of either a debilitating ethos of professionalization and specialization and/or a parochial atmosphere of denominationalism and dogmatism. In influential places like Harvard, Yale, Chicago, and Union, the "double consciousness" of being of the Academy but not in it, or of being in the church but not of it, has resulted in a nearly wholesale capitulation to the system of rewards and sensibilities, prestige and status of the university. In the more populous places like Fuller and Southern Baptist and Catholic seminaries, the "single consciousness" of being suspicious of the Academy and proud of it, or of being entrenched in the church and limited by it, has yielded a virtually thorough subordination to the doctrines and dictates of church bureaucrats. In this way, the very *character* of our seminaries and divinity schools prohibits and precludes an adequate preparation for the vocation (not the profession) of ministry to the people of God (not the denomination).

Second, the major post–World War II developments such as the de-

An address presented at a symposium in Minneapolis sponsored by the Association of Theological Schools, July 1987.

centering of Europe, the demystifying of European cultural hegemony, the deconstruction of European philosophical edifices, and the decolonization of the third world has left theology with hardly an autonomous subject matter (hence a temptation to be excessively frivolous and meretricious in its enactments) and with little intellectually respectable resources upon which to build. The point here is not simply that the giants of the past decades—Barth, Brunner, Tillich, the Niebuhrs—are no longer with us; but rather that the kind of world, culture, and society that produced and sustained them is no longer with us. The old consensus, along with the tribal civility, snobbish gentility, and institutional loyalty of male WASPs that circumscribed it, now merely limps and lingers in small pockets of our educational landscapes. Its adherents still wield much institutional power in our seminaries and divinity schools—yet they have not revised and reformed the work of the giants in a refreshing and refined manner. So it is not surprising to see so much nostalgia for the golden age of U.S. theology in the higher echelons of theological education.

A major watershed occurred in the sixties with the entrée of significant numbers of black and women students—only later to be accompanied by Latinos, older students, and self-identified gays and lesbians. In this turbulent period, it became fairly clear that the riches of the past theological giants were not brought to bear on the new realities in ways that could seize the imagination of the new students (who would soon constitute a majority in our theological schools). Leading liberal and neoorthodox male WASP interpretations of the Christian faith fell more and more on deaf ears. In some ways, this was unfortunate in that many profound insights were overlooked. Yet the relative silence and/or outright complicity on such crucial matters as racism, gender oppression, or U.S. militarism made it difficult for many students and faculty to take these interpretations seriously in the sixties and early seventies. The emergence of liberation theologies and the upsurge of conservative evangelical and fundamentalist perspectives were, in part, responses to the vacuum left by the liberal and neoorthodox male WASP interpretations. Yet neither responses have allayed the protracted crisis in theological education.

Liberation theology indeed has injected a sense of relevancy and urgency in theological education regarding the social and political dimensions of the Christian faith—forcing even those conservative Christian thinkers riding the tide of Reaganism to accent these dimensions in interesting and revealing ways. Yet the social and political aspects of the Christian faith are inseparable from though not identical with the spiritual and personal aspects of the Christian faith. Politics always has and always will be a poor vessel for healthy and longstanding transcendence

274

for persons who undergo illness, dread, despair, and death in any social system.

Conservative evangelical and fundamentalist perspectives disclose the degree to which the hunger for meaning and value, community and authority, still lurks among the general populace. But, like all forms of dogmatism, it runs the risk of backlash owing to the hypocrisy of its leaders, the narrowness of its scope, and the hollowness of its message. In this way, the very *content* of what is taught and transmitted in our seminaries and divinity schools impedes and obstructs an adequate preparation for the multidimensional practice (not solely the political praxis) of the Christian ministry to the people of God (not the nation, party, or group).

The last source of the crisis of theological education—besides the institutional and intellectual ones—resides in the constituencies of seminaries and divinity schools. Students and the prospective congregations they will serve present formidable obstacles for solid preparation for Christian ministry. Students are, like all of us, products of a culture. Advanced capitalist culture—with its consumer sensibilities, flashing images, and quick information—simply does not provide the kind of exposure to and appreciation for the spiritual discipline, biblical grounding, and church ritualistic practices requisite for a vital and vibrant Christian ministry.

Therefore theological schools must first expose most students to these phenomena while they also attempt to shape students into serious Christian ministers of various sorts. Needless to say, this process of exposure is difficult in that students must be convinced that a particular tradition is worth being exposed to and shaped in. Sometimes the result is a rejection of any tradition—a rejection which paradoxically fuels a more intense quest for spirituality that can end in a self-manufactured mythology and superficially constructed community. This quest, though possibly motivated by noble aims, may simply mirror the very individualism and voluntarism (including a typically American gesture of refusing the past and casting the present in Edenic terms) that led to the rejection of other traditions.

Furthermore, because theological students are so diverse—a more broad array of colors, ages, genders, and sexual orientations than students in law, business, and medical schools—it is more difficult for them to create the kind of supportive networks necessary for a rich educational experience. The combination of attending school, working for a living, raising a family, and serving a church presents an enormous burden on theological students. It leaves little time for nurturing empowering relationships among each other—relationships that are the very yeast of any genuine pedagogical endeavor. This is even rendered more complicated in university-related seminaries and divinity schools where theological students are often looked down on by their university peers, partly owing to the relatively easy entrance requirements for seminarians and partly because of the mild secular snobbery toward religious people rampant in the Academy.

The congregations who receive these students are often perplexed—and for good reasons. For instance, the historical-critical methods of reading the biblical texts add little to the religious sustenance of most Christians, and few biblical professors at seminaries provide the interpretive tools required to contribute to this sustenance for congregations. This tremendous task often falls upon the shoulders of students. And the congregations suffer for it. Without some close relation with a working pastor—a valuable apprenticeship that becomes pivotal for most students—this burden can prove devastating. Yet such apprenticeships have their price, including the promotion and cultivation of views that highlight the irrelevance of seminary education yet accent the instrumental prestige-value of seminaries for career purposes.

Similarly, most courses in philosophy of religion, theology, and ethics present materials to students as if they were preparing for graduate work in the respective fields rather than for Christian pastoral ministry. This is not surprising since most of the professors have little or no experience in (and a few have little or no appreciation for) the Christian pastoral ministry. Hence, many fine prospective ministers are seduced into graduate work principally on grounds of prestige and status. This is a loss for the church—and in no way a gain for the Academy.

It is inexcusable that the faculties of seminaries and divinity schools should continue to teach as they do with little reflection or consultation about what they do, why they teach what they do, and whether what they teach aids their students in preparation for Christian ministry. The relative absence of collective conversation among seminary faculties about the aim and purpose of their curriculum, the circumstances and challenges of their students, the perplexities of the congregations, and the academic pressures on themselves reveals the depths of the crisis in theological education.

What Is to Be Done?

If my sketchy and schematic description of the crisis in theological education has any validity, full-scale reform is imperative. The best place to start is with the most delicate and difficult: *the self-images and self-identities of seminary professors*. The sense of vocation and purpose of seminary professors sets the tone of theological education. To the degree to which this sense is captivated by that of the secular Academy—with its present-day downbeat Alexandrian cynicism and backstabbing careerism—the seminary will be simply a marginal imitation of mediocre professionalism. To the degree to which this sense is guided by that of the church bureaucracy—with its myopic preoccupation with growth and quantity—the seminary will be merely a backwater site that produces insular ecclesiastical clones.

An appropriate starting point for reform in theological education is seminary professors creating for themselves a sense of vocation and purpose that revels in the life of the mind—always in conversation with the best that is being thought and written regarding their intellectual concerns—yet puts this at the service of the people of God. Seminary professors first and foremost must view themselves as servants of the kingdom of God and thereby resist the lucrative temptations of a flaccid careerism and a flagrant denominationalism.

Such a vocation means that seminary professors will be marginal to both Academy and church. But it will be a marginality that bears fruit, an enabling marginality aware of its limits and mindful of its strengths. Need we remind ourselves that the great seminary professors of the past (who were neither careerist nor technicians but rather ecumenical intellectual figures with which the larger culture had to reckon) had this sense of vocation. And they were able to gain the respect of their secular peers, the attention of their fellow Christians, and the admiration of their students. In fact, many middle-aged seminary professors and pastors still pull from the vocational inspiration and existential mileage they received from such seminary professors. In this way, seminary professors can change the character of theological education by giving students a new and novel sense of what it means to have a vocation as a Christian intellectual in our time.

This shift in vocation must be accompanied by a shift in curriculum. The fourfold division of biblical studies, theology, church history, and practical matters derived from the "theological encyclopedia" movement of eighteenth-century Germany must go. For theology is no longer the queen of the curriculum that puts all the biblical, historical, and practical pieces together. Theology in our time can no longer aspire in a serious manner to be the tribunal before which other fields must come. The days of wholesale theological synthesis are over. To be a Christian theologian today is to be a learned proponent of an interpretation of the Christian faith in conversation with other disciplines: anthropology, sociology, philosophy, history, etc. It means to be a critic of culture and society from the vantage point of one's location within the rich though flawed history and tradition of the Christian church. Of course, the history of theology is crucial as one source of one's Christian perspective. But one's perspective is always already shaped by other sources—Weber, Marx, Du Bois, Stanton, et al. Theologians must be relieved of the burden of holding the seminary curriculum together.

This burden must be relegated more and more to historians— but historians of a certain sort. Church history must break out of its ecclesiastical cocoon and become the hermeneutical activity it once was. The grand legacy of church historians like Ernst Troeltsch and Walter Rauschenbusch or philosopher-theologians turned historians like H. Richard Niebuhr must be appropriated for our own day. If we in theological education take seriously our commitment to prepare self-reflective and self-critical Christian ministers, we must become fellow hermeneutical thinkers and doers putting forth diverse interpretations of the texts and traditions of the Christian heritage in light of our understanding of the new challenges in the present. To be fellow hermeneuts is to be conversational comrades in pursuit of a Christian meaning of and response to history (understood as past and present). In this sense, the former burden of theologians is equalized and democratized; that is, it rests upon all those who partake of the conversation in the seminary.

This conception of theological education entails that we view traditional distinctions between fundamental theology, dogmatic theology, and practical theology as mere heuristic devices that help us grasp what we are doing in relation to the way in which theologians once talked. Philosophical questions concerning the grounds and bases of our claims indeed persist, theological attempts to render coherent and consistent the dogmas and intuitions of the church must continue, and training for preaching, counseling, and ritual remains crucial. Yet these activities should be informed by a profound and pervasive historical consciousness; that is, a recognition that they are provisional, tentative, and revisable human practices shot through with interests and prejudices, regulated by operations of power, and guided by Christian ideals to which they never fully conform. And, as Hans-Georg Gadamer reminds us, to acknowledge historical contingency is not to overcome it. Rather it is to render our methodological orientations more suspect, our interpretations more open-ended, and, most importantly, our Christian lives more humble.

To put hermeneutical historical consciousness at the center of theological education means not only that seminaries become beacons of light in the present linked to an empowering past within an amnesiac society; it also means that forms of social analyses come to the forefront. This is so because history is what human beings born under circumstances not of their own choosing do with those circumstances in specific times and in particular spaces. The dialectical interplay of how human beings appropriate what is transmitted and bequeathed to them by institutions and traditions and how these institutions and traditions are shaped by this human appropriation links historical consciousness to social analysis. For too long theological education has specialized in transmitting beliefs, ideas, and thought-systems to students and overlooked the ways in which these beliefs, ideas, and thought-systems emerged, developed, and declined in relation to social conflicts over language, identities, territory, goods, and services. For us Christians, the history of Christian thought is more than the history of religious ideology; the history of Christian churches is more than the history of institutional hierarchy and social subordination; the history of canon-formation of the Scriptures is more than the history of textual conflict and hermeneutical violence; and the history of Christian preaching is more than the history of societal legitimation. Yet as Christians who recognize our finitude and fallenness, we are aware that we never fully escape our own complicity in ideologies, institutional hierarchy, social subordination, textual conflict, hermeneutical violence, and societal legitimation, even in our most prophetic moments. A fundamental task of theological education is to transform this awareness into an enabling source to resist our complicity with these idols. Secular folk would call this "criticism"; we Christians can call it the love ethic in its pedagogic mode. For its aim is to empower us to better serve the kingdom of God, its motivation is to aid and abet us in our becoming fuller Christians despite our faults and blindnesses, and its institutional function is to make our seminaries and divinity schools contexts in which reflection and learning become effective means of enhancing the quality of service to the people of God.

This conception of theological education—still in need of a more detailed delineation of curricular and extracurricular activities—requires paradoxically a much *closer* relation of seminaries to the conversations in research-oriented universities and a more *distant* relation of seminaries with the ethos of specialization in these universities. Seminaries cannot possibly provide adequate education in economics, sociology, psychology, literary studies, etc. Yet seminaries can be the place where Christian ministers-to-be are in close dialogue with these disciplines in light of their Christian heritages. This dialogue cannot and should not take place in the university because its ethos is first and foremost secular. To imitate this ethos (as ought departments of religious studies in universities and colleges) is suicidal for seminaries and divinity schools. Mature Christian ministers should not feign objectivity or value-neutrality, but rather be self-invested and self-involved advocates of the Christian gospel genuinely open to criticism and counsel.

The current crisis in theological education is not to be confused with

Epilogue
Sing a Song

For they who fashion songs must live too close to pain,
Acquaint themselves too well with grief and tears;
Must make the slow, deep, throbbing pulse of years
And their own heartbeats one; watch the slow train
Of passing autumns paint their scarlet stain
Upon the hills, and learn that beauty sears,
The whole world's woe and heartbreak must be theirs,
And theirs each vision smashed, each new dream slain.

But sing again, oh you who have heart,
Sweet songs as fragile as a passing breath.
Although your broken heartstrings make your lyre,
And each pure strain must rend the soul apart;
For it was ever thus: to sing is death;
And in your spirit flames your body's pyre.

Frank Yerby

I

I love music. I don't think it's in my genes, so it must have something to
do with my upbringing.

As a youth, I went to nightclubs every weekend. I never understood
the real significance of this weekly routine until I left Harlem.

We moved from our place on Lenox Avenue not long ago. We lived
across the street from Harlem Hospital. Over the past months, my hearing has begun to fail me. My wife convinced me that the almost constant
sirens of the ambulances weren't helping matters. So we moved out to
Queens, nowhere near a hospital. It's a neighborhood without gang
fights, shootouts, or loud sirens. Better for my eardrums, but the quiet
annoys me.

This story, written in 1975, was first published in the black student journal of Williams College in 1982.

II

One night, while I slept, my hearing failed me for almost thirty minutes. I was furious—and frightened. One whole episode in my dream was like a silent movie. No sound, just body movements.

The next morning, Saturday morning, I made my biweekly trip back to Harlem to Johnny's barber shop. I could see Jackson, Hook, and Brother Will through the large front window.

Jackson was an old high school classmate of mine. Now he has a good job with the city. He drives a garbage truck—and makes almost twice as much money as my wife, who is a nurse.

Hook is a bonafide hustler. He makes money any way he can. And somehow he seems to have a lot of it. I first met Hook two years ago at his brother's service station. His brother was sick at the time, so Hook was managing the station. During the Arab boycott, just when all the other gas stations were raising their prices, Hook started a gas war. His challenge lasted two days. He made a mint during the challenge, though his middle men cut off his gas supplies after the first day. The next day Hook filled at least forty cars with a mixture of gas, water, Kool-aid, and any other fluid he could find. My car was one of those forty.

But it worked out well for me. When my car stalled on St. Nicholas Avenue it was demolished by another car—luckily, I was out of it. So my insurance and I bought a new car. And believe me, the assistance was heaven-sent.

I really do like Hook, even aside for this selfish reason. I like him because of his independence. He listens only to himself. The length of his jail record is the best testimony for that. Hook believes in autonomy. Nobody tells him what to do, be it the police, his wife, or his best friend. He's unemployed right now—but living comfortably.

Brother Will is the pastor of Guiding Light Apostolic Church of God in Christ. My wife tells me that he can drive the devil out of Satan himself by the sheer volume of his voice. I've known Brother Will for over twenty years and still have no desire to hear him preach. I guess I've seen too many of his sermons to take his oral ones seriously. But he's basically a good man, with a quick mind and a quicker eye.

As I entered Johnny's, Brother Will, sitting in the high chair, said loudly, "Ah, look who the wind blew in! That educated sinner, Zek!"

I must explain here that my real name is Ezekiel. Ezekiel Clifton Satterfield. My father gave me this burden-bearing name. I never did like it; sounds too important. So I tell folks to call me Zek. Just Zek.

Johnny exclaimed, "My man Zek, haven't seen ya' in a while! How's life on the island been treatin' ya'?"

"Not too bad, Johnny," I replied, "Cain't complain at all."

Jackson and Hook exchanged similar greetings with me as I took my seat.

I grabbed the *Amsterdam News* and glanced at the headline. It read:

THE DUKE OF MUSIC IS GONE

I yelled, "Duke Ellington, the Duke, died? My Jesus!"

Hook interjected, "Yeah, Zek. The Duke is gone, man. It's a shame."

Johnny mumbled, "Old Duke was the King. Our King. Cool, suave, and always down-to-earth. We seem to be losing all our kings these days."

"Yeh, but is he really the King these days, Johnny?" asked Jackson.

"Whatchu mean, man! 'Is he really the King these days?' You know damn well he's the King!" hollered Hook.

"Naw, I ain't sayin' he *ain't* the King. I'm sayin' that young folks today might not think he's the King like we do," retorted Jackson.

"Well shit, oh, 'scuse me Reb, forget young folks, they ain't got no taste. Their James Brown or Barry White cain't touch the Duke. Damn, don't let me get ta talkin' 'bout the greatness of the Duke 'cause I'll be here all night!" shouted Hook.

"Please watch your tongue," Brother Will remarked. "I cain't stand the truth to be put in such unclean language."

"Glad y'a agree with me, Reb," said Hook, with a smile.

Brother Will continued, "Ya' know, that's what's wrong wit' the church today. The young folk don't 'preciate the music of the past. They always want ta jazz up the spirituals and gospels, like they in some night-club. I don't mind the guitars, but I cain't stand that fast, funky beat of those boys who play the drums for that youth choir of ours. I truly believe that's the main reason why the Holy Ghost don't come to Guidin' Light as much as it use' ta."

I remained silent. The death of the Duke had shaken me. My head sunk in sadness. My idol had succumbed to Nature. His music from now on would be the spiritual extension of a man now but dust. It frightened me. I was scared of losing my hearing. I realized then the power of music, its sustaining and redeeming power. I wondered whether silence was a kind of death.

Jackson was still defensive. "Just like we think the Duke is King, so my kids think that James Brown or Barry White is King. Who are we to say who's really the King or not? Times change. We got to realize that."

Hook shouted back, "If change means goin' from the Duke to what young folks like, I ain't gon' change! Change ain't just change, Jackson. There's change from bad to good and from good to bad. Ya' gotta' take your pick!"

Johnny added in support, "That's right Jackson. Ya' know that the Duke is King. Why make his crown less worthy by lettin' anybody who young folks like wear it?"

"A-m-a-n!" said Brother Will. "That's like lettin' any man be Christ just 'cause some folks say he is the Christ. Ya' see, there's true prophets and false prophets. And ya' know the false ones when ya' see 'em! Just like I know that the true Christians love those old spirituals and gospels and the false ones love that jazzed-up stuff."

"Settle down Reb or ya' ain't gon' have no sideburns left. I cain't shape 'em when ya' get excited like that!" cautioned Johnny.

Hook sat back in his chair and said, "Ya' need to stop bendin' the Holy Book your way Reb. 'Cause singin' or listenin' to the spirituals or gospels ain't never made nobody no true Christian. Christ in the flesh ain't never even heard 'em. I like 'em and I don't even believe in Christ outside the flesh, wit' my hell-bound self. Respectin' good music ain't got nothin' to do wit' no religion. It all comes down to a matter of 'preciation. Young folks don't 'preciate nothin', the spirituals, the Duke, nothin'! They been spoiled rotten. I was down at City College the other day messin' around. I asked this young brotha' what he was studyin' to be. He told me he wasn't even interested in studyin.' He said he was just playin' along with the game. Then I asked him why in the hell he was in college? He said, 'That's your problem, old brotha', you still believe games are played only on these petty streets in Harlem. Well, let me clue you in, these streets have only low-level games, with everything to lose and hardly nothin' to gain. The real games are played on different streets, like Wall Street and Pennsylvania Avenue.' Then I told him, 'Well, since ya' ain't studyin' nothin', it looks like ya' gon' be stayin' here wit' me playin' these low-level games on these petty streets!'"

Hook went on, "I was about to go upside the little bastard's head, but it looked too hard to knock some sense into! Ya' know, he really got me warm! Like I don't know that them big corporations and the government are bloodsuckers. Shit, he ain't never even paid no taxes yet!"

Hook seemed delighted as usual to speak his mind on the young folks' issue. His usual diatribe against the young was one form of enjoyment for him. Since his last four-month stint in jail, he frequently would air his hostility toward young folks, especially men under thirty. He complained that they were soft. They had no courage. They succumbed to the wishes of their friends and submitted to the rule of pseudo-leaders.

As Brother Will stepped down from the high chair, Johnny said, "Come on Hook! It's your turn to get your beard trimmed and thank God it didn't rain yesterday on your conk, 'cause I ain't in no mood to cook no hair today!"

When Hook was seated in the high chair, he turned to me and said,

"Why ya' so quiet this mornin', Zek? With your educated mind, I'm sure you got somethin' to say 'bout these issues."

I looked at Hook with a friendly frown. I had been following the conversation closely; I also had glanced further down in the newspaper article and observed that James Brown, Barry White, and many others publicly mourned the loss of the "late, great Duke of music."

So I said to Hook, "It's true that young folk don't 'preciate things like we do. I see it in my own Bessie Mae. But there's no clear-cut reason for it. Jackson, you try to understand young folks, but you lose your own views in the process. You act as if their ways are automatically worth endorsin'. As if the mere march of time is the march of truth. Hook, you want everybody to be as independent as you, but don't realize that most folks, young and old, just ain't like that. To be independent is not only to be free but also lonely. Most folks cain't stand loneliness. Only a select few have the courage to endure such pain. To be independent is to be an outsider. Such persons possibly enrich the lives of others, but they usually live self-destructive lives themselves. To be truly free is to clearly see the true depths of life. This demands that you step to the edge of a slippery cliff. Few avoid fallin' over and the bottom down below has no cushion. I personally . . ."

"Wait a cotton-pickin' minute, brotha' Zek!" Hook said, politely interrupting me. "I know you're educated and all that. And I respect ya' more for it 'cause you're a self-learnet' man. But at the moment I only wantcha' to answer the questions on the table, Is the Duke really the King for all, young and old? And are young folks soft?"

I continued, "Oh, yeh. Duke is definitely the King. Young folks simply have no one who can compare with him. Just as there is no one today who can compare with Ellison in writin' or Du Bois in learnin'. Ya' see, the young folks today lack discipline—and ain't nothin' worthwhile been produced without discipline. But discipline is based on authority, and what authority is worthy of their loyalty? Corrupt governments, status-ridden churches, the suspicious media, adulterous parents, manipulative peers? To whom or toward what can they turn? Solely to music. So they have turned to music. Music has become the air they breathe, the very sunlight they absorb. They imitate its rhythms in their walk, their talk. Yet they are soft, for they have never really suffered. That's why so much of their music lacks depth."

I stopped and was quiet. I could hear Jackson snoring a bit. He had begun to doze sometime after I separated the march of time from the march of truth. Aside from Jackson, the only noise in the barber shop was the clicking of Johnny's scissors on Hook's mustache. As usual, no one replied. It is assumed, for some odd reason, that I have the last word.

285

I never knew whether this custom arose out of deference or indifference to me. I did know in regard to Jackson though.

When the time came for me to take my seat in the high chair, Brother Will, Jackson, and Hook had left. Two young men entered just as they walked out the door. After my haircut, I paid Johnny and said good-bye. As I was leaving, Johnny scratched his head and said, "I tend to think ya' spoke words of wisdom this mornin', Zek. But if what ya' said is true, then what happens to young folks who can't hear no music? Ya' know, my sister Essie got a pretty little girl who can't hear a word. She's deaf." Johnny looked perplexed and continued, "Well, I guess she probably just reads, writes, or does somethin' else, but don't mind me, Zek. Take it slow, and tell Phyllis I send my hello."

III

Whenever Phyllis stands with her hands on her hips on the front porch looking down the street for my car, I know she's mad. Whenever she decides to attend the Saturday night meeting of the church missionary society, I *know* she's upset.

She greeted me with a medium holler, "Ezekiel, I don't know why we have to go through this every time you go to Johnny's. With all the things that need to be done 'round this house, you go and spend the whole day there! I know all y'all doin' is talkin' trash!"

She became even madder when I didn't get mad.

"Well, I'm goin' to Motha' Hinton's for a missionary society meetin'. Tell Bessie Mae to warm up that chicken in the oven," she said. "And there's some salad in the icebox," she added, in a low and reluctant soft voice.

I knew she was mad. So I just let her release her steam, a technique that has worked well for eighteen married years now. But as she left, I momentarily wondered why she was so upset.

I was really quite hungry, though I hadn't realized it until Phyllis mentioned that chicken in the oven. When I entered the house, Bessie Mae shouted, "Is that you Dad? I know you must be starvin'. The food will be ready in a minute."

I must explain here that Phyllis and I had a little girl eighteen years ago. I named her Bessie, after my favorite blues singer. Phyllis named her Mary, after her Savior's mother. So we compromised and that's how Bessie Mae got her name.

Bessie Mae's voice was always like music to my ears. Not any particular words, but the soft sweet tone of their sound. The legato style of her expression. The enchanting rhythm of her delivery.

I walked into the kitchen mentally waltzing to syncopated thoughts.

Bessie Mae gave me a big hug and a kiss on the cheek.

I said jokingly, "Since when do I get all this good sugar! You must've broken up with Raymond again, so that now I get all that surplus affection!"

She blushed. "Come on now Dad, don't play like that. You know I've always been and always will be your Bessie."

Though I could hardly hear her words, I chuckled in reply, "I'm just not used to that much sugar from such a sweet young pretty girl!"

"By the way," she said, "Raymond will be over in a few minutes. He told me this morning he wanted to talk to you about his job."

I would not have heard her remarks about Raymond had she not repeated them when I returned to the kitchen with my highpowered hearing aid.

We sat silently, ate, and watched "The Jeffersons." In the middle of the program, Bessie turned to me and asked, "Dad, why do you think black folks talk so loud? Not only on TV, but also in real life. We always seem to shout or holler when we speak to one another. Why?"

"It's tension, honey. Nerves. We got a lot of tension to release."

The doorbell rang, and Raymond joined us in the kitchen. After the program, Raymond and I retired to the den. He seemed a bit shy and began to speak in a low tone of voice.

"Mr. Satterfield, I've been wantin' to talk to you for a long time. I told Bessie it had to do with my job, but it's really more than just that."

I interrupted, "You gotta' talk a little louder, Raymond. My hearing's been fading on me lately."

"Oh, OK," replied Raymond. "What I really want to talk about is you. Your life. Ya' see, I ain't never had no man around the house, only women. You're kinda the first man I really respect and look up to. Plus I'm thinkin' 'bout quittin' my job and maybe goin' back to school. And I know you're a man of a lotta' education. So first, how'd ya' ever get interested in learnin'?"

"I'm honored that ya' think so highly of me, really 'preciate it, son. To tell ya' the truth, I never got interested in learnin', I just always was interested as far back as I can remember. It's like tryin' to remember your first memory. Ya' see, my father was a Baptist preacher down South for a while, so I had all kinds of religious books around. Since my mother died in childbirth, havin' me that is, it was only me and Pops. After he quit preachin', he came on up to the city and got a job at Penn Station downtown. When he came home from work, he taught me everything he knew. And believe me, that was a lot. We read and talked 'bout everything. Oh, how he loved that story about Gilgamesh! Ya' know, his dream was to start a bookstore on 125th Street and Seventh Avenue."

"I guess it never came true," said Raymond, with sympathy.

"Yeah, it was just a fantasy and he knew it. He knew wigs would be more popular than books in Harlem for years to come. He used to always say, with a grin, 'I may be educated but I ain't no fool!'"

"Why did he quit preachin'?"

"He quit 'cause he thought there was enough preachers around talkin'. He believed God had sent him here to write. Pops thought that some preachers were called by God to speak and others to write. In his last days, he became a kind of self-styled atheist. He said he couldn't believe in a God that only called black preachers to speak and none to write. He came to believe that he could be saved only by leaving volumes of books behind 'im. He longed for immortality, but only in the form of the written word."

A beam of puzzling dismay flashed across Raymond's face. He asked, "What did he write?"

"Nothin'," I softly replied, "Not a word. He died an alcoholic, distressed over his failure to gain his salvation. Ya' know, Pops could really speak, he was an absolute master of the spoken word. But, for some odd reason, he hated his gift. He thought God had called him for another mission, a mission for which he had no gift."

"Do you have this gift, Mr. Satterfield?"

"I'm not really sure. But let's not call it a gift. It's really a capacity. Ya' see, that's where I think Pops was wrong. He had a gift for speaking, it came natural. It flowed like water from a faucet. But writin' ain't no gift, it's a capacity. It takes time and long, lonely hours to develop this capacity. Pops couldn't accept this, and that's what killed him in a sense. He hated solitude and silence, but that's what you need to develop the capacity of writin'."

"Did you ever preach?" Raymond asked.

"Naw, naw. I'm not a religious person, though I value what religious folks are searchin' for. What they and Pops try to find in religion, I find in music."

"Oh, so you're a musician or composer?"

"Yeah, I guess you can say that. But I've become one only within the past few weeks. That's when I began to write. Ya' see, I believe writin' is a kind of music composed for those who no longer hear the sweet music of persons, for those who live in silence. I write in order to sing for those who live in this silence."

We heard a loud door slam in the next room.

"Bessie Mae, Ezekiel, where are you two?" called out Phyllis, as she entered the house out of breath.

"Dad is talkin' to Raymond in the den. I'm here in the kitchen watchin' TV, Momma," Bessie called back.

"Ya' know, Raymond," I said, "I don't know how we got on this tangent 'bout Pops, but let's drop it and talk for a moment 'bout your future plans. Ya' say ya' might go back to school?"

"I'm really not sure, Mr. Satterfield. But I am sure that I want to be respected in the community as an educated man, somethin' like yourself. Everybody wants to be respected for somethin'. Folks in Harlem are respected for havin' fine women and cars, for bein' a good musician or athlete. I'd like to be respected for my learnin'."

"Oh, I see. Ya' really want praise and fame. Ain't nothin' wrong with praise and fame if ya' can find what ya' really need to enjoy 'em. And what ya' really need to enjoy 'em is peace of mind. Without peace of mind, ain't nothin' worth nothin'! Ya' have peace of mind when ya' have what ya' really need to enjoy what ya' really want, even if ya' never get what 'chu really want. And peace of mind ain't nothin' but being in harmony with yourself and others, like harmonious notes in a melody."

Phyllis knocked on the door and whispered softly, "Ezekiel, it's almost ten o'clock."

"Thanks, darling. I 'preciate your concern—for your daughter," I replied, saying the last phrase under my breath.

"I really should be goin', Mr. Satterfield. I enjoyed it, believe me," said Raymond, humbly and with appreciation.

He and I went into the kitchen. Bessie and Phyllis were watching TV. Phyllis still seemed a bit upset, though no longer mad. So I planted a juicy kiss on her big brown cheek. Just as I began to relay to her Johnny's hello, the phone rang.

IV

"Brotha' Zek," said Hook, "they're havin' a special tribute to the Duke tonight down at Sam's club. Some of the best jazz and blues singers in the country gon' jam there tonight. Like Count Basie, Lionel Hampton, Billy Eckstine, Sarah Vaughan, Nancy Wilson. All the stars, man. Why don't ya' meet me down there and we can pay our respects to the King together."

"Um . . . it does sound like it's gon' be quite a tribute. All those big folk gon' be at Sam's?"

"Yeh, man. It's a special Harlem tribute to the Duke. It's a private community tribute before the press and media make their big splash at Carnegie Hall on Monday."

"Alright, I'll meet'cha there, Hook."

"Where ya' goin' this time of night Ezekiel?" asked Phyllis.

"Darling, there's a special tribute to Duke Ellington tonight down at Sam's. You know how I idolized the Duke and all. So I thought I'd go pay my respects."

"'Pay your respects?' At a nightclub? How can you pay your respects in a worldly nightclub to someone whose soul is now being judged? I tell ya', I've been married to ya' for eighteen long years and I don't understand your ways more now than I did when we first got married!" she exclaimed.

"I should be back around three or so. There's quite a slate of performers, like Eckstine, Vaughan, Basie. . . ."

"Ezekiel, you watch yourself now," she said, with a worried voice. "I've been feelin' funny 'bout 'cha since last night when ya' kept singin' that verse of Bessie Mae's record over and over in your sleep.

Wake up ev'ybody, 'no more sleepin' in bed
No more backward thinkin', time for thinkin' ahead

"You must have said those lines at least ten times last night. You seemed either to be dream singin' or just unable to hear your own voice. I told ya' to hush three times but ya' totally ignored me. I figured somethin' was wrong and I've been prayin' hard ever since."

"Don't worry, darling. That episode last night was a fluke. But I sure love ya' for lovin' me so much. I could never do without your love and prayers."

I bent down and gave her a sentimental kiss. I then walked slowly into the bedroom. I was frightened at her revelation. But I knew my false lack of concern would calm her down.

I had trouble choosing the appropriate clothes to wear to Sam's club. I hadn't gone to a nightclub since my youth. My slacks were all cuffed. I was pretty sure the fashion had changed from cuffed to uncuffed to bell-bottom cuffed. Well, at least I would be a little in style with my cuffs. My shirts were alright. But my ties were ridiculous. They were all as thin as licorice and as wrinkled as leprous skin. Even an iron was useless. So I threw on my old navy-blue sports coat over a purple turtleneck, slipped into my black pimp socks, the only stylish part of my outfit, tied my brown side-winding shoes, and put on my dark hat. I was sharp! Or at least felt so. And isn't feeling so what it's really all about?

V

I jumped into my car and headed toward the Harlem River. I love to drive along the Harlem River, down Harlem River Drive, just to see the calmness of the water. As I approached the river, I could see the glistening ripples of the strong current. Suddenly I realized I was still wearing my high-powered hearing aid. For a moment, I decided to stop and take it off. But I changed my mind. Since I wasn't going to the club to impress some beautiful young lady with my sexy ears and since I wanted to hear the music of the great stars, I decided to keep it on. I took one last look at the river, then went directly to the club.

I parked on 138th Street across from Harlem Hospital and a few blocks down from Sam's club. After locking the car, I pulled out the only relic of my youthful nightclub days, my old mauve-colored shades. I must have looked like a clown walking down the street with those shades and my outdated clothes. I did hear a few brothers and sisters giggle as I passed. But it was a giggle of acceptance and accommodation.

As I drew closer to the club, I could hear the syncopated beat of the drums and the uptempo of the guitar from the music inside. At the door of the club, the collective chant of the dancers inside resounded in my ears.

> It ain't what'cha know,
> It's how ya' feel!
> Don't worry 'bout being right,
> Just be fa' real!

Before entering, I noticed a sign on the door. It read:

> For those who want to groove
> We got the music that moves and soothes!

At the door I was told the entertainment tonight was downstairs. On the way down the steep stairs leading to the dance floor I wondered whether the tribute was over, or if it just had not yet begun.

The stairway was lined with curvacious females, consciously and unconsciously soliciting lustful male glances. Young men, sporting the latest fashions and conked hair, posed as if for portraits, their Kools dangling from their mouths. They stood staidly, partly blocking the stairway.

As I worked my way past the line of women, I overheard a cute swarthy young lady whisper to her friend, "Look at this old dude—he's as cool as he wants to be, with his old-time rags and purple shades!"

Her friend giggled.

But from behind, I heard a familiar voice exclaim, "This brotha' is sho'nuff sharp tonight! Good to see ya' made it, Brotha' Zek!"

It was Hook. We greeted each other with a rhythmic handshake.

"Come on, Zek. Let's push our way through this crowd and pay our respects to the Duke!"

As we forged ahead, Hook looked around and said, "I bet we're the only ones here who can really 'preciate the Duke like he should be 'preciated."

By the time we reached the lower level, I had begun to believe him. There were no pictures of the Duke, no signs of the tribute, and definitely no jazz band or blues singers providing the music. It was undeniably a disco party.

I asked the bouncer whether there was to be a tribute for Duke Ellington. He replied indeed there was. Tomorrow night. I turned and stared at Hook.

That damn Jackson told me it was tonight!"

I said to myself, "Where the hell is Jackson? I see he's not around." I thought of turning back, but the ensuing uphill battle discouraged me. I figured it would be easier to pay, have a quick drink, and exit through one of the doors from the lower level room. So I paid and went in. Hook followed, but I sensed that our companionship for the night was over. He went his way and I went mine.

The murky room was jam-packed. The music was loud yet overshadowed by vociferous outcries and visceral shouts. Many of the dancers blew whistles which sounded like small sirens. The clamorous crowd began to dance around in a ring and chant in cadence with the offbeat,

> Shit!
> Got-damn!
> Get off your ass and jam!

The chant was ironic; there was no room to sit anywhere.

People of all sizes and shades of the Negroid spectrum filled the misty, sweltering room. Flashing fluorescent multicolored lights shone just bright enough to see who was wearing what and who was with whom. The floor was filled with banana-skin females dancing with jet black men and chocolate-colored women dancing with paperbag-brown males.

The weekly routine of my youth had really not changed for these young people—or Hook, for that matter. The Party still revolved exclusively around music. It was still a release of tension, of nerves. A kind of cathartic ritual, the Party still served as a comforting place of retreat, a precious secular sanctuary in which to lay one's burdens down. It remained a kind of homecoming for people chasing after the carnal grail.

Watching the vivacious dancers, I could see my former Self. There I was, finger-popping and ass-twitching. But I also could see me now through my former Self. There I was, wall-flowering and analyzing.

But just then the cute swarthy young lady asked me to dance. I was delighted. I did the "Popcorn," a dance Bessie had taught me a few years ago. The young lady did something else. But my backwardness was unimportant. We were both having great fun. I felt so good and even racially proud as I watched this young lady move. You should have seen her! She was so enchanting, so masterful in her movements, so graceful in her steps, so sexy with her hands.

Gradually I began to notice smoke coming from the room above. The disc jockey turned the music up full blast to combat loud sirens outside and the small sirens inside. But the dancers seemed to take little notice of the smoke.

They began to stomp on the floor and shout,

We gonna turn this motha' out!
We gonna turn this motha' out!

The collective chant must have sounded like voices singing out of empty cisterns and exhausted wells. I'll never know. I could no longer listen.

The louder they shouted, the less I heard. The less I heard, the more pain I felt. And the deeper the pain, the more I could see. Clearly see.

VI

I saw a dark, somber light in the midst of the fire-covered Party. Live corpses fell to the ground and stretched their hands toward the dark light.

I said to the corpses, though I did not hear it, "Why persecutest thou thyselves so?"

They could not feel the grief in my heart nor see the tears in my eyes. My words made them tremble.

When I looked closer, I could see female apparitions, resembling fading petals on a fiery bough of darkness, grasping for breath in time with the fast, funky beat of male drummers. The drummers were blind. They could not see the ghastly dancers nor their gasps of exhaustion. They beat the drums with dry human bones, as the sultry faces of the women ghosts became covered with perspiration of blood. Yet the ghosts continued to dance and pointed to a crude poster hanging over the drummers. It read:

Party! We don't need no music!
Party! We got soul!

The apparitions had visible shadows of luscious female bodies. The few yolk-colored bodies stood out clearest under the dark, somber light. My mauve-colored shades allowed me to detect this. I also noticed that the shadows of the male drummers had no necks. There was no link between their bodies and their heads.

VII

Hook never did attend the special tribute for the Duke at Sam's. Nor did Sam's ever hold the special tribute for the Duke. Most of the club burned down that April night. Hook was one of the many fatalities. It must have been one of Phyllis's prayers that spared me a similar fate.

But I am in Harlem Hospital, partially burnt and permanently deaf. I no longer can hear loud sirens, nor Bessie's pleasant voice, nor Duke's melodies. Yet I love music more than ever. In fact, now I sing.